THE STORY OF
SILK

To
My silken-haired daughter, Zoë

THE STORY OF
SILK

Dr John Feltwell

ALAN SUTTON

First published in the United Kingdom in 1990 by
Alan Sutton Publishing · Phoenix Mill · Far Thrupp · Stroud · Gloucestershire

British Library Cataloguing in Publication Data

Feltwell, John *1948–*
The story of silk.
1. Silk industries, history
I. Title
338.476773909

ISBN 0-86299-611-2

Title page illustration: A lady on a cocoon-reeling machine, from Handbook of the Collection
Illustrative of the Wild Silks of India *(1881) by Thomas Wardle*

Endpapers: front: Black mulberry leaves; Back: White mulberry leaves.

Maps by Ethan Danielson
Typeset in 1113 Garamond.
Typesetting and origination by
Alan Sutton Publishing Limited.
Printed in Great Britain by
The Bath Press, Avon

Contents

List of Illustrations

I would like to thank Her Majesty the Queen for permission to photograph and publish plate 12; the Marquess of Salisbury for permission to use plate 11; Folger's Shakespeare Library of New York for plate 1; the Medici Society Ltd for plate 16, which is in a private collection; David Evans Ltd for plates 15, 22, 23 and 24; the Musées Nationaux des Chateaux de Versailles et de Trianon for plate 5; the British Library for plate 10; the Gainsborough Silk Weaving Company for plate 21; the Antique Textile Company of London for plate 19; the Trustees of Macclesfield Museum for plates 17, 18 (which was illustrated by Sean Purcell of Blackpool and Fylde College) and 26; Hermès of Paris and London for plate 27; Spink & Son, St James's, London for plates 2, 3 and 4; Topham Picture Source for plates 20 and 28; Valerie Baines ARMS for plates 6 and 7; The Mount Vernon Ladies Association for plate 13; and Miss Elsie Feltwell for plate 25. Plates 8, 9 and 14 by John Feltwell: Wildlife Matters.

As for black-and-white illustrations, the following have been kind enough to grant permission: The Savannah Historical Society, Savannah, Georgia, for plate 7; Worldwide Butterflies and The Lullingstone Silk Farm for plates 77–81; Mr R. Currie of the International Silk Association in Lyon for plate 76; Peter Caruth of Derby for plate 74; Guy Hart Dyke for plate 58; Photo Michel Sinic of St Jean du Gard for plates 14, 19, 24, 25, 27, 29; The Conway Library, Courtauld Institute of Art, for plate 63; Wandsworth Borough Council for plate 70; David Evans & Co. of Crayford for plates 54–5; The Spitalfields Trust for plates 72–3; the National Trust for plates 25, 60–1; Valerie Baines ARMS for plates 5, 11, 18, 20–1, 34–6, 39–40, 45, 75; Mary Evans Picture Library for plates 6 and 59; Dr Alan Morton of Imperial College for the novel DMAP software for generation of map 5; The Linnean Society of London for plate 22; Topham Picture Source for plates 3, 10, 26 and 62; Robert Gooden for plates 4, 77–81; The remainder are by the author or as credited in the captions.

T
H
E
·
S
T
O
R
Y
·
O
F
·
S
I
L
K

List of Illustrations

List of Illustrations

T
H
E
·
S
T
O
R
Y
·
O
F
·
S
I
L
K

List of Illustrations

List of Illustrations

Maps

Foreword

D espite the comprehensive bibliography shown at the end of this book, there is very little literature currently in print on any aspect of silk and Dr Feltwell is now fulfilling a great need, both for the textile student and the enquiring reader.

The author has put impressive research into the whole subject of silk. In particular, his coverage of historic events connected with silk, over some five thousand years, provides a useful concise reference that has hitherto been accessible only by visits to numerous libraries.

The story of how silk is produced is one that is not well understood generally. John Feltwell gives a good overall picture of the origins of silk and the countries in which it is produced. He describes the different species used for silk production, and the species of mulberry silkworm, which are numerous and very different. Mulberry is a study in itself and we have an insight into some of the interesting facts and differences that exist.

An interesting trend in the development of sericulture is leading to production coming mainly from developing countries. France and Italy led the world in sericultural research and development from the middle of the last century until after the Second World War. Japan has modernized both rearing techniques and quality control of the fibre to an unprecedented degree of excellence. However, both European and Japanese silk industries have had to cut back both on production and research for reasons of simple economy. Both have developed industrially and must pay economic wages. Silk production, however much it is technically advanced, is still a labour-intensive process, ideally suited to cottage industry. Consequently we see India fast becoming the number two producer after China and moves, just beginning, to establish silk industry in Africa and Indonesia. There will surely always be a demand for silk – no artificial fibre replaces it – so maybe, without the advantage of cheap labour in any country, we will find, long after we have passed on, that sericulture will spread again throughout even more of the world than we have known in the past.

ROBERT GOODDEN
Lullingstone Silk Farm
Sherborne, Dorset
September 1990

Preface

T his book has been written mostly in a restored *magnanerie* or silkworm-rearing room within the National Park of the Cévennes. It is now my studio. For ten years I thought about the old silkworm beds stacked up dustily in the granaries and the old cocoons which fell out of the metre-thick stone walls – forgotten casualties of over-active silkworms. It took another ten years to write the book during sojourns in France.

My curiosity extended to the intriguing social history of how silk arrived in Europe and shaped the daily lives of thousands, how the Huguenots and Flemish weavers influenced European society, and how weavers' cottages and silk mills dominated communities.

For me the silk road did not end in Europe, as popularly thought. It bridged the Atlantic, reached the Pacific and it finally met up with its 'roots' coming the other way round the world – the Chinese galleons which plied the Pacific to the west coast of America, effectively circumnavigating the world with silk.

I was also keen to find out how silk is produced from such a simple caterpillar and how it was transformed into such a sought-after material through spinning, weaving and dyeing.

Silks have been covetously guarded by kings and queens, archbishops and emperors for millennia; commoners have been denied silk for centuries. Ingenious industrial espionage eventually spirited silk technology out of the East and the commodity continued to attract intrigue – a whole silk community was once kidnapped specially at the whim of a king. The trend among present-day English royalty to wed in home-produced silks is nothing new; this is an ancient tradition.

'Men of the Cloth' have always been 'Men of the Silk Cloth' in my eyes. The evidence is overwhelming. Cathedral precincts, abbeys, monasteries and priories abound in mulberry trees.

In this book I have explored these fascinating aspects of the intimate association between man and this domesticated insect. For a decade it has always been my driving enthusiasm and an intriguing journey. I hope you enjoy it too.

JOHN FELTWELL
St Martial, France
Battle, England
September 1990

Acknowledgements

I am greatly indebted to the Ducros family at Cabanevieille, St Martial for their warm nature – Rolland, Georgette, Marie-Louise and Patrick – with whom I have talked about their cottage silk industry on and off for twenty-four years. Their personal experience in silkworm-rearing and filature stretches back to the end of the last century, and has been invaluable in piecing together some of the finer points of French sericulture. As always my good friends, Dr Jacques and Denise Lhonoré of the University of Maine (France) have always offered generous encouragement with this project and provided an overview of the subject. I have watched with interest the development of the silk enterprise at St Hippolyte du Fort in Hèrault, where I have been a frequent visitor for over ten years. Many thanks to all those involved there for answering my constant queries.

My thanks are due also to Geoff Burton of Sheppey, who read the entire manuscript in fine detail, and with his linguistic expertise guided me through otherwise pitiful translations, and to the Mairie of La Salle (Gard) for permission to reproduce 'House Rules for Silk Workers' in its translated form. Claude Rivers at Oxford gave me the benefit of his entomological background in also reading the entire manuscript. Mr L. Rheinberg of the Silk Association of Great Britain has kindly helped with my enquiries.

Elsie Feltwell and Kevin Fulcher read those chapters with historical slants and Lee Ann Feltwell in Philadelphia assisted with the American section. My wife, Carol, has patiently lived with all too many drafts of this book which she has also read and provided the calligraphy items.

There have been hundreds of correspondents over the years who have responded to requests in magazines for information on mulberry trees, silk mills and Huguenot information, often ferreting out titbits of fascinating local information. To all of those people, again, many thanks.

I would like to make special thanks to Brocklehurst Fabrics Ltd of Macclesfield for so generously supplying the Royal Blue dyed shot silk used for the special editions.

Mrs Brenda Leonard, formerly Librarian of the Royal Entomological Society of London has been very helpful and understanding with my long-term interest in silk. Miss Gina Douglas of the Linnean Society, and Mr Alan Clark of The Royal Society have been of great assistance too.

Finally I would like to thank Jaqueline Mitchell and Peter Clifford of Alan Sutton Publishing for smoothly guiding this book through publication.

Introduction

In the Ages of Old,
We traded for Gold,
Our Merchants were thriving and wealthy
We had silks for our store,
Warm wool for our poor,
And dregs for the sick and unhealthy.

From Weaver's complaint against the
Calico Madams 1719 -1721

The history of silk begins over five thousand years ago, yet the art of drawing out silk from a moist cocoon has changed little since its original discovery when a wayward cocoon was carefully retrieved from a princess's cup of tea, to much excitement and interest.

Since then stories, myths and legends have grown up around silk. This marvellous material, a natural product which is simply the secretion from the mouth of a moth caterpillar, was so sought after that methods of production were secretly and jealously guarded for thousands of years. Stories became distorted, exaggerations rife. Gradually the know-how crept across the hazardous silk road until it reached Europe only comparatively recently. The rest is a credit to the skill of French Huguenots.

Rearing thousands of hungry silkworms on special beds has been made easier by the caterpillars's total lack of inclination to wander far –unlike other caterpillars – and the moth's inability to fly induced by thousands of years of domestication. Today, scientists have produced a synthetic diet enriched with all the necessary dietary ingredients so that multitudes of 'test-tube' caterpillars can be produced all year instead of relying on the annual flush of mulberry leaves. While millions of Japanese and Chinese cocoons are still being produced by an industrious work-force, there is a modest revival in the

Introduction

An ancient legend is repeated here in this figure from an 1887 book on silk (Wardle, T., *Silk, its entomology, history and Manufacture*). It was widely believed that silk came from worms which issued forth from rotten calf meat which was allowed to fester for some days

French silk industry which is now supported by government. In Britain silkworm-rearing remains a curiosity.

People still marvel at the incredible two kilometres of silk thread that can be drawn off from just one silk cocoon. Methods of reeling, twisting and weaving silk have hardly changed since earliest times. A revival of silk production in Western Europe in recent years reflects the hard work of Spitalfields, Macclesfield and Lyon weavers all united as fellow Huguenots. Some of the old methods of dyeing silk with wild plants have been replaced with synthetic dyes but there is now a renewed awareness in this old craft of natural dyes.

Silks have always been coveted, admired and worn through the ages by the highest in society from Chinese rulers, the Egyptians and Romans to present-day royalty, especially in Britain. Long before silk was actually produced in Europe both the French and British kings were always very proud of their imported silk stockings, showing them off at court. Such was the unusual spectacle that many instances of the wearing of silk stocking are recorded for posterity.

Mary Queen of Scots was an excellent needlewoman with a strong French tradition, whose fine works in silk survive. The marriages of Princess Diana

Introduction

The annual ceremony of blessing the silkworms was organized by Lady Hart Dyke at Lullingstone Silk Farm. The 'Silk' banner shows three mulberry leaves and cocoons, while a tray of cocoons carried by the first lady in the procession is offered for blessing. Members of the local community turned out to enjoy this ceremony in the grounds of Lullingstone Castle, Kent

and The Duchess of York have revived interest in silks, recalling the tradition among the monarchy back to Henry I in the twelfth century, who wore fine silks. The ceremonial dresses of archbishops and bishops too have been carefully made from home-produced silks; mulberry trees were often grown within the ecclesiastical walls of abbeys and monasteries. Lawyers

Introduction

'taking the silks' to aspire to the Queen's Court is yet another example of court members being touched with silk's esteem.

One who fostered the cause of silk was James I of England (VI of Scotland). Stimulated to do something for the thousands of refugees fleeing the Continent after the Massacre of St Bartholomew, James I tried to set up a silk industry not only in England but later in Virginia. Both efforts failed but today many gardens in England have 'genuine James I mulberry trees' planted by this passionate king. The Huguenot settlements in England such as Spitalfields, Wandsworth, Greenwich and Canterbury can often be identified by ancient mulberry trees, weavers' cottages or silk mills – a unique feature found nowhere else in Europe.

Mulberry trees have a memorable effect on those who have encountered them: everyone seems to remember where they last saw one, or where they sampled some of the luscious fruits, or what happened under them. Where Buckingham Palace now stands was the site of a James I mulberry orchard described by John Evelyn in his diaries as rather a 'seedy' meeting place – but the mulberry tarts were good!

Shakespeare too is associated with mulberry trees and cuttings from 'his trees' have crept into many gardens, as indeed have those from Hardy's house in Dorset. Milton's mulberry stands in Cambridge. Lord Nelson is said to have amused Lady Hamilton under a mulberry tree and Keats to have written 'Ode to a Nightingale' beneath one.

More recently one of the protagonists for home-produced silks in England was Zoë, Lady Hart Dyke who single-handedly pioneered the industry at Lullingstone in north-west Kent. She was the first to do so since James I and his wife three hundred years before. Some of her Lady Hart-Dyke's silk was used in making parachutes for the Royal Air Force during the Second World War and other silk went into precision instruments in the Royal Greenwich Observatories around the world. Today, her enthusiasm for silk has been continued by Worldwide Butterflies and the Lullingstone Silk Farm in Dorset which acquired her reeling machine.

The qualities and mysteries of silk will always remain irresistible to man: the softness of the natural product next to the skin, its lightness, suppleness and penchant for holding lively colours give it vibrant quality that will never be matched with synthetic fibres and chemical dyes.

Other less obvious benefits of the silk industry are the Jacquard loom with its punched cards, which was the forerunner of the computer, and the fact that in the 1990s we have silk to thank for experiments in genetic engineering.

CHAPTER 1

The Silk Road: China to England

Spain shall hence forward keep her silks at home,
And Italy disperse hers where she may;
The Merchant shall not need to farre to rowe,
Since thou hast shewen a short and cheaper way.
The silken fleece to England thou hast brought,
There to endure till Doomes Day cut her clue.

From George Carr in Stallenge 1609

The common conception of the silk road is that of a route[1] which spanned the stony wastes from China to the Mediterranean, a link between East and West. It was first established at least four thousand years ago, was about 5,000 km long and stretched from Xi'an in Shaanxi Province in China, crossing the bleak wastes of Central Asia to Antioch and Tyre on the Mediterranean and Rome. Trading boats in the Mediterranean carried silks to other parts of Europe.

But the silk road did not end in the Mediterranean; its threads spread slowly through Spain, across the Atlantic to Latin America and ventured into the southern parts of North America. Here, silks are 'met' coming the other way, eastwards, so that in the splash and spume of Pacific breakers on the beaches of present-day California, the silk road finally ends having successfully circumnavigated the globe.

Few walked the entire length of the silk road and the predominant travellers were monks and pilgrims anxious to spread the religious word. There were also spies disguised as religious converts eager to find out more about the mysterious East. Traders soon began to bring their caravans on the

6

Traditionally, the silk road starts in China and ends in Europe. However, here the silk road is further traced from the Old World to the New World and meets up with the silk route going in the opposite direction, from the Philippines and China to the Americas, both routes meeting on the Pacific beaches of North America

The Silk Road:

silk road, exchanging goods and paying taxes at various places. The Soviet Union was crossed via a network of stage-traders, but hardly ever did the same traders journey the whole distance. The seventh-century Chinese traveller Hsuan-tsang noted in Turkistan (now part of the USSR) on his way to India that the people of Kucha (then K'iu-chi) dressed themselves in ornamental silks and embroidery.

One of the few who did travel the entire route was the trader and explorer Marco Polo (1256–1323). He was welcomed by aristocracy wherever he went and was in a superb position to note fine silks, but these were not high on his list of priorities. His real interest was in gemstones and trading them on. When he did put quill to paper he showed an eye for detail, but some say he tended to exaggerate! His journeys through the area covered by the present-day USSR, Persia and China reveal that silks in markets and bazaars had been well established in the communities for a long time before he was there. Silks were being produced in great abundance in Georgia (USSR) and the bazaars had some of the finest silken fabrics and cloths of gold he had ever seen. Baghdad (now Iraq) was a city with silks, cloths and gold while at Yazd (in the centre of Persia) silk was the principal export. Silk was not the only fibre spun and woven in these parts; the Tartars of Kalachan wove camel hair, and, incredibly, asbestos fibre.

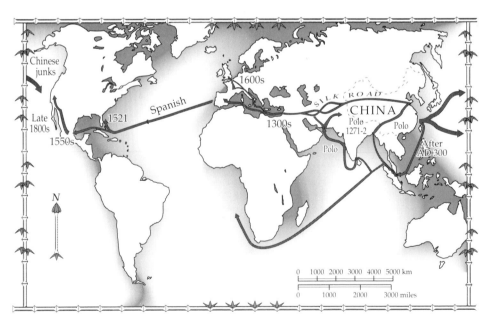

帝元妃西陵氏

The Chinese
empress Hsi-Ling-Shi
(2,640 BC), who is
thought to have first
discovered the
potential of the
silkworm, stands by
her tiered trays of
silkworms

The Silk Road:

The creature at the centre of attraction along the silk road was of course the silkmoth, *Bombyx mori*, which produced the precious commodity. There were always other silkmoths, such as the Tusseh silkmoth, whose 'worms' also produced silk, and their silks were also traded along the silk road, probably from before *Bombyx* silk was ever traded.

But it is in China, over 4,500 years before Marco Polo's travels, that the story of silk really begins. China was the undoubted origin of all *Bombyx* silk products, for it was in China that the white mulberry, the only food plant of the *Bombyx* silkmoth, and the silkmoth naturally coexisted. The Chinese had the unparalleled and exclusive claim to a tradition of at least five thousand years of silk production, and it was a happy coincidence which led to the discovery that a silk thread could be drawn off from one of the silkmoth cocoons. Consequently, its potential to be spun and woven was realized too.

Just where and when this natural product was exploited in the wild for domestication in China is not known. Its discovery is a subject of many myths and legends. One person, however, is singled out as starting silk production, the Chinese Empress Hsi Ling-Shi (otherwise known as Te-ling-she), the principal princess of Hwang-te, in 2,640 BC. She went to retrieve a cocoon which had accidentally fallen into some hot water (some say a cup of tea) and on withdrawing it, much to everyone's amazement, it came out on a delicate thread of silk. It was not long before its potential was fully appreciated. The empress's enthusiasm for this natural fibre impressed the emperor who was encouraged to have silk robes made from it.

Silk reeling is thought to have started in China a century before the Biblical flood, during the time of Fouh-hi. The invention of the loom is generally attributed to Empress Si-ling-chi, the wife of the celebrated Hoang-ti (2,602 BC).

Some of the oldest silks known in China today are threads and embroidery in the Summer Palace Museum of West Lake in Hanzhou, estimated as being 4,500 years old. Weaving patterns and designs have been found on a bronze urn of 1,300 BC and a late Stone Age cocoon is known. Ancient silks from a Chu tomb in the Hubei Province have been shown to date from 300 BC. Silks, quilts, gowns and skeletons swathed in silks have frequently been found in burial vaults.

China held the key to silk production and maintained its monopoly over the rest of the world for at least 2,500 years. During the reign of the Ptolemies, who ruled Egypt from 330 to 323 BC, China was regarded as 'The land of silk (Serica)' since silk was produced in several provinces (hence sericulture[2] – the production of silk today). The Chinese emperors did very

China to England

well in collecting taxes from silks. The productive provinces, in decreasing order (and in old names), were Xanting, Peching, Nanking, Huquang, Kiangsi, Honan, Suchan and Xansi.

The Japanese did not acquire the art of silk production until at least two thousand years after the Chinese but soon learnt the skills. It is thought that silkworm eggs reached Japan from Korea in the fourth century.

In India *Bombyx* silks have been produced for at least the past two thousand years, and their own silks from their native wild tusseh silkmoths for about five thousand years. Early Sanskrit inscriptions of around AD 150 mention a separate class of people whose sole occupation was to attend to silkworms. The practice still continues today.

As soon as the *Bombyx* silkmoth was introduced along the silk road westwards from China to India the silkworms could have eaten the leaves of the black mulberry, *Morus nigra*, – a native of Persia. It is more likely though that the white mulberry – a native of China – was transported along the silk road to India at the same time as the silkworm eggs.

The art of silk production was therefore the exclusive prerogative of the Chinese for 2,500 years, until the year AD 552. It was then that China's precious trade secrets were apparently purloined. Two Persian monks, under the encouragement of Emperor of the East, Justinian I (483–565 AD), cleverly brought the eggs of the silkmoth back to Constantinople (now Istanbul, Turkey) hidden in their hollow canes. This was apparently their second attempt, having returned empty-handed the first time. Justinian had an ailing economy and wished to prop it up with silk revenue. He was desperate.

The two monks' missionary duties obviously stretched far beyond religious interest, into the fields of industrial espionage, perhaps the first of its kind. It was, though, a plan which would benefit the people and Justinian. The monks stayed on at Constantinople to supervise the whole process, and the silkworms were fed on wild mulberry leaves, probably the black mulberry. This act of bravery – for they were likely to lose their heads if caught red-handed – was a turning point for Western Europe since it opened the door to silk production there.

Production of silk in Persia subsequently reached record levels. Annual production was about 10,000 zooms (a zoom equalled two bales, each of 0.91 kg or 2 lb) and in a fruitful year the greatest production came from Kilan province (8,000 bales). Other provinces producing silk were Schirawan and Chorazan (3,000 bales each) and Mazanderan and Caraback (2,000 each). Three types of silk were produced; the first was entirely made for girdles, the second, called 'Mileck', was adorned with Persian figures of men, women, beasts and plants, and the third, 'Zerbas' or 'Milechzerba', inlaid with silver and gold, was used only for the clothes of 'ladies of first rank and quality'.

It was after Alexander the Great (356-322 BC) conquered Persia that the Greeks gained 'the knowledge' of silk production. Aristotle maintains that 'Pamphila the daughter of Platis was the first who spun or wrought silk' in his *Historia Animalia*, but by that time the Chinese had surely been spinning for two thousand years.

The archipelago of Greece provided a thriving silk economy. The island of Morea, so called because it had so many mulberry trees, produced fine silk worth 100 'fols' a pound. The island of Scio produced 13,608 kg (30,000 lb) of silk each year and nearly all was made into velvet and damask and sold to Egypt, the Barbary coast, Turkey and France. Tinos's silk was not too fine but was strong enough for stockings, ribbons and gloves. Its annual production was about 7,258 kg (16,000 lb), each pound selling for a 'sequin'. Tiny Thermias' production was 544 kg (1,200 lb) each year. The island of Cos had, since the Roman empire, produced very fine silks.

The Romans were always keen to travel with their herbs, vegetables and fruits and they were probably responsible for moving mulberries around their extensive empire. It is possible that they introduced the black mulberry to Britain, along with the vine, pear, cherry, damson, quince, peach, fig and medlar. Pliny the Younger said that he could see mulberry and fig orchards in the countryside around the bay of Ostia, near Rome, where he lived.

During the time of the Roman Empire, silk commanded a very high value, equal to gold and pearl. It was considered effeminate for men to wear silk; in fact, according to Tacitus, Tiberius passed a law forbidding any man from defiling or dishonouring himself by wearing silk – *Ne Vestis Serica Viros Soedaret*. There were two sorts of silk garments in use: *holosericum*, made of 100 per cent silk, and *subsericum*, where the warp was either linen or wool. So expensive was pure silk that only empresses or princesses could wear *holosericum*.

It is not until late in the tenth century that we find the next reference to silk, and therefore mulberry trees, in Italy. A unique event happened which emphasizes the great importance people placed on the commodity. Roger I, King of Sicily (1031–1101) was a great campaigner and captured a complete group of silk-workers in Athens and Corinth and set them to work for him in Palermo and Calabria. The religious crusaders frequently came into contact with silks on their travels and those they brought back to western Europe were highly prized. So the seed of silk was sown in southern Italy. The

China to England

climate was soon found to be conducive to silkworm-rearing and the country was destined to become a leader in European silk production.

Silk from Sicily and Sardinia was always acclaimed for its high quality. The mulberry was chosen as the symbol of prudence by the Duke of Milan, Ludovico Sforza (1451–1508), whose name was appropriately 'Il More'. Although the Latin name of the mulberry tree, *Morus*, comes from the Greek word meaning stupid, the duke had every good reason to choose the mulberry for his emblem since the mulberry has very good survival qualities. In 1493 the Duchess of Milan, Beatrice d'Este Sforza wrote in a letter that she was having dresses embroidered in silk designed by Leonardo da Vinci.

It was during the Han dynasty (202 BC–AD 220) that silks were traded across the silk road to Roman Asia. Not that silks were the only products moved. Silks were more important as prestigious items in society to those in Roman Asia than to the Chinese, who often sent them as embassy gifts. The peak flow was probably in the late Han period.

Probably more silk passed overland than by the sea route of Ceylon and Arabia. Chinese ships began to sail the Indian Ocean with silks and ceramics and in the eighth and ninth centuries, the seaports of Yangchow and Canton were said to have foreign populations (mostly traders presumably) of over 100,000. The typical junk ships traded with the Philippines and thus on to the Americas in the Ming (1366–1644) and Ch'inng (1644–1912) dynasties. Late in the seventeenth century there is still evidence of silks being brought to the California coast from the Philippines.[3]

Peking remained the silk centre of the world for several centuries, long after the greatest traffic along the silk road was recorded in the Tang Dynasty (AD 618–907). When Marco Polo was there he witnessed incredible scenes; every day over a thousand cart-loads of silk entered the city from the surrounding countryside where the peasants were presumably growing silkworms, and spinning and reeling silk.[4] This was the city of Kublai Khan (1216–1294), then called Khanbalig, who was extravagant with his wealth. More than ten days' journey to the west of Peking was the silk centre of T'ai-Yuan-Fu which Polo visited.

Kublai Khan's banquets were attended by over forty thousand people, and the lords-in-waiting to the khan had their mouths and noses 'swathed in fine napkins of silk and gold, so that the food and drink are not contaminated by their breath or effluence'. On the khan's birthday (28 September) twelve thousand barons and knights paraded in clothes of gold and silk in imitation of the khan's own solid gold robes.

However, Marco Polo's journeys, during the Mogol Yuan dynasty

The Silk Road:

(AD 1274–1368) were really an exception, since most traders were Asian. The rulers of China used a lot of silk for their ceremonial dresses and special documents, the latter up to the third and fourth centuries. With the Treaty of Shan-yuan between the warring Sung and Liao, the Sung were assured of a good supply of silk, some 200,000 bolts, as well as 2,834 kg (6,248 lb) of silver. In 1402 this was raised to 300,000 bolts and 5,664 kg (12,487 lb).

China traded with Japan in 1392, selling copper coins, silks and ceramics in return for sulphur and swords from the Shogunate. This may have been the earliest time silk was traded between these great nations. In the fifteenth and sixteenth centuries Soochow was the largest city in the world and was famous for its fine silks and cottons. Wu-hsi, in the Lower Yangtze region of China, was also an important silk centre. The products of these cities made their way to Japan, to Europe and to the New World. In the sixteenth century silks were exchanged with the Russians for fur and, later, for tea.

Stories brought back by English, Russian and German explorers, in pursuit of the archaeological booty of cities 'lost' to the deserts, reveal much of our knowledge of how active people were hundreds of years ago in the Gobi Desert. At this time the climate was obviously different to today and civilizations prospered, with irrigation systems and the cultivation of fruits, until they were overcome by the encroaching sand. The Englishman Sir Aurel Stein found the remains of apple, plum, peach, apricot and mulberry trees sticking up through the shifting sands of Niya. Albert von Le Coq

The Japanese have taken up the art of enticing caterpillars into artificial pupation sites by providing them with little cells, like matchboxes, in which the caterpillars spin themselves up. These artificial nests are called 'Mabushi'

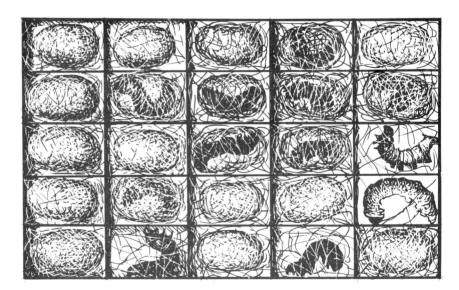

China to England

(b. 1860), the son of a wealthy Huguenot wine merchant, found silk manuscripts employing excellent calligraphy and illuminated manuscripts on various textiles at the lost city of Karakhoja (just inside China's border with Mongolia). Col. Petr Koslov's early 1900s expedition to Karakhojo discovered twenty-five Buddhist paintings on silk and linen, as well as paper, in the tomb of a princess. These now reside in the Hermitage Museum in Leningrad.

Part of the silk road also passed through the province of Uzbekistan, to the west of China. This semi-arid area had produced silk (and cotton). The Armenians also became enormously successful traders and would carry silk bales great distances on horse or camel caravans, risking robbery, ambush and local taxes en route, but their profits were worth the risk. They would buy silk 'batmen' at 20 crowns a piece, and sell at 30 crowns (one 'batman' equalled a bale of 18 lb 12 oz). One horse could carry 272 kg (600 lb) and a camel 454 kg (1,000 lb), so the trader stood to gain 500 crowns per camel once delivered. The Persian caravans carried about 2,000 bales annually during the months of May and June.

In particular they traded with Tocat and Angora and with Nosava on the Caspian Sea, a great trading centre. Silks from the Mogul Empire made their way here too. Silks then went to all parts of Muscovy and as far north as Archangel on the North Sea. Here the English and French bought directly and the Dutch shipped via Stockholm and the Straights of Elsinore to Holland. Frederick II (1712–86) (The Great) built Frederickstad in Holstein especially as a 'silk port' to accommodate the trade but the venture was not successful, despite him setting up an embassy in Muscovy.

By the fifteenth century silk was also being produced in France. In fact, the person credited with introducing mulberry trees and silkworms to the country (as well as roses, carnations, muscat grapes and peacocks) was Rene, Duke of Provence. He had connections in Italy, and probably imported his silk technology from there. However, his Italian connections were not that strong, for he had relinquished his title as King of Sicily by 1442. Provence provided the right climate for growing mulberry trees and rearing silkworms. Later, the know-how moved north, up the fertile plains of the Rhône Valley to Lyon, and westwards into the Cévennes.

Heartily sickened by the loss of revenue to the French by the importation of foreign silks, Louis XI proposed in 1466 that Lyon should establish its own silk industry. This was the beginning of Lyon's five centuries of association with silk. Louis curbed trade with Italy and encouraged French-produced silk by placing several royal orders for silk with weavers in

Tours. He also instructed a certain Maufrain de Carmisolle to set up silk mills in Tours and Lyon.

Silk was still an expensive commodity in the reign of Henry II of France (viz. 1547). It was not until about 1589, during the reign of Henry IV, that silk production was started further north in places like Orléans. This pleased Henry IV since it employed a lot of 'poor orphans and widows and many lame and old' and kept money in France instead of it going to Italy. Henry, as leader of the Huguenots before he was made king, may have had a special interest in sericulture as the Huguenots were often skilled in silkworm-rearing and working silk. He might have wished to keep alive an industry in which his kinsmen were skilled artisans.

Henry also employed a Monsieur Colbert who then employed a Monsieur Isnardes to go into silk production near Paris. This project was so successful that in 1664 he presented the king with a large amount of French silk that was better than any that could be obtained from Messina (Italy).

Henry IV's grandson, Louis XIV, also encouraged mulberry plantations throughout France and this in turn encouraged James I to boost his own economy in England, where the silk industry had yet to become established.

Silk had of course been used by English royalty, prior to James I, but it was always acquired at great cost from abroad. It is said that in the reign of Henry VI (1422–71) there was a silk society flourishing; this during the most acute phase of the Wars of the Roses.

In France, Napolean sponsored much silk production in Lyon from the Tessinari family, who are still in business today. They made items like the king's bedchamber in Versailles which took seventeen years to complete. He also patronized the Paris-based firm of Prelle, another company still in business today.

Throughout Europe experiments continued with silk production. The word was spreading but it was only the rich who could manage large production just for the sake of a pair of silk stockings. A gentleman in Germany in 1653 boasted that he had produced enough silk to make two pairs of silk stockings. The quality of German silk was claimed to be as good as any from Persia or Italy at that time and he was hoping that the Emperor of Germany would do the same as the King of France in banning Italian imports in order to stimulate home production.

Silk technology had taken a few centuries to move around the Mediterranean countries, north and west to Western Europe. The big secret that the Chinese has coveteously guarded for four thousand years was out. Everyone now wanted silk. From the eastern Mediterranean the knowledge spread to

This is a Babylonian love story first told in *Metamorphoses* by Ovid. Pyramus and Thisbe, the hero and heroine, were young lovers but their parents did not approve. They arranged to meet under a mulberry tree and Thisbe arrived first. However, she was surprised by a lion and in fleeing dropped her veil under the tree. The lion picked the veil up and tore it to pieces with his teeth, bloodied from having just attacked an ox. Pyramus then arrived on the scene, found the bloodied veil, assumed that Thisbe had been eaten by the lion, and stabbed himself. As illustrated here, Thisbe returned, threw up her arms in desolation at finding Pyramus dead under the mulberry tree and then killed herself. Thereafter the fruits on the white mulberry changed to black, which has the blood-coloured juice. A lot of detail, with artistic licence, is included in this work published by Hieronymus Bosch in 1552

A large and important woven silk temple hanging depicting a central standing figure of Mahakala, known in this form as Mgompo, the protector of the tent, holding a gri-grug (flaying knife) and a kapala (skull cap) in his hands and a magic baton supported across his forearms. The figure is wearing a five-pointed crown set with skulls and with snakes entwined around his neck, wrists and ankles; around his waist there hangs a cord of death heads. Within the nimbus of fire surrounding the deity are, from left to right in ascending order, Vajrapani and Lhamo, riding an ass; two carrion animals, Legsldan nag-po (another form of Mahakala) and Ekajata (Consort of the main figure) holding an Amritsa vase; two crows and two apsaras. To the lower edge seven yoginis hold offerings to the deity. The upper right-hand border is brocaded in gold with the four-character mark of Yongle

China to England

Italy and the western Mediterranean. The Spanish around Granada were adept at producing silk, the French prospered, and finally the possibilities of producing home-grown silks attracted the monarchy in England.

Silk manufacture may have been established in England as early as the twelfth century, since fresh mulberries (which do not travel well) were being traded on the London market from 1170. However, the first real documentary evidence that silk production was in operation does not occur until the seventeenth century when James I undertook his extensive, perhaps romantic, adventures into silk production.

NOTES

1. The silk road is also called the silk route, but in fairness it was really just an all-purpose trading route going westbound from the orient and eastbound from the Middle East. Everything was carried along its tracks; lapis luzuli, Baltic amber, jade, cobalt, rugs, porcelain, tea and silks. The only reason it was actually called the silk road (and not for instance the tea road) is that silk was was one of the finest and most expensive commodities carried.

2. This is also known strictly as *sériciculture* in France but in modern French parlance it is increasingly being shortened to *sériculture*.

3. Robert F. Heizer and Albert B. Elsasser, *The Natural World of the Californian Indian* (California, 1980).

4. Richard Humble, *Marco Polo* (London, 1975).

CHAPTER 2

The Silk Road: England to America

Where wormes and food doe naturally abound
A gallant silken trade must there be found
Virginia excels the World in both
Envie nor malice can stay this troth!

Alice G.B. Lockwood, 1934 in *Gardens of the Colony and State*,
1934 Scribners.

J ames I was the first person to try seriously to establish a silk industry in England. Mulberries had been known at the English Court for over four hundred years before James ascended the throne in 1603, so one part of the silk technology – the mulberry tree introduced from the Continent – was already present in England. But what of the little 'worms'?

James I had a logistical problem at the beginning of the seventeenth century: what to do with the huge influx of refugees from the Low Countries and France. Religious strife in Europe, especially following the Massacre of St Bartholomew in 1572 instigated by Catherine de Medici, resulted in a mass exodus of protestants from France. Some sought refuge in the Low Countries before joining ships to England. Tens of thousands arrived by boat in London and at places like Sandwich and Rye in Kent and other locations around the coast of south east England.

James I's enthusiasm for silk was thus born out of his immediate concern to find employment for the immigrant weavers, and of course to produce

The most High and Mighty Monarck IAMES by the grace of God king of Great Brittane France and Ireland Borne the 19 of Iune 1566. The most excellent Princese ANNE Queene of Great Brittaine France and Ireland Borne the 12 of October 1574.

James I and his wife both tried hard to establish a silk industry in England. They too, enjoyed wearing silks. Although trying very enthusiastically, beyond the call of normal State business, the English adventure with silk still failed. So too did James's silk experiments in America where he had a financial interest. Today England is left with a legacy of black mulberry trees resulting from these seventeenth-century experiments, quite unlike the rest of Europe where the white mulberry abounds

English silk for the first time. His wife liked silks too, and this may have influenced him considerably. James also saw the establishment of an English silk industry as a source of income, for he must have envied the way in which the French had already established a well-organized silk industry. It was in 1604 that James I anonymously published his vehement attack on the evils of tobacco in *Counterblaste to Tobacco* and it may be that his abhorrence of tobacco fueled his enthusiasm for silk which he thought provided gainful and more worthwhile employment. The skills of the Huguenot spinners and weavers were put to good use in England and many a master tradesman was employed to establish the English silk industry.

Three years after taking the throne James I had already established a silk industry down the River Thames from London at Greenwich. Charlton House was built by Sir Adam Newton, schoolmaster to Henry, the Prince of Wales, James' eldest son. It is thought that Newton built the house for his royal charge, but the prince died in 1612, the year it was completed.[1]

It was here that James employed a married couple, John and Frances Bonnell, to make 'Greenwich silk'. They were hired from 1606 to 1613 for an annual stipend of £60 out of the royal purse and were awarded 'The survivorship of the Office of Keeping Silkworms at Greenwhich and Whitehall'. Perhaps James wanted to enthuse his son in rearing silkworms. The son was, in any case, far more interested in boats, and Greenwich was a fine place for him to pursue that venture.

Probably the first documented mulberry orchard in the United Kingdom was established at Charlton House at this time and the importation, planting and management of the mulberries was put under the direction of Monsieur Vetron from Picardy. This silk venture was a modest success, furnishing at least some royal clothes. Today Charlton House still stands and is now open to the public; it claims to have a genuine James I mulberry by the front door. The orchard is long gone, however, grubbed out 200–230 years later.

James I's interest in the silkworm grew quite obsessive. He appointed special attendants as well as a Governor of the Chamber whose duty it was to carry the insects 'withsoever his Majesty went'. One can imagine the king's entourage complete with guardians of the silkworms. James also had a garden in Whitehall, possibly in the present St James's Park which backs onto Whitehall in London, where he also planted mulberries.

Close to his palace at Westminster, he had an orchard of mulberries put in by one William Stallenge, later commissioned by James to write a major book on sericulture. At the time the site was an area of wasteland but after the orchard was established it became a well-known London meeting place, as John Evelyn the diarist recalls:

10th May 1654. My Lady Gerrard treated us at Mulberry Garden, now the only place of refreshment about the town for persons of the best quality to be exceedingly cheated at; Cromwell and his partisans having shut up and seized on Spring Garden, which till now, had been the usual rendevous for the ladies and gallants at this season.

This mulberry garden aroused quite a deal of attention; the poet William Dryden ate mulberry tarts there and Sir Charles Sedley was inspired to write a play, *The Mulberry Garden*, which alluded to its less respectable aspects. The garden and silk experiments were continued in 1628 when Lord Aston was paid £60 a year out of the royal purse to maintain the project.

James I's silk industry slowly gained momentum, and preparations for a massive programme of establishing mulberry plantations and rearing silkworms came to a head in 1609. William Stallenge's book was published, the nursery stock of mulberry trees was ready, and mulberry seeds were available for an assault on the English aristocracy, who had big estates suitable for plantations, and the general public. The mulberry species chosen by James's advisors was the black mulberry, an unusual choice since it is the white mulberry which is much preferred throughout Italy and France, a tradition which continues today. It is possible that the black was selected for its greater tolerance to colder weather. James I then wrote to all his lord lieutenants requesting them to plant mulberries. To each he offered ten thousand trees which could be collected in London at the rate of 3 farthings a plant or 6s. per hundred. James also offered seed to be sold at the same time, during March and April 1609:

19 January 1609

James Rex
Right truly and well beloved we greet you well.

It is a principal part of that Christian care which appertains to sovereignty, to endeavour by all means possible, as well to beget, as to increase among their people, the knowledge and practice of all arts and trades, whereby they may be both weaned from idleness, and the enormities thereof, which are infinite; and exercised in such industries and labours as are accompany'd with evident hopes, not only of preserving people from the shame, and grief of penury; but also of raising and increasing them from wealth and abundance; the scope which every freeborn spirit aims at: not in regard of himself only, and the ease which a plentiful estate brings to every one in his particular condition; but also in regard of the honour of their native country, whose commendation is no way more set forth, than in the people activeness and industry. The consideration whereof having of late occupied our minds, who always esteem our peoples good, our necessary contemplations, we have conceived as well by discourse of our own reason, as also by information gather'd from others, that the making of Silk might as well be effected here as it is in the kingdom of France, where the same hath of late years been put in practice; for neither is the climate of this isle so far distant or different in condition from that country, especially the higher parts thereof; but that it is hoped, that those things which by industry prosper there, may by the like industry used here have like success.

Any many private persons, who for their pleasure have bred of those Silk-Worms have found by no experience to the contrary, but that they may be nourished and maintained here in England, if provisions were made for planting of mulberry trees, whose leaves are the food of the silkworms; And therefore we have thought good hereby to let you understand, that although in suffering this invention to take place, we do shew ourselves somewhat an adversary to our profit, by diminishing our royal customs for silk beyond the Seas; nevertheless when there is question of so great a public utility to come to our kingdom and subjects in general; and whereby besides, where multitudes of poor people of both sexes and all ages, such as in regard of impotency are unfit for other labours may set on work, comforted and relieved (by being employed in the Silk-Work). We are contented that our private benefit and interest should give way to the publick. And therefore being well persuaded that no well affected subject will refuse to put a helping hand to such a good work, as can have no other private end in us, but the desire of the welfare of our people.

We have thought good in this form only to require you, as a person of greatest authority within that country, and from home the generality may receive notice of our pleaure, with more coveniency than otherwise, to take occasion either at the quarter sessions, or at some other public place of meeting, to pursuade and require such as are of ability, (without descending to trouble the poor, for whom we seek to provide) to buy and distribute in your county the number of ten thousand mulberry plants, which shall be deliver'd to you at our city of London, at the rate of three farthings a plant, or at six shillings the hundred containing five score plants; and because the buying of the said plants at this rate, may at the first seem chargeable to our said subjects, whom we would be loath to burthen, we have taken order that in March or April next there shall be delivered at the same place a good quantity of mulberry seeds, there to be sold to such as will buy them by means thereof the said plants will be deliver'd at a smaller rate than they can be afforded, being carried from hence; having resolved also in the meantime, that there shall be published in print a plain instruction and direction both for the increasing of the said mulberry trees, the breeding of Silk-worms, and all other things needful to be understood for the perfecting a work everyway so commendable and profitable, as well to the planter, as to those who shall use the trade.

Having now made known unto you the motives as they stand with the publick good, wherein every man is interested; because we know how much the example of our own deputy lieutenants and justices will further this cause if you and others of your neighbours will be content to take some good quantities hereof to distribute upon your own lands; we are content to acknowledge thus much more, in this direction of ours, that all things of this nature tending to plantation, increase of science, and works of industry, are things so naturally pleasing to our own disposition, as we shall take it for an argument of extraordinary affection towards our person, besides the judgement we shall make of the good disposition, in all that shall express in any kind their ready mind to further the same, and shall esteem that in furthering the same, they seek to further our honour and contentment; who having seen in few years space past, that our brother the French King has since his coming to that crown both began and brought to perfection the making of Silk in his country, whereby he hath won to himself honour, and to his subjects a marvellous increase of wealth. We should account it no little happiness to use if the same work which we have begun among our people with no less zeal to their good, than any prince can have to the good of theirs, might in our time produce the fruits which there it hath done. Wherefore we nothing doubt if ours will be found as tractable and apt to further their own good, now the way is shewed then by us their sovereigns, as those of France have been to conform themselves to the directions of their king.

The garden did not close until the land was granted by Charles II to Bennet, Earl of Arlington in 1673. Later Goring House, Arlington House and Queen's House were built on this site, only to be pulled down to make way for Buckingham Palace, quite a change for this convivial gathering place to become a royal residence.[2] The three mulberry trees which survive in the present gardens of Buckingham Palace are thought to be direct descendants of those in James I's Mulberry Garden.

On his excursions through the countryside James used every opportunity to encourage his hosts to plant mulberry trees on their estates and we are now left with a legacy of old mulberry trees outside fine country houses which usually have notices stating: 'This is a genuine James I mulberry tree'. They are not always the original trees but are often second or third generation cuttings from the original James tree, but they exist on the same spot. One so-called genuine James I mulberry tree survives at the Mountbattens' home, Broadlands, in Hampshire, said to have been planted in about 1607.

James I's enthusiasm in trying to establish a viable silk industry in England was completely thwarted. His grand plan failed. It is popularly thought that the reason why the venture foundered was because the silkworm does not like black mulberry leaves. In choosing the 'wrong' mulberry species instead of the white mulberry, productivity of cocoons was theoretically reduced and the projects ground to a halt. There is no evidence to show this, and thousands of people in Britain can attest to rearing healthy caterpillars through to good cocoons on their own back garden black mulberry leaves. There must have been other factors to explain this misadventure: lack of organization, lack of silkworm eggs. We will perhaps never know.

The same year that James I was furthering silk production in England via his lieutenants he also began the first of several shipments of silkworms to Jamestown, the village named after him in Virginia in 1607. This was the first English settlement in America and the seat of government of Virginia resided here until it moved to Middle Plantations (now Colonial Williamsburg) a little inland in 1699. James thought that Jamestown might benefit financially if it engaged upon silk production, though it suffered a setback when it burned to the ground in 1608.

Between 1609 and 1622 attempts were made to establish sericulture further inland and down the coast where the early settlers had cut their way into the pine woods. The Virginia Co. was set up to exploit the new territory, and there was much two-way trade from Virginia to England. Both

England to America

James I and John Tradescant the Elder (Royal Gardener) had financial interests in the company. The New World was full of opportunities.

Thus began the American silk industry, the beginning of a costly experiment which eventually failed, completely wiped out by the importance of the tobacco, rice and indigo crops. Silkworm shipments of 1609 and 1622 perished at sea, but others got through. Curiously enough it is thought by some that Shakespeare had his inspiration for *The Tempest* from James's ships perishing in the Atlantic. Enough drama, however, to colour any literary tale, would have come from the *Mayflower* pioneers who crossed the high seas in their frail boats, the seeds of useful plants carefully wrapped in their pockets.

By 1619 the occupants of the Jamestown colony had turned their attention exclusively to sericulture and there were penalties for not planting mulberry trees. It was normal at the time to employ slaves to do all the work in the plantations, both tobacco and mulberry, for it was the government of Virginia which started the slave trade there in 1619. The popular air of the time was:

> Where worms and wood doe naturally abound,
> A gallant silken trade must there be found.
> Virginia excels the world in both,
> Envy nor malice gaine say this truth.

In 1623 James thought fit to order the members of The Virginia Co. to rear silkworms and set up silk mills. He wrote to his cousin, Henry, Earl of Southampton, who was also the company's treasurer:

To our right trusty and right well beloved cousin and councillor,
Henry, Earl of Southampton, treasurer of our plantation in Virginia,
and to our trusty and well beloved the deputy, and others of our
said plantations.

James Rex
Right trusty and well beloved, we greet you well.

Whereas we understand that the soil of Virginia naturally yieldeth store of excellent mulberry trees, we have taken into our princely consideration the great benefit that may grow to the adventurers and planters, by the breed of Silk-worms, and setting up of Silk-works in those parts. And therefore of our gracious inclination to a design

The Silk Road:

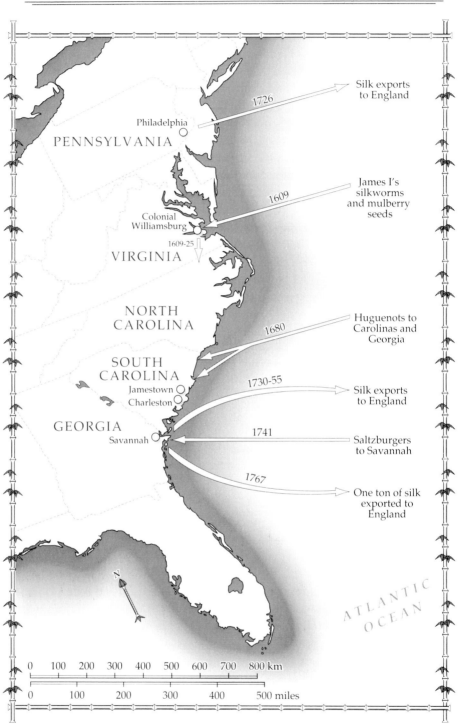

Associated silk traffic along the eastern seaboard of America in the seventeenth and eighteenth centuries. At the time when there were more native Indians in the Americas than Europeans, the pilgrims and colonists who originally settled in Virginia and Pennsylvania gradually spread southwards into the Carolinas and Georgia trying new crops. The native mulberry trees were tried as a suitable food plant for imported silkworms and soon limited quantities of American raw silk were being exported to England. The exchange did not become extensive, since rice, indigo and tobacco won out as important cash crops

Silk exports to England

1726

James I's silkworms and mulberry seeds

1609

Philadelphia

PENNSYLVANIA

Colonial Williamsburg

1609-25

VIRGINIA

NORTH CAROLINA

1680

Huguenots to Carolinas and Georgia

SOUTH CAROLINA

Jamestown

Charleston

1730-55

Silk exports to England

GEORGIA

Savannah

1741

Saltzburgers to Savannah

1767

One ton of silk exported to England

N

ATLANTIC OCEAN

0   100   200   300   400   500   600   700   800 km

0   100   200   300   400   500 miles

of so much honour and advantage to the public, we have thought good, as at sundry other times, so now more particularly to recommend it to your special care, hereby charging and requiring you to take speedy order, that our people there use all possible diligence in breeding Silk-worms, and erecting Silk-works, and at that they rather bestow their travel in composing this rich and solid commodity, than in that of tobacco; which besides much unnecessary expense, brings with it many disorders and inconveniences. And for as much as our servant John Bonoeil[3] hath taken pains in setting down the true use of the Silk-Worm, together with the art of Silk-making, and of planting vines, and that his experience and abilities may much conduce to the advancement of this business; we do likewise hereby require you to cause his directions, both for the said 'Silk-works' and vineyards, to be carefully put in practice throughout our plantations there, that so the work may go on cheerfully, and receive no more interruptions nor delays.

Given under our signet, at our palace at Westminster, the ninth day of July, in the twentieth year of our reign of England, France and Ireland, and of Scotland the five and fiftieth.

It is apparent from James's letter that the French vignerons had already been over to Virginia to advise on vine production before 1609. Silk production would have been commonplace to them, since viticulture and sericulture were ordinary occupations for thousands of Frenchmen in the south. James also sent copies of a pamphlet on sericulture[4] by Mr John Bonoeil which maintained that if enough hands were available 'much silk might be raised in Virginia as to supply all Christendom'. James's letter is written with such strict command that those who did not abide by the instructions for the silkworms would certainly receive the king's displeasure.

Bonoeil also mentioned that he had written the pamphlet from first-hand observation of how silkworms are reared (sometimes under 'primitive conditions') in the Languedoc, Cévennes, Provence and around Avignon and in parts of Italy. There were already mulberry trees growing in Virginia, presumably the native American red mulberry, 'the tallest and the broadest that anyone had ever seen, some were big enough to bring forth six pounds of silk per annum from cocoons'.

Several people in Virginia heeded James's order to start silk production but were hindered by the scarcity and high cost of Negro slaves. Eventually tobacco won as an economic crop since, in comparison, it did not require much labour.

One person who did set up mulberry orchards in Virginia was Sir Robert Murray who planted at least ten thousand trees. He perfected a way of growing mulberries quickly from seed and established hedges of bush mulberries 'like currants or gooseberries', a novel idea for the time, and similar to the modern method of apple-growing.

Other dignatories set good examples. For instance Edward Digges, Governor of the Virginia colony from 1655 to 1656, raised silkworms. So too did his colleague, Col. Thomas Pettus, on the Littlejohn plantation on the banks of the James River. Silk from this particular enterprise was presented to Charles II. A little later, the Governor Sir William Berkeley ordered more planting of the imported white mulberry and one plantation owner in Gloucester county planted seventy thousand trees in 1664–5. The burgesses rewarded the Berkeleys with 9,072 kg (20,000 lb) of tobacco for the silk they produced.[5] But by the end of the seventeenth century Virginian silk production had seriously diminished.

James I certainly whetted the appetite of some American colonists who tried their hand at sericulture. But after his influence ebbed, some pursued silk production and failed, while others managed some sort of living.

It has been suggested that one of the contributory reasons why sericulture failed in the New World was because James I's interest in it waned and he did not see the project through, 'but as soon as they thought that they had engaged the planters to begin upon it, instead of promoting it heartily, and sending some able and skilful person to direct the undertaking, they threw all upon the planters.'[6] Establishing any new crop would have been difficult for the settlers. Apart from Indians they had innumerable difficulties with understanding their new climate, with its extreme temperatures and different soils, quite apart from having to forge somewhere to cultivate in the native pine forests. If perhaps the settlers had been given continual assistance and support from England, the adventure may have succeeded.

Huguenot silk-weavers were probably among the first colonists at Jamestown. They certainly were elsewhere, since a party of them settled in Georgia and the Carolinas in 1680. The government gave them free land to settle in the Carolinas and to plant mulberry trees. Their productivity was not high, the total silk produced and exported to England between 1731 and 1755 being only 113 kg (249 lb). In 1765, still only 74 kg (163 lb) of silken goods were sent back to England.

Silk was not entirely cast aside for the benefits of tobacco. The fine

England to America

materials had already made their name as prestigious fabrics, and American silks had already crossed the Atlantic to attire English royalty.

When the fortified colony of Savannah was cut out of the riverbank by Governor James Oglethorpe's men in the 1730s, silk production was seen as a real means of generating income. Savannah *was* Georgia then since nothing else of this forested country had been explored by the white settlers.

On Oglethorpe's initiative the Saltzburgers, some 1,200 of them in 1741, fleeing from religious persecution in Europe, diligently became involved in agriculture and sericulture and established colonies at Ebenezer, Bethany, Goshen and on St Simon's Island. The trustees who tried to establish a government in Savannah, and to promote silk production, ruled that no-one could serve on the assembly unless they had a hundred mulberry trees and produced 6.8 kg (15 lb) of silk from each of their 20 ha of land. The trustees also instructed that on each 4 ha of land one hundred white mulberry trees should be planted.[7] The plantations had to be managed for ten years. The trustees ensured that supplies of mulberry seed, even trees and eggs of silkworms, were sent over from England.

The trustees in London who governed Savannah worked to a strict rule of law. One of their advisors was the notable Sir Thomas Lombe who wrote a strong testimonial in support of the colony, described by some 'as rich in enthusiasm as it was poor in first-hand knowledge'. Lombe reckoned that forty thousand people in Georgia (which was hardly more than Savannah and it environs) could be otherwise employed in this industry. When the laws

The silk industry fulfilled a lot of aspirations when Governor James Oglethorpe, an Englishman from Godalming in Surrey, established the first English colony in Savannah, Georgia. The silkworm, silk cocoon and black mulberry leaf still figure in Savannah's seal whose motto *Non Sibi Sed Aliis* means 'Not for themselves but for others'

against holding Negroes were revised, each plantation was required to possess one female Negro well trained in silk-culture to every four male Negro slaves.

A technical advisor, one Nicholas Amatis, was sent from the Piedmont district of Italy and, not surprisingly, found the climate of the Appalachians (Carolina, Virginia, Maryland and Pennsylvania) much to his liking and well suited for sericulture. The grand plan was to have mulberry plantations stretching from the river bluff well inland, and sketches were made of this. The seal of the trustees of Savannah appropriately incorporated silkworms and cocoons with the motto *Non sibi sed aliis.*

Silk production did not proceed as fast as it should have done under the guidance of Nicholas Amatis, for it seems he or his workers may have been guilty of sabotaging the venture. It is reported that Amatis's assistants may have broken silk-making machinery, burnt silkworm beds, destroyed mulberry seeds and fled to another state. Curiously, the débâcle with Amatis may have stemmed from him being denied a Catholic priest by the magistrates during his last illness.

Amatis's unfinished job fell on one Jacques Camuse and his wife who attempted to teach the Georgians the art of sericulture and silk-winding. But this project did not progress as well as anticipated since Mrs Camuse was afraid to teach the ladies of the colony too well, lest her own services became dispensable. It is said that all the professional skill of silk production lay with the old Mrs Camuse in 1740, so much so that if she died the whole industry would collapse with her. It did not.

Despite these problems Savannah gradually became the focal point for the export of silk from the colony. The first Georgian silk exported to England was in 1735, though it had probably been produced locally for a few years and a government mulberry nursery had been established in 1732. There were obviously disease problems which could attack the silkworms at any time, and 1742 is recorded as being one in which half the Savannah silkworms died. However, productivity was high on the Saltzburger's estate and from the Whitfield orphanage, since in 1751 all but 137 kg (302 lb) of the 286 kg (630 lb) of silk produced that year came from these two places.

A filature factory was established in Savannah in 1753, as the plaque on the original site records. Here Georgian silk was reeled until 1771 but the original filature was destroyed by fire in 1839. Previously, in 1732, Oglethorpe had tried the imported Indian Tusseh moth as a source of silk, using a work-force of Italian immigrants, and 3.63 kg (8 lb) of silk was exported to England between 1734 and 1735. *Bombyx* silk production in

England to America

1739 was 4,536 kg (10,000 lb) with a value of $75,000, all from locally produced cocoons. The filature factory later opened to meet the growing demand. During the years 1755–72, just over 4,000 kg (8,818 lb) of silk, representing local production, was declared to the custom-house in Savannah. The climax of production was probably about 1767 when almost a ton of silk was exported to England. However, the War of Independence (1776) eventually curtailed silk production.

Silk had been seen as a saviour to the new economies and colonies throughout the eastern seaboard states. Silk production had failed in Virginia due to tobacco, failed in South Carolina due to rice and indigo; Georgia was its only chance. Oglethorpe's influence over the silk industry in Georgia slowly waned, taking over a hundred years to finally disappear. He had made a brave attempt at sericulture in a wild country against countless odds and he did well. There were several contributory factors to the decline of this silk industry. The climate, although warm, is very thundery, hot and sticky and not exactly the kind of climate that silkworms 'enjoy'. Labour became too expensive, bounties were withdrawn by the government for silk production and, probably most significant of all, rice was being increasingly cultivated.

William Bartram, the celebrated English botanist and naturalist, could not help at some stage observing silk production in the eastern states through which he regularly journeyed. Bartram was twenty-five miles from Charleston (South Carolina) in April 1776 when he recorded in his book[8] a large orchard of the European Mulberry (*Morus alba*) some of which was grafted on stocks of the native Mulberry (*Morus rubra*). He was correct in believing they were for the culture of silkworms.

The silk industry in Pennsylvania (the colony's keystone state) started in 1725 and within a year was exporting to England. William Penn's vast land grant stretched from the port of Philadelphia to Lake Erie. By 1750 serious production was in full swing. Bounties were offered for silk cultivation in Pennsylvania and in 1765 one hundred weavers emigrated from London to take up the offers. If it were not for the presence of statesman Benjamin Franklin in London during this time, the promotion and temptations of working in Pennsylvania would not have materialized. Although Franklin was born in Boston (Massachusetts) he established his business in Philadephia (Pennsylvania) and did much to promote trade and industry in his home state.

The nineteenth century saw quite an amazing enthusiasm and boom in planting mulberry trees in an endeavour to raise silk in America. There had already been a 'tulipomania' in the seventeenth century and Americans were

Typical of many such rural mills the 'Old Oil Mill' at Florence, Massachusetts was used by the New York & Northampton Silk Co. in 1834. The illustration is taken from L.P. Brockett's 1876 book entitled *The Silk Industry in America*

always keen to try other ventures in this new land of opportunity. Later, there were to be chrysanthemum, aster, sweet pea and cactus manias.

Six north-east states (Maine, New Hampshire, Vermont, Rhode Island, Connecticut, Massachusetts) participated in silk production and a surfeit of silk companies was established, such as the North-east Silk Co., the Rhode Island Silk Co. and, in the middle states, the Albany Silk Growers' Co., the Queen Anne County Silk Co. and the Talbot Silk Co.

The first American silk mill was opened in 1810 in Mansfield (Massachusetts), by the Mansfield Silk Co. A white mulberry bush variety called *M. alba multicaulis*, originally from China, was introduced via France to America for the mulberry boom. Shipments arrived at the Linnaean Gardens in Flushing on Long Island, a well-known nursery owned by William Prince & Son. The US government lent its support, and in 1828 published a 220 page report on silk production.

In the north-east the silk industry was still active in Pennsylvania. The Society for the Promotion and Culture of the Silk-worm had a special meeting at Indian Queen in April 1828 to promote the culture of the mulberry tree and the raising of silkworms. Members resolved that it would provide 'an important source of wealth to the state, be highly advantageous to the agricultural interest and give employment to women and children'. Premiums (or prizes) were offered for good production: $60 for the greatest amount of sewing silk of the best quality produced in Pennsylvania, $50 for the greatest quantity of silk and $50 for the largest number of best white

England to America

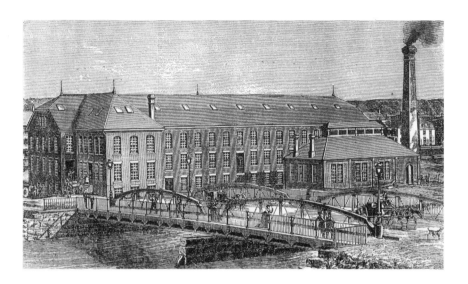

The Unquomock Silk Mill in Holyoke, Massachusetts is typical of many of the larger silk mills in America and Europe in the nineteenth century. In the 1850–60s Unquomock became the largest in the state, but on the morning of 16 May 1874 a catastrophe befell it. A reservoir upstream, containing six million gallons, burst, the mill was destroyed, 148 people lost their lives and the mill boiler was washed 1,000 ft down the river

mulberry trees raised. It may have been this enterprise which exported fine silk to Liverpool in 1831, said to be the equal of any Bengal silk. It was produced by a Monsieur Duponceau in Pennsylvania.

The enthusiasm for silk production was to last only a decade. It peaked in 1839 and by 1840 it was almost dead. Five dollar mulberry trees could be bought for five cents. The millions of mulberry trees planted between 1832 and 1839 were left abandoned. The situation was worsened by a blight of mulberry trees. Mansfield's production of cocoons gradually dropped off through the following decades, falling from 140,616 kg (310,000 lb) in 1840 to 2,268 kg (5,000 lb) in 1880. Some parts of the southern states, however, maintained rural silk crafts for a long time after silk was originally introduced and had become commercially unviable, since premiums were being offered for silk production in Georgia.[9]

If James I is thought to have been responsible for introducing sericulture to the eastern seaboard, the Spanish were certainly there before him, but a long way to the south. Sericulture had been blossoming in Mexico one hundred years before James's exploits. The Spanish, with their expertise in sericulture from Granada, had promoted the industry in 'New Spain' (Mexico) and had profited well from the abundance of wild mulberry trees which grew there.

There were many attempts at introducing silkworms across the Atlantic and several counter-claims as to who actually carried the first shipment. Certainly Columbus is attributed with this in 1492 but a few years later in

The Silk Road:

1501 Ferdinand and Isabella of Spain sent Fray Nicolas de Ovando to the West Indies. Here he carried out a schedule of tithes, one provision of which required the islanders to pay one tenth on all silk cocoons produced back to Spain. A further shipment of silkworm eggs was sent from Granada together with skilled silk-workers in 1517 but the project was later abandoned. A later voyage of 1521 located suitable land for raising silkworms north of Florida in the region of present-day South Carolina, but no records exist of their successes or failures.

There were later claims for introducing the silk industry to Mexico, especially between Hernan Cortés and his rival Diego Delgadillo. Producing silk was a prestigious indulgence and secrecy was often courted. It is probable that Cortés's requests to Spain for silkworms, cuttings, seeds and eggs in 1522 were answered and that silk production started at his palace at Coyoacan, a few miles south of Mexico. All this is substantiated in the marvellous book of Borah (1940) who has identified over fifty towns raising silkworms, apart from Mexico City, in the 1540s. However, Delgadillo believed he was the first to introduce the silkworms to the country. He also described the burgeoning Mexican silk industry in the 1580s where many Spaniards had up to eight silkworm houses over 200 ft long, all very wide and high, and saw over ten thousand sand trays per house loaded from floor to ceiling with cocoons.

The western seaboard of America was one of the last places to be opened up by European settlers. By the time the colonists were well established on the east, the west was still a rugged, unexplored land, highly populated with native Indians. Capt. Cook and Capt. Vancouver had left descriptions of colourful coastlines on this desert landscape. The west was a land which was first tamed by Indians, colonized from Mexico by Spanish missionaries (who knew how to grow mulberry trees, among many other useful fruits from Granada), and finally by waves of settlers who walked across the 6,437 km (4,000 miles) continent from the east. The chain of mission gardens extending up the Californian coast, each a day's ride from each other, served to educate the local Indians into how to grow exotic fruits such as citrus, olive and pomegranate, and probably mulberry. Several of the mission gardens are still open today.

Apparently the first plantations of mulberry trees in the west were established by Ozro W. Childs (born *c.* 1824) at her nursery just off Main Street, Los Angeles, in partnership with W. Huber. Later, another attempt to establish a silk industry further south was made by Louis Prevost, a French nurseryman, who bought part of the San Gabriel Mission in San Bernardino

England to America

in 1869. This movement worked well during his lifetime but expired after his death. According to Frank Mason in his 1910 book, California produced 113 kg (250 lb) of silk cocoons in 1865, the industry having started here in 1860. It would have failed completely if it were not for an Act of Californian legislation that offered bounties of $250 for everyone who planted five thousand mulberry trees and $300 for one hundred thousand trees. There followed a sericulture spree but this was short-lived since the bounties were retracted. The maximum silk productivity for California was 861.9 kg (1,900 lb) in 1868, but by 1878 the industry was virtually dead. There followed other short-lived attempts in other places including Kansas and Salt Lake City, Utah in the 1880s. Some sericulturalists hung on in desperation; Mrs Carrie Williams of Minneapolis Beach, San Diego County[10] published a book in 1895 on how to rear silkworms, and offered that The Minneapolis Beach Colony Co. would buy all cocoons raised in California. We assume she was not successful after this.

By the turn of the century the industrial city of Peterson in New Jersey became the silk centre of America. Immigrant silk-workers arrived from Europe, and silks were imported from Japan, ready for dyeing in the soft waters of the River Passaic. In 1913 there was a strike among silk-workers and a thousand of them paraded in Madison Square Gardens under the direction of the idealist John Read.

It is within sight and sound of the breaking waves and spuming surf of the Californian coast that the silk route finally ends. The route from China westwards through Asia and Europe to Spain and across the Atlantic to 'New Spain' had eventually made its way northwards up the Californian coast. At the same time trade routes had been established eastwards across the Pacific to the shores of California; perhaps bolts of silk were spilled on the shores from wrecks. Here the circumnavigation of Chinese silks is concluded. The silk route was not simply from China to Europe. It stretched right round the world, but was particularly strong from Europe to the Americas via Spain and Mexico.

NOTES

1. T.L. Jenkins, *A History of Charlton House* (c. 1980).
2. D. Bellamy, *The Queen's Hidden Garden, Buckingham Palace's Treasury of Wild Plants* (1984).
3. John Bonoeil, one suspects, might be the same person as John Bonnell of Greenwich who helped James I so much, but who is spelt differently here.

34

THE · STORY · OF · SILK

The Silk Road:

4. This leaflet has proved impossible to locate.

5. J.P. Dutton, *Plants of Colonial Williamsburg* (1979).

6. Joshua Gee, *The Trade and Navigation of Great Britain & Ireland* (1760).

7. K. Coleman, *A History of Georgia*.

8. William Bartram, *Travels of William Bartram*.

9. I am very grateful to Mrs Florence Griffin of Atlanta for drawing my attention to these premiums being offered for silk in Georgia. They definitely prove that silk was still being produced as late as the 1850s when silk was sent from Elbert County to Charleston for weaving. Mrs Griffin's researches have been published in *The Transactions of the Central Agricultural Society*.

10. Minneapolis Beach may well now have been renamed like so many other places.

CHAPTER 3

From Silkworms to Silk

The silkworm will feed on occasion upon the leaves
of elm, oak, apple-tree, crab-tree, cherry and
plumb-tree, bramble leaves, other trees, shrubs and leaves.

Henry Barham 'An Essay upon the Silkworm' 1719

The most labour-intensive period in silk production is the rearing of silkworms. And it is all a question of timing. In the wild, the silkmoth lays its eggs on mulberry twigs where they overwinter until the buds open in the spring, thus assuring survival. This single generation, with a resting stage over the winter, was the basis for domesticated silk production for thousands of years. However, in some countries silkworms are now bred continuously throughout the year.

Rearing silkworms at home, for instance as a hobby or combined with school studies as is the case in France, is a completely different matter from rearing them commercially. In a silk-rearing room incubation of the eggs has to be carefully monitored so as to coincide with the opening of the mulberry leaves.

The silkmoth life cycle described here is of the wild silkmoth of China and Japan, *Bombyx mori*. It is commonly thought that the original species does not now survive in the wild and that its continued existence is assured only by its culture by man. The setting described here is principally that of southern France, which would have been similar to that in Italy where ideas were copied anyway. Apart from the endeavours of James I there has never been a cottage silk industry in England, so there is no real comparison to be drawn between the two countries.

From Silkworms to Silk

Zoë, Lady Hart Dyke inspects her fully grown silkworms. They are being reared in the traditional way on silkworm beds arranged in tiers. Photographed in 1952

There are certain characteristics of the present-day silkmoth which give clues to its four thousand years of domestication. The adult moths cannot fly; although they have wings, these are short and broad and flight is not attempted. Curiously, the shape and small size of the wings are not relevant to their inability to fly. The wings are just as good as those of other silkmoth

From Silkworms to Silk

species which can fly, including the wild mulberry silkmoth, *Bombyx mandarina*, which may be a close relative of *B. mori*.

Caterpillars have also lost any real power of locomotion. They rarely wander far and so they are reared together on uncovered 'silkworm beds'. The silkworm is therefore a most obliging caterpillar and easily reared, unlike most other caterpillars which wander off at the first opportunity.

Like the other wild silkmoth species of the Indian sub-continent the silkworm passes through the same four stages of metamorphosis, i.e. egg, caterpillar, chrysalis and adult, or to give them their scientific terminology, ova, larva, pupa and imago.

All caterpillars must shed their skin in order to get bigger, a process known as ecdysis, and they have to do this four times. Each stage in the caterpillar's life is called an instar and there are five of them between the egg and the chrysalis. It is the fifth stage caterpillar which spins the precious silk cocoon. What attracted people to the silkmoth initially was its protective cocoon thickly spun in silk. It is a characteristic of all caterpillars (butterflies and moths) to produce silk to secure themselves on a leaf. Many moths also use silk for making a cocoon which protects them from bird and lizard predators. The superior nature of the *B. mori* silk was a natural choice; and the natural fibre a much coveted raw material.

Commercial production of silk relies on three advancements today. First, fooling the silkworms that it is perpetually summer; second, using artificial diets; and third, providing a continuous supply of food plant. Supply of enough leaves at the right time is often the most limiting factor in silk production. In Taiwan today they are able to have eight generations of silkworms a year, and four flushes of leaves off their mulberry trees. For the trees this is the result of selective breeding. For the silkmoths this is the result of giving the caterpillars more than twelve hours of daylight each day. In this way the caterpillars are in a continuous breeding mode.

Establishing a good source of mulberry leaves is essential before rearing silkworms and it will take a minimum of three years to have an adequate supply of leaves from an orchard. Bush mulberry trees can be grown effectively and quickly in a polythene tunnel, otherwise an orchard may take several years to reach optimum productivity.

There is not much free time when silkworm-rearing commences. The caterpillars have to be kept warm if the early summer weather deteriorates, and the cocoons have to be harvested and marketed.

The supply of mulberry leaves must be available at the right time. One large single tree may support a thousand hungry caterpillars sufficient for a

Synthetic diets

In Europe the culture of silkworms relies upon the natural cycle of plants and insects. The mulberry produces only one flush of leaves and the silkmoth one generation of eggs and caterpillars each year. So under natural conditions there are limits to reproduction. Research was therefore undertaken to find ways of boosting production. One of the earliest experiments was performed by a Dr Lodovico Bellardii of Turin in the early nineteenth century. He collected mulberry leaves in the summer, dried them in the sun, powdered them and stored them in an airtight and dry bottle. This mulberry leaf powder was reconstituted in the spring with a little water and the caterpillars were said to eat it immediately and avidly.

The essence of a synthetic diet is that all the elements of a normal diet of leaves such as vitamins, proteins, carbohydrates and fats are incorporated into a suitable medium for the caterpillars to feed upon. In practice a perfectly synthetic diet of ingredients brought together by man is frequently rejected by caterpillars. If a little of the powdered foodplant to which they are normally accustomed is added to the mixture this makes all the difference and the caterpillars begin to feed. This is then called a semi-synthetic diet. At least twenty species of moth caterpillars have been successfully reared on semi-synthetic diets.

The advantages of a semi-synthetic diet are that it can be used independently of a supply of fresh mulberry leaves. These are gathered at the appropriate moment, dried and stored. Preparation of the diet as a sort of stiff porridge mixture can be done several months before it is needed, and stored in a refrigerator. Small doses of antibiotics are added to the mixture to prevent bacteria and fungi living on the rich medium under storage. Small quantities of the diet can be poured into test tubes and these are used to rear tiny caterpillars. The caterpillars are then transferred to larger vessels containing the diet. Adequate ventilation is required to prevent condensation and waterlogging of the vessel. Keeping the jars upturned on blotting paper absorbs much condensation.

Some sort of chemical imprinting is evident in caterpillars. If they have nibbled mulberry leaves first of all, they will very rarely accept a dietary mixture thereafter. If they are offered a dietary mixture as soon as they hatch from the egg, they will feed on this exclusively thereafter.

small-scale production. In the Cévennes there is now a silk cooperative which recommends a suitable holding of about two hundred large-leafed mulberry bushes ('Kokuso' cultivar), grown as a modest vineyard or orchard. This would be sufficient to produce about ten thousand cocoons. These fresh 'green' cocoons can then be sold to the silk cooperative.

There is a very common myth that silkworms much prefer the white mulberry (*Morus alba*) to the black mulberry (*M. nigra*). This is not so. Caterpillars will not starve to death on *nigra*, although they might possibly take a few extra days to develop, have higher mortality and lighter cocoons, with less silk.

The life cycle of the silkmoth starts with the emergence of the female and, after mating, her laying eggs. When she emerges from her cocoon she dissolves a passageway through the maze of silk fibres embracing her in the cocoon, crawls out and expands her wings to dry. Once the moths have hatched from these cocoons, the silk threads of the cocoon are broken and cannot be used for recovering any valuable silk.

EGGS

The newly hatched female moth is so laden with eggs that her abdomen is basically an extended swollen sac containing between three hundred and five hundred eggs. She disperses sex scent into the air which attracts the males to her. Emerging into a domesticated world with other males and females in close proximity, it is only minutes before she is engaged in a prolonged period of copulation, 'tail' to 'tail' with her partner. They may stay like this for several hours.

Replete with fertilizing sperm from the male, the female commences to lay her eggs all over the cocoon from which she has just emerged, or on branches or twigs. Her wings useless for flight and her abdomen cumbersome, the female rarely moves far from her cocoon.

It was customary in the nineteenth century in southern France and the Piedmont region of Italy for cooperatives to distribute batches of eggs to peasant families. These were reared in all available premises, dark cellars, outhouses and the like, the amount of space available limiting production. It was thought that 1 oz of eggs would produce young caterpillars requiring 3 sq ft of space. Thereafter three times the area was required for each successive stage. An Italian experimenter went further and noted that from 1 oz of

From Silkworms to Silk

Female silkmoths have extended abdomens which accommodate large numbers of eggs. After mating and fertilization, the eggs are laid on the first convenient surface, such as the leaf, stem, box or surface on which the insect is resting. The pale yellow eggs are glued to the surface and soon change to a darker hue

eggs, the first stage caterpillar needs 8 sq ft, the second 15 sq ft, the third 35 sq ft, the fourth 82 sq ft and the fifth 200 sq ft. He noted how the peasants of Italy tended to cram in their caterpillars; this was not good for them since they are very susceptible to disease in overcrowded and high humidity accommodation.

Traditionally, each household in the Cévennes asked for a specified weight of eggs from the local cooperative. These were given free, and the weight would indicate the total number of silkworms that each household could handle from its available mulberry trees. Shortly before Easter requests would go in for eggs. Delivery was often via the visiting *boulanger*. On delivery the eggs were looked after every hour of the day and night. Sometimes they were entrusted to the lady of the house who would put them in a special pouch suspended between her breasts to keep them warm. Examples of these little pouches may be seen in some regional museums. [1] At other times the eggs were wrapped in a handkerchief and kept behind the wood burner or stove, even up in the warmth of an inglenook fireplace. At night they would be transferred to the bottom of the bed or under the pillow. Other people tried utilizing the warmth from a manure bed. In commercial production eggs were often placed in a small heated stove, or in a special room where only eggs were incubated. Artificial incubation was essential since cool weather was sometimes experienced in the spring, especially in the mountains. Considering the importance of silk in the economy of the typical cévenol (perhaps 80 per cent of the annual income was generated from the sale of the cocoons), care of the eggs was taken very seriously. It was generally considered that whoever had the charge of looking after the eggs

From Silkworms to Silk

should not indulge in any 'violent exercises', lest the eggs be damaged.

Incubation took about ten days, as it does today when silkworms are reared at home in Europe or the USA. The warmth of an average home is sufficient to incubate the eggs. Under semi-natural conditions eggs normally hatched six to twelve weeks after being laid, after a critical intervening cold spell, i.e. winter. For those buying-in silkmoth eggs, there was always the problem of premature hatching before mulberry leaves were out. One old remedy was to seal them in perfectly dry glass phials and place these in a pot of cold water. Kept cool like this, or in ventilated boxes in cellars, outhouses and the like, the eggs will not start to develop and can be kept for six to ten months. A suitable place today would be a cellar, spare room with a constant cool temperature, or the bottom section of a refrigerator. Once incubation commences it cannot be stopped; the skill is to start the incubation so that the newly hatched caterpillars will have fresh leaves to eat. In Europe, the mulberry is one of the last trees to come into leaf. When there are 2 cm long buds on the mulberry trees, the ten-day incubation period can begin.

The eggs are inspected daily until hatching. Healthy eggs are a bluish-grey colour; these are the ones which will hatch. Yellow eggs and black eggs never hatch. Italian peasants used to have a trick of washing batches of dead eggs in wine to give them a bluish-grey colour, and to put these on the market. It took a good eye to detect the differences. The caterpillars, too small to handle, are fed on small pieces of finely chopped mulberry leaf, which is placed on the material used for wrapping up the incubating eggs. Once the caterpillars have transferred to the leaves they can be looked after in small boxes with adequate ventilation.

CATERPILLARS

'Caterpillars should always be fed leaves of their own age,' wrote William Stallenge in 1609, 'young caterpillars fed tender young leaves, older caterpillars the larger and tougher leaves.'

Looking after caterpillars is a demanding occupation, especially in the hot Mediterranean. Rearing silkworms in pots is a method the Spanish had perfected at the end of the sixteenth century, according to Stallenge. Caterpillars were kept in special vessels woven from straw, osier, rushes or other similar light material. The surfaces of the vessels were smeared with ox dung which was allowed to dry and cake. This method seemed to be excellent for preventing attacks from rats and mice, preventing dessication of mulberry leaves and keeping the caterpillars in a cool environment.

Caterpillars are essentially non-stop eating machines with voracious appetites. They have one purpose in life, that is to pass to the next stage all the essential nutrients required for a successful life as a moth. Vitamins and minerals are passed from the caterpillar to the adult via the chrysalis and in order for the caterpillar to collect together all these essentials for life, it has to eat fast and furiously. Only a small proportion of the vital nutrients are retained from the food they eat; they jettison the unused part of the food as droppings. Silk rearers will recount how a shed full of munching caterpillars is quite a sound – it can be heard up to several metres away – like that of torrential rain falling on leaves.

Picking enough mulberry leaves to feed the caterpillars every few hours throughout the day and night was often a problem for the cevénol. There was always the possibility that the supply would run out and the right to any neighbour's unused tree leaves would have to be negotiated and bought. Carting sacks of mulberry leaves over increasing distances became a major difficulty without mechanization; mules were the main means of transport.

Another of the principal difficulties in looking after caterpillars is that they are very susceptible to disease. One particular problem arises at feeding time. When mulberry leaves are plucked from the trees and collected in bags, heat is generated among them. This is most pronounced on hot sunny days, especially when the bag might have to be in the sunshine for half an hour or so. If the caterpillars are fed these warmed leaves, they will almost certainly die. Many cévenol rearers can attest to this. Perhaps a mild form of fermentation is to blame. To avoid this, leaves are left in the shade for two hours to cool before feeding. Modern rearers of silkworms in France are aware of this, while in England, where the climate is cooler, mulberry leaves are generally brought straight to the caterpillars without any adverse effects.

In the past the diseases of silkworms were mysterious to those who looked after them, and vivid descriptions of various ailments were noted in the eighteenth century. There was the *scarlet* disease which afflicted moulting caterpillars. They would emerge with a reddish tinge and die, perhaps after the fourth moult. The *yellow* disease was typical of caterpillars whose skin became tight over the swollen head and a yellow liquid would ooze from the mouth. The disease was also called the 'glow' since the body soon assumed a transparent glowing appearance.

Yet even in the seventeenth century there were curious antidotes to prevent disease. The well-respected chief druggist to Louis Le Grand of

From Silkworms to Silk

France (Louis XIV, 'Le Roi Soleil', 1638– 1715), a Monsieur Pomet, cited a certain Monsieur Isnard, on how to improve the breeding stock of silkworms by countering disease, in a very peculiar operation:

> At the time when the mulberry leaves are ready to gather, which should be five days after their budding, in the beginning of the spring, they take a cow which is almost at calfing, and feed her wholly with mulberry leaves, without giving her any thing else to eat of herbs, hay, etc. or the like, till she has calved; and this they continue for eight days longer, after which they let the cow and the calf both feed upon this some days together, without any other mixture as before. They kill the calf after it has been filled or satiated with the mulberry leaves and the cow's milk, then chop it to pieces to the very feet, and without throwing any thing away, put all together, the flesh, blood, bones, skin, and entrails, into a wooden trough, and set it at the top of the house, in a granary or garret till it is corrupted; and from this will proceed little worms,

The house in which Louis Pasteur lived when he stayed in the Cévennes last century to sort out the *maladie du vers à soie*. The house is now a private school and is not open to the public. It stands in an undistinguished back street of St Hippolyte du Fort, not too far from Monoblet, and is marked with a simple historic marker

which they lay together in a heap with mulberry leaves to raise
them afterwards, just as they do with those which are produced
from the eggs; so that those who deal considerably in them, never
fail, every ten or twelve years, to raise them this way.

Without any scientific knowledge of what caused diseases there was little
that peasant rearers could do to protect or cure their caterpillars. It is
mentioned in *Silk Manufacture* (1840) that Abbé Eperic of Carpentras (Rhône
Valley) had a method well proven over twenty years of experience, of
preventing caterpillars from getting the 'jaundice'. He recommended
sprinkling quicklime over the silkworms with a silk sieve and then giving
them mulberry leaves moistened with wine. This, it was said, was adopted in
the *département* of Vaucluse. As for the dangerous 'nephitic air' which was
produced by decaying mulberry leaves, this could be countered by using
chloride of lime.

Another more potent problem loomed, however. Considerable heart-break
and anxiety struck the French silk-rearers at the beginning of the nineteenth
century when their entire population of caterpillars went black, began to
stink and died overnight. This was the result of the dreaded *pèbrine* caterpillar
disease. The problem was so severe that the peasant people of the Cévennes
mustered enough money between them to pay for the leading expert on
microscopic disease, Louis Pasteur, to travel from Paris to try to sort out the
problem.

Pasteur came to the Cévennes and stayed at a small house at St Hippolyte
du Fort (near Ganges), where he held conference and visited the important
silk centre of Monoblet, a little village up in the mountains not far away.
Today there is a plaque indicating where he stayed, though the house is not
open to the public. Pasteur studied the *maladie du vers à soie*, pronounced it to
be a virus, and recommended improving sanitary conditions in selecting
stock: eggs should be taken only from healthy females. Unfortunately other
problems were lurking on the horizon for the cévenols, more potent ones
which would put them all out of business. This was the flooding of the
market with cheap Italian silks, as well as the introduction of synthetic
fibres, rayon and nylon.

Silkworms were reared in a *magnanarie*, a traditional building which was
used and copied in Italy, France and later in the USA. Sometimes they were
specially built, but mostly they were adapted rooms and outhouses, such as
granaries, chicken sheds and wood-sheds. During the 'Golden Age' of silk
production in the Cévennes at the end of the nineteenth century many

Marcello Malpighi (1628–94)
Insect anatomist

The Italian Marcello Malpighi was one of the first people to give an account of the structure of an insect. In fact, some excretory vessels in the body of insects are now known as Malpighian tubules. In his research he used the silkworm and described the spiracles or air tubes found along the sides of the caterpillar chrysalis and moth. He also described the multi-chambered heart, the nerve cord, the ganglia and the silk glands.

In fact the Dutchman, Johann Jacob Swammerdam (1637–80) had already described the Bombyx silkworm with ten sets of spiracles, but the more meticulous Malpighi showed there were actually nine pairs.

Malpighi was not the first to describe the silk glands of Bombyx, however, since this was credited to an earlier anatomist, Andreco Libavius, in 1599.

So interesting was Malpighi's original research that in October 1667 the joint secretary of the Royal Society of London, Henry Oldenburg, invited him to submit his work. A number of his letters were published and Malpighi became a Fellow of the Royal Society in 1668. The following year he published his memoire on the silkworm De Bombyce.

Hard pressed by his every-day medical practice Malpighi wished he could devote more time to his researches. In a letter written from Bologna to the Royal Society dated 15 July 1669, Malpighi describes the tubules in the abdomen of the silkworm thus:

. . . I set about further observations of the silkworm when spring was gone by, and came to the further conclusion that the little yellow guts which I had formerly observed to be inserted in the lower part of the body cavity probably take the place of the vessels of the gall bladder and pancreas, and I ascertained that they still exist in the chrysalis and the butterfly, so that the resistant texture of the outer skin is dissolved by the liquour contained within, as by aqua regia.

Silkworms busy eating mulberry leaves. Young caterpillars are given chopped-up leaves but later they eat whole leaves. The noise of thousands of caterpillars eating has been described as 'the sound of torrential rain playing on leaves'. Silkworms have to be fed every three or four hours, day and night

country folk added an extra storey to their houses to accommodate the silkworms. Today, many of these single-storey additions are in decay as they were built rather hurriedly just for silkworms.

Magnanaries had to be well ventilated with tiny fireplaces in each corner to maintain the right temperature. Cold weather and piercing north winds after Easter were feared since high mortality was likely. Fires were kindled if the temperature dropped below about 20 °C.

It was also the firm belief of the peasants of Italy that any violent noise would disturb the caterpillars. Today there is still a great tradition among the cévenols in taking seriously the threat from thunderstorms. Caterpillars are very sensitive to heavy thundery weather (to which this mountainous region is particularly prone) and will stop feeding. This is perhaps due to changes in atmospheric pressure; whether the quality of the silk cocoons is impaired is another matter.

Tradition dictated that if there was a thunderstorm a live coal had to be carried around the *magnanarie* to drive off the evil spirits and calm the caterpillars. Extraordinary lengths were taken by some scientists to ascertain whether silkworms were really sensitive to noise. Messrs Rozier and Thome fired several pistol shots in a *magananarie*, and decided that none of the healthy caterpillars were disturbed – only a sickly one! There was also some preoccupation with the possible benefits of having some object made of iron in the *magnanarie*. Either iron objects were suitably placed around the room, or in the case of some experimental *magnanaries*, the silkworm beds were all wired up to a sink. This must have acted as a lightning conductor for all the silkworms in the event of a storm!

Each room was filled with tiers of silkworm beds or trays from floor to ceiling, each separated by a few inches, perhaps stacks of ten trays in each room. Tiny passages divided stacks of beds and allowed distribution of

An unusual panel of silk brocaded with coloured silk and metal thread, depicting a repeat mirror image of trees, exotic fruit and a bird perched on the top of a branch, with much of the design outline in black. Other examples of this silk are in the Musée des Tissu, Lyon and the Abegg Stiftung in Berne. Another design from the same group is in the Art Institute of Chicago.

Length: 176 cm; Width: 57 cm.
Possibly Spanish (1720–30)

*T
H
E
·
S
T
O
R
Y
·
O
F
·
S
I
L
K*

A kutcha woman's garment of red silk embroidered in silk chain-stitch with stylized flowers and roundels enclosing flowers; waves and Chinese cloud bands around the hem and sleeves and a small purse hanging below the neck. It is Chinese Turkistan silk, possibly Yarkand or Khotan, from the second half of the nineteenth century. There is a pair of matching leather boots, embroidered with silk chain-stitch in a style similar to the garment, the upper part being covered with printed cotton, and lined with white leather from Chinese Turkistan, Yarkand origin. A virtually identical pair of boots was given to the Victoria and Albert Museum by Sir Douglas Forsyth in 1875

From Silkworms to Silk

Collecting the foliage for the hungry caterpillars was often a family affair, youngsters playing the pipe while the relatives worked hard. The leaves, or branches with leaves, were collected in sacks which were then brought back to the *magnanerie*. The leaves would begin to heat up in the sack in warm weather and would have to be laid out on the floor for a few hours to cool down. Feeding warm leaves to caterpillars invariably killed them. If your own source of leaves ran out, rights to neighbours' leaves would be bought and a journey of a mile or two to bring in leaves was frequently the case

mulberry leaves. Attention also had to be paid to excluding birds and vermin.

The *magnanarie* also had to smell sweet, according to Stallenge in the seventeenth century. The floor had to be sprinkled daily with vinegar and strewn with herbs such as lavender, rosemary, thyme, savory and penny-royal, among many others.

Woven cane silkworm beds were specially made by craftsmen in southern France and were for sale to all those who kept silkworms at home in their *magnanaries*. They were prepared from split lengths of Provençal cane (*Arundo donax*), a very common species which forms dense stands along rivers and ditches. Banks of four split canes were interwoven with others, to make a bed 1.4 m wide by 3 m long. The rim and supports below the bed were made of chestnut.

Feeding the voracious caterpillars is an acutely busy period which lasts about a month. During this period the caterpillars increase their body weight tenfold, growing from 1 mm to 70–80 mm in just five weeks. To give some idea of the quantity of mulberry leaves required to feed caterpillars, twelve thousand caterpillars would need twenty sacks of mulberry leaves a day. It is also estimated that 220 kg (485 lb) of leaves is sufficient to make 1 kg (2.2 lb) of silk. It has been said that a man and a boy in Sicily were able to tend in two months as many silkworms as would produce 27 kg (60 lb) of silk. This may have been their only annual employment, but it was hard work.

The fully-fed caterpillar is quite an impressive sight. It is a pale slate blue, almost oyster-white colour with a retractable head. Sometimes the caterpillars are oyster-white interspersed with black bands. Occasionally brown caterpillars occur and these may indicate their wild ancestry. When disturbed the head and first few segments retract into the body which then swells up, giving a menacing appearance. It has eight pairs of legs of three different types: three pairs of 'true legs' which will eventually become the legs of the adult moth, four pairs of 'prolegs' slightly towards the front of the middle of the body, and a pair of claspers at the rear. The caterpillar breathes by way of nine pairs of air tubes (spiracles) situated on the sides of the body. Contractions of the body as it moves help to waft air into the body for oxygen to be extracted and circulated to all parts of the body. It is very difficult to sex a caterpillar from external characteristics, but at this stage the sex is already determined and the sex organs already in place in the body. Sometimes it is possible to see a pair of purple testes through the body cavity of the male caterpillars, on the underside near its rear.

Once fully grown the caterpillars have to find a place to make their silk cocoon. Like other caterpillars or butterflies and moths they do not have to go through the period called 'wandering', when they walk several metres in search of a suitable site. However, they do become very restless and fidgety, moving around in a small area. They readily utilize whatever is available to make their cocoon.

In France the traditional way to encourage the caterpillars to make cocoons was to provide them with branches of broom stood up like stooks on the silkworm beds. The broom would have been cut the previous year and stored and dried so that all that was left was a mass of dark twigs. Once in position, these branches would soon be smothered with caterpillars and cocoons. One old custom to encourage all the caterpillars to move off their food and go to pupate was to walk round the *magnanarie* with fried onions. The smell was enough, apparently, to encourage them to take to the broom. Alternatively, reducing the room temperature was another trick. Yellow caterpillars were always known as wanderers or *cochons* and they never made cocoons. A modern version in the plastic age, is a plastic 'hedgehog' rather like a bristley

French (Cévennes) sericultural patois

Patois varies according to locality, even between hamlets within sight of each other. These patois words are from the environs of St Martial, near Sumene in Gard. 'Lo' or 'Lou' means 'the' in English. Most of these patois words have never before been put down on paper; they were only used verbally. The Ducros family, who have spent so much time sorting them out with me, can only suggest that the following spellings are the closest to what they took for granted as everyday words.

Patois	French	English
De Foureille	Action d'élever les cocons de dessus la bruyère	Taking the cocoons off the broom twigs
Éruguer	Chenille	Caterpillar
Lou Gabiette	Tente	Broom tent
La Trinque	Une hache pour ramassage de la bruyère	Special axe for cutting broom
Lo Mourié	Mûrier blanc	White mulberry
Lo Ramme	Rameau du mûrier	Mulberry shoot
Lou Boulan	serpette	Sickle
Lou Bruc	Bruyère	Broom
Lou Fourel	Cocon	Cocoon
Lou Granne	Oeufs (La graine)	Eggs
Lou Jort	Branches	Branches with leaves
Lou Magnac, magnan	Vers à soie	Silkworm
Lou Sede	Soie	Silk
Lous Canisses	Les lits d'élevage	Cane silkworm beds
Lous Parfuma	Casette avec sucre	A diffuser for sweetening the air
Ma Gna Gueire	Magnanerie	Silkworm breeding room

Part of a 'plastic hedgehog' used in place of a tent of broom twigs. Caterpillars make their cocoons in it with ease, since the bristles of plastic are sufficiently dense to simulate plant material

broom, with adequate places for caterpillars to climb into. An even more efficient method is with trays of tiny cubicles, each the required size for one caterpillar to enter and start to make its cocoon. All the methods are very efficient, but the great advantage is that the caterpillars pupate (make their chrysalids) close to where they fed as a caterpillar.

In constructing the broom tents in the Cévennes it was customary to make a pointed tent (*lou hespital* in patois), wigwam-shaped, on the topmost silkworm bed. On all other levels the tent was curved all round (*lou gabiette*). The tents were erected a few days before pupation which meant that the almost full-grown caterpillars with their voracious appetite is still had to be fed. This was one of the worst jobs since it required delicately pushing mulberry leaves down the inside length of the tunnels without injuring the caterpillars.

COCOONS AND METAMORPHOSIS

The object of the caterpillar constructing a cocoon is to have a safe place in which to turn into a chrysalis. Chrysalids cannot defend themselves and would make a good meal for a bird or a mouse. Thus the tough nature of the intermeshing silk is to form an effective barrier. Once transformed into a chrysalis the cocoon is a safe place to prepare for the next stage of the metamorphosis, the formation of the adult insect which has to escape from the silken enclosure. To change from a chrysalis into a moth is a true form of

From Silkworms to Silk

This photograph shows typical 'tents' of broom in which cocoons have been formed. When the caterpillars are close to finishing their feeding, they seek a place to spin a cocoon. 'Tents' of broom twigs are carefully arranged on the beds so that the caterpillars can crawl in and find a secure place to attach the silk threads. When the caterpillars have spun themselves inside their safe cocoon they change into a chrysalis. When this is completed the cocoons have to be disentangled from the broom and cleansed of any debris. Note that the young boy and girl are both wearing clogs. Photographed in the *Magnanerie des Cambous* at La Vallée-Française.

metamorphosis. If we were to look inside a newly formed chrysalis, all we would see would be a mass of yellow liquid. From this mass would soon be formed all the sophisticated hormonal, nervous and respiratory systems of the insect, some more complicated than those of man.

Spinning a silk cocoon is a lengthy and presumably energetic process for a silkworm; it takes about two to three days. Someone worked out that one caterpillar moves its head 150,000 times from side to side spinning its silk out, just to make its cocoon.

Silk is a natural product secreted from two pairs of spinnerets or silk

In England fully-fed caterpillars might be enticed on to much-divided stalks and twigs, carefully arranged in the silkworm-rearing room. This over-simplified illustration comes from Mrs Whitby's 1848 book on rearing silkworms and is typical of her production procedures carried out at Newlands, near Lymington, Hampshire. Instead of broom stalks (as used in France), she recommends that 'the boughs of the seedstalk of the turnip, or asparagus, dried and cleared of seed, should be thinly spread out in the form of a fan'

glands below the mouth of the caterpillar. It is produced as a liquid but hardens on contact with air. Silkworms spin silk from their spinnerets using a side-to-side motion of their head, carefully covering the twigs around them with a fine web. Gradually they entomb themselves in silk, first a transparent web of fine silk, then other layers which obscure the caterpillar from view. After two to three days the caterpillar rests, its job complete. Sometime later, the caterpillar slips off its skin unseen, and reveals the chestnut brown chrysalis shell. This then hardens in a few hours.

The length of the silk in a single cocoon has been often debated and studied. Distances range from up to 9.6 km (6 miles) to a more accurate figure of about 300–400 m. The International Sericulture Committee mentions 500–2,000 m. The average length probably does not exceed 600 m for the finest cocoons. Various calculated lengths range from about 400 m (Miss Rhodes of Yorkshire) to a maximum of 600 m in Italy (Count Dandolo). The width of the silk thread straight from the caterpillar is about 30 microns (one micron is a 1,000th of a millimetre).

The colours of cocoons vary between races and among individuals. Some of the finest-looking cocoons are a rich yellow-orange. The pigment is mostly carotenoid, with some flavonoid, extracted and stored from the mulberry leaves by the caterpillars. Its function in the silk is thought to help in protection from harmful effects of ultra violet light. These pigments

From Silkworms to Silk

 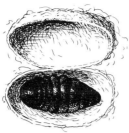

There may be up to 600 m of silk thread in the tough cocoon; here it has been cut open to show the dark-coloured chrysalis inside. Without the protective silk cocoon the chrysalis would be defenceless against predators. In emerging from the chrysalis the silkmoth dissolves a passageway out of the maze of silk threads

contribute to the natural colours of raw silk and are only in the sericin which is removed in the degumming.

Cocoons brought in bulk to the silk-reeling factories were sorted into different grades, at a special place within the factory for handling the cocoons, the *coconiere*. Nine grades of cocoons were recognized:

1. Good cocoons
2. Pointed cocoons (useless for reeling as thread would break)
3. Cocalons (larger than normal)
4. Duppions (double cocoons, where two caterpillars have pupated together)
5. Soufflon (loosely meshed silk and often transparent)
6. Perforated (pierced, broken)
7. Good choquettes (a dead chrysalis stuck to the inside, i.e. the cocoon does not rattle)
8. Bad choquettes (rotten)
9. Calcinated cocoons (contain petrified chrysalids which rattle inside)

These different forms reflect the problems and diseases that caterpillars suffer from, and in some cases, the quality of silk. The calcinated cocoons were actually held in great esteem by the silk-workers of Piedmont where these 'confit' cocoons commanded a higher price than others.

Only a small proportion of the millions of processed cocoons was actually kept for breeding purposes, to ensure a supply of silkworms for the following year, and only the finest cocoons were selected. The male and female cocoons were easily sorted according to weight, the female cocoons being heavier. (It was an easy matter for a weighing machine to be calibrated so that a male

From Silkworms to Silk

Men bring their fresh cocoons to the *place* in the little village of Monoblet, near St Hipployte du Fort to be officially weighed. Louis Pasteur worked in this village to sort out the problems of the mysterious illness which afflicted the Cévennes silkworms last century. Women look on; they have much harder work to do later. The old mulberry tree on the left is the same as that on page 106. Today the *place* is for cars and vans, not horse carts. Photographed in the 1920s

cocoon did not alter the balance, but female cocoons made one side drop.) These cocoons kept for breeding were called *queen cocoons*, regardless of sex. A group of women could sort several hundred cocoons every hour.

Cocoons ready for sale had to be *joli* with no bits of broom adhering. There was a communal weighing station in the local village and by reputation it always underweighed: if one had 100 kg (220 lb) of cocoons *Le Poids Publique* always showed 99 kg (218 lb)! In the 1950s in the Cévennes there were fifty families who brought cocoons for sale prior to the fête day. They were paid either immediately by the middlemen or within a month or so. The cocoons then made their way to Nîmes and perhaps Lyon. The rate for 100 kg (220 lb) of fresh cocoons was 3,000 French francs (30,000 FF ancien). Cocoons weighing 100 kg (220 lb) were sufficient for one family with four hands to produce on twenty-three silkworm beds in a season.

Carrying out various duties in the countryside very often had to be done in synchrony with the phases of the moon or seasons. This was a custom well recognized by Stallenge and is still known in some parts of rural France. The best time to cut mulberry leaves (when there was any choice) was during an increasing moon. Then long shoots of mulberry with their complement of leaves could be cut and offered to the caterpillars. During a waning moon much shorter branches could be cut. It was thought that the silkworms 'desired to hatch and spin their silke during the increase'. The recognition that plants have certain virtues at different times of the month or year was far more evident then than now. In fact a lot of homoeopathy and herbal medicine is based upon the virtues of plants collected at precise times when sap is rising or not and when certain secondary plant substances are in the leaf or not. The ancients, having a greater understanding of the ways of plants, perhaps knew various benefits that escape us today.

In the Cévennes, silkworm-rearing was always completed by 23 June, *La Fête de St Jean*. By this time all the cocoons would have been amassed together and sold. The fête day was to celebrate the completion of all the back-breaking and arduous work. The old branches of broom from which the cocoons had been laboriously plucked were burnt at a ceremonial bonfire. This was obviously good for hygiene control, since if used the following year the broom would have carried disease organisms to the next generation of worms. The first part of the cévenols' year was now completed: silkworms in June, onions in August, sweet chestnuts in October and November, olives in December and January, and cutting winter fuel and broom for next year's silkworms in February and March.

THE *BOMBYX* SILKMOTH

The sex of the moths is determined as soon as the eggs are fertilized. Though visible signs are hard to find in the caterpillar, they become more obvious in the chrysalis, and very obvious in the adult. On emergence male and female moths look completely different. The female is always larger, with a swollen abdomen full of eggs. The male has a pair of feathery feelers (antennae) essential for detecting the female in the wild, but in the case of domesticated silkworms this is a superfluous characteristic.

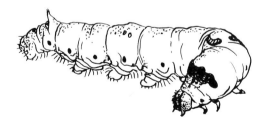

The *Bombyx* silkworm is as large and as fat as a thumb when fully grown, with a greyish-blue colour. It has three pairs of true legs which will eventually become the legs of the moth, and four pairs of prolegs which have suckers and hooks to grip on to leaves. The front end of the caterpillar is larger than the rest of the body and it can retract its forward segments, presenting a menacing stance to predators

Insect hormones or pheromones

The whole of the silkmoth family of moths throughout the world are notorious as producers of sex scents, otherwise called insect hormones or pheromones. Both sexes produce these hormones but greater interest has focused on those of the female since she produces a large, potent amount. Unlike conventional hormones produced inside the body, as in insects or in vertebrates like man, these hormones are secreted to the outside of the body and are dispersed in the wind. Their function in the female is to attract males. Typical of most hormones, they alter the behaviour of the target animal.

Insects have amazing senses of smell, far superior to those of man. In some species, males can detect the female's pheromones up to 5 km (1.9 miles) away downwind. Insects' 'noses' are their feelers or antennae and the more feathery — or pectinated — they are, with divisions and sub-divisions like a radio aerial, the greater the surface area on which the highly volatile pheromones can be detected. Thus, the more elaborate the structure of the antennae the greater the sense of smell, and with two antennae a directional fix can be determined to ascertain the correct position of the female in the dark. Flying upwind towards a greater concentration of pheromones, the male eventually finds his target, rather like a trout swimming upstream following a familiar scent.

The structure of silkmoths' pheromones is complex and has posed biochemists a great many problems.

Females produce a massive amount of scent, undetectable to the human nose, and the male picks this up with his feathery antennae. In silkmoths it is not long before the sexes copulate, soon after emergence. The life of the silkmoth under perfect domesticated conditions is about three to four weeks at low temperatures. It is interesting that as long ago as 1792 John Hunter, the noted surgeon-naturalist, tried to control the genetics of the silkmoth by experimenting with *in vitro* fertilization, i.e. artificial fertilization, not by copulating moths, which would be *in vivo*. He claimed to have successfully hatched caterpillars from a batch of eggs but this has been disproved recently.[2]

From Silkworms to Silk

The wings of the adult silkmoth are small and never used. Their disinclination to fly has been brought on by years of domestication. When excited, especially in males, the wings are often vibrated as if preparing for flight, but nothing ensues. This is merely to raise the metabolic rate of the body so that the insect can become more active. Like all butterflies and moths the wings of the silkmoth are covered with tiny scales which fall off in contact with other insects and cocoons.

There is normally only one generation of silkmoth each year, a characteristic of the genus known as being univoltine. However, in the temperate regions of India, in Jammu and Kashmir, and in the sub-tropical regions of Uttar Pradesh, Himachal Pradesh and Punjab, two generation (bivoltine races) *Bombyx* silkworms have been selected. The Central Silk Board of India evolved four new bivoltine races in the early 1970s. In other parts of India multivoltine races are traditionally reared where mulberry leaves are produced continuously. The recent dramatic rise in silk production in Brazil is partially attributed to them using a multivoltine race with six generations a year.

The number of generations a moth will have during a year often depends on its physiological state, which is governed in turn by the number of daylight hours (photoperiod) and temperature. If the insect goes into

The male is the diminutive sex and does not have the larger wings or abdomen of the female. When excited by the female – which is most of the time – the male will flutter his wings continuously while trying to engage in copulation. Eventually he rubs most of the scales off his wings, and those of his mates

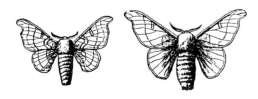

diapause, it is sometimes very difficult to break this dormant period. The *Bombyx* silkmoth naturally goes into diapause in the egg stage, but this can be broken artificially by dipping the newly laid eggs in weak hydrochloric acid for a few minutes and then washing them. The eggs start to develop, change colour and the caterpillars emerge in ten to fourteen days.

The *Bombyx mori* silkmoth is now extinct in the wild. It has been domesticated for over five thousand years and we are unable to say what it really looked like and where exactly it lived, before man took it from the wild and domesticated it. It now survives only courtesy of its commercial use.

Michael Tweedie[3] proposed a plausible theory to account for the demise of the silkmoth in the wild. The silkmoth clearly originated somewhere in China, was domesticated and, through successive generations, was selected for docility in both the caterpillar and the moth. Some of the wild *Bombyx* silkmoths mated with the domesticated races and incorporated this docility gene. As the docility gene was dominant it effectively suppressed the capability of the insect to survive in the wild. An analogous situation has occurred in mammals with the aurochs (the ancestor of domestic cattle) and the Arabian camel. Robert Goodden[4] is also of the opinion that *B. mori* originated in China and other East Asian countries. It almost certainly resembled *B. mandarina* and very probably stems from that species.

OTHER SILKMOTHS

The *Bombyx mori* silkmoth rules supreme for sheer productivity and quality of silk, compared with other silkmoth species. It is, though, part of an extended family of 'silkmoths', which includes the *Saturniidae* and the *Bombycidae* (True Silkmoths), to which it belongs. They all produce silk, but in different proportions.

The 1,200 species of true silkmoths are grouped by scientists into seven moth families spread across the New and Old Worlds. Eighty per cent of the saturnids live in the tropics. We know a little more now than when Thomas Wardle wrote his handbook on the wild silkmoths of India in 1881 in conjunction with the British Museum of Natural History in Kensington. About four hundred species and varieties of silkworm were then known,

From Silkworms to Silk

Major Silkmoths of the World

Antheraea assamensis	Muga silkmoth
Antheraea mylitta	Tusseh silkmoth
Antheraea peryni	Chinese oak silkmoth
Antheraea polyphemus	Polyphemus silkmoth
Antheraea yamamai	Japanese oak silkmoth
Attacus atlas	Atlas silkmoth
Automeris io	Bullseye silkmoth, Io silkmoth
Bombyx mori	Bombyx silkmoth
Callosamia promethea	Spicebush silkmoth
Hyalophora cecropia	Robin or cecropia silkmoth
Hyalophora gloveri	Glover's silkmoth
Pachypasa otus	Syrian silkmoth
Samia (Eri) cynthia	Eri or Ailanthus silkmoth

grouped as mulberry-feeding silkworms (domesticated), atlas and eri group, Actias group, Tusseh and Muga group and a miscellaneous group. The silks from some of these were exhibited by Wardle at the Paris Exhibition of 1878. A recent revision of some important silkmoths by Brian Gardiner (1982) is a useful guide.

The *Bombyx mori* silkmoth has lent itself readily to domestication although it is a relatively small moth and has a small cocoon compared with some of the much larger silkmoth species. No other silkmoth species produces the quality and quantity of silk of the *B. mori* and there is much variation between species. For instance, *C. prometha*, *H. cecropia*, *H. gloveri* and *P. otus* are all poor silk producers, while *A. io* has almost unusable silk. The moth which comes second in importance and commercial application is the Tusseh silkmoth.

India leads the world with research into sources of silk, other than from *B. mori*. These include Tusseh, Muga and Eri silks, otherwise called wild silks because of their cultivation in the rainforest or jungle, rather than in controlled conditions. Its Inter-State Tasar Project (ISTP) is funded by the Swiss Development Cooperation (SDC) and there is currently a Muga Seed Development Project (MSDP) underway in Assam.

From Silkworms to Silk

Tusseh silkmoth

No book on silk would be complete without details of the second major source of silk, that from the Tusseh silkmoth (*A. mylitta*). This is a large Indian moth with a wingspan of 15 cm (5.9 in).

Some authorities include two other closely-related silkmoth species as producers of Tusseh silk. These are the Chinese oak silkmoth and the Japanese oak silkmoth.

The Chinese silkmoth occurs throughout China including the province of Shantung where 'Shantung silk' is produced. Furthermore, Tusseh silk may be obtained from a hybrid between the Chinese oak silkmoth and *A. roylei* — the Himalayan oak silkmoth.

In most cases the cocoons produced from these silkmoths are at least twice as large as those of *B. mori* and are usually greyish-brown in colour. Those of *A. yamamai* are bright green and the silk is difficult to reel without prolonged boiling in potash.

The silk produced is variously called Tusser, Tussar, Tusar, Tusseh, Tussah or Tasar, all of Indian origin. In the Burbham Hills of Bengal the native Indians call it the 'Bughy' silkmoth. Tusseh silk is durable, coarse, dark-coloured and much worn by the Brahmins and other Hindu sects.

Unfortunately Tusseh silkmoths cannot be domesticated. However, a traditional way of looking after and guarding the silkworms in the jungles was practised by the hill people (the Parieahs). They would look for tell-tale droppings on the jungle floor initially to locate the caterpillars. Then they would keep watch over them and protect them from the attentions of crows and bats. Male moths were often marked with identification marks particular to each district, since the Parieahs believed that they migrated, sometimes over 161 km (100 miles). Such detail is described in Roxburgh's 1802 account of the Tusseh silkmoth. The natives of Bengal and many other places in India still rear the Tusseh silkmoth in the wild.

The sorts of jungle plants on which the wild silkworms are tended include *Rhamnus jujuba* (the Byer of the Hindus), *Terminalia alata glabra*, the mangrove, *Sonneratia acida* and the beautiful crape myrtle, *Lagerstroemia indica*.

The harmless exploitation of this natural resource of wild silkmoths from the jungles continues successfully today, without any signs of domestication or deleterious effect on natural populations. In 1877 Tusseh silk from all the Indian villages produced a considerable amount for export. The London market was consuming an average of 238 bales of Tusseh silk, and this

From Silkworms to Silk

Cocoon

Male Moth

The stages in the life cycle of the Tusseh silkmoth are shown here as drawn in Roxburgh's 1804 manuscript, published in the *Transactions* of the Linnean Society of London

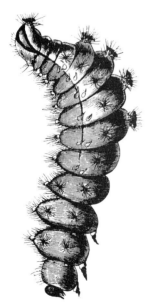
Fully-grown silkworm

Female Moth

Cocoon cut open to show crysalis

increased threefold in 1879 for the Paris Exhibition. There must have been quirks in the market, since in 1878 Wardle records that two thousand bales of Tusseh silk could not find a market, even at 2s. 3d. to 2s. 9d. per pound.

Eri (Ailanthus, Arrindy, Arrindi) silkmoth

This Indian species is indigenous to the Dinagepore and Rungpore districts of Bengal. Its relatives, however, are all found in the New World. There are several distinct races of the Eri silkmoth, regarded by some as true species. The two major races or subspecies are *S. cynthia ricini* and *S. cynthia canningi*. These can be found in areas stretching up into Assam and into Megalaya.

The species is very hardy and has been introduced to many parts of Europe and the USA, where in places it has naturalized itself in city parks. Its Ailanthus name recalls one of the caterpillars' food plants, the tree of heaven, *Ailanthus altissima*, a widespread species of urban environments in Western Europe.

In India the 'arrindy' silkworm was especially cared for by workers in the field. The silk is not as uniform as *Bombyx* silk and cannot be reeled. This means that Eri silk has to be carded, like wool. Woven, it makes tough garments, which Roxburgh found were in constant use for up to twenty years by both men and women.

The Eri silkmoth was introduced to Italy in 1856 and was brought to Spain a few years later for domestication. It now lives in the wild at sea level in the region of Barcelona on the Mediterranean coast, where it breeds as one generation on *Prunus, Ilex, Ligustrum, Sorbus,* and *Viburnum*. It flies in April and May.

Muga (Moonga, Mooga) silkmoth

The Muga silkmoth is a native of the Himalayan foothills of Assam, where up to three generations of the moth can be obtained each year, though in most parts only one generation is the rule. India holds the world monopoly in the production of Muga silk.

The golden-yellow Muga silk was much used by the Ahom kings for ceremonial dresses. Today, the old and the respectable classes in Assam wear dhotees, chapkans, turbans and mekhalas – a kind of shirt made from about a metre of silk, elaborately embroidered – made from Muga silk.

Francis I made sure
that the celebrated
meeting between
himself and Henry
VIII at The Field of
the Cloth of Gold in
1520 on 7 June was a
most lavish affair,
even to the point of
embarrassing Henry
with such French
indifference of
largesse. It is
reported that the
impromptu palace
and grounds
between Guines and
Ardres in northern
France covered 1,672
sq m (2,000 sq yd)
and that sixteen
thousand books of
silk were used to
make the tents.
Henry was escorted
by five thousand
followers dressed in
sumptuous velvet,
satin and cloth of
gold, and Cardinal
Wolsey was escorted
by two hundred
gentlemen dressed
in crimson velvet

THE · STORY · OF · SILK

ABOVE: Two types of flowers are found on the black mulberry (*Morus nigra*), male and female, but neither are particularly striking. Female flowers which later develop as fruits are covered with tiny 'hairs', whilst the male flowers have tiny anthers

BELOW: Fruits of the black mulberry are red before they become dark red, almost black prior to falling – hence their name. The luscious fruits make plenty of mess if left unpicked but many find them delicious to eat. Non-bearing mulberry species have now been developed so that one can enjoy the nature of the mulberry tree without its attendant mess

ABOVE: *Bombyx* silkworms are gregarious by nature and are disinclined to wander far. Their colour can be variable according to the strain, and they may or may not have a dark band between their segments. The silkworms can telescope their first few segments together in times of danger, thus giving an appearance of a much larger 'head'

BELOW: The *Bombyx* silkmoth has been domesticated for five thousand years and both the male and female have lost the power of flight. Males have larger antennae ('feelers', but actually they are used as noses) than females and use their sense of smell to locate their mates. The featheriness of the antennae gives an indication of the detection of smell; the more feathery, the greater the sense of smell. Typically the males of silkmoth species around the world have more feathery antennae than females. After mating, the female silkmoth lays eggs either on her cocoon or on twigs

Collecting cocoons and weaving silk, from Giovanni Boccaccio's *Declaris mulieribus*, a fifteenth-century French manuscript in the British Library

From Silkworms to Silk

Chinese oak silkmoth

A. peryni is a native of northern China, but it too has been introduced to Europe and the USA. It was introduced to Europe for silk-rearing at the end of the nineteenth century. In about 1875 it was introduced to Spain in the regions of Navarra and Guipuzcoa, having previously been on the Balearic islands of Mallorca and Menorca. Like the Eri silkmoth it is now naturalized in the region of Barcelona as well as Castellon de la Plana.

Atlas silkmoth

The Atlas moth, *Attacus atlas*, is the largest moth species in the world, with a wingspan of 28 cm (11.02 in). Its caterpillar is large too, and produces sufficient silk in its cocoon for it to be used in sericulture. Silk produced from the Atlas moth is called 'fagara silk'. India is the only place where the silk from the giant Atlas moth is collected and processed, albeit on a small scale. In fact India is the only place in the world where all four types of silk – Tusseh, Muga, Eri and Faraga – are home-produced.

The insect with the largest wingspan in the world, the Atlas moth, *Attacus atlas*, has a large caterpillar which produces a silken cocoon of use to man. Silk from the Atlas moth, known as 'fagara' silk, has been used by the natives of India, possibly for thousands of years. The moth does not lend itself to domestication commercially and thus does not contribute significantly to world silk production

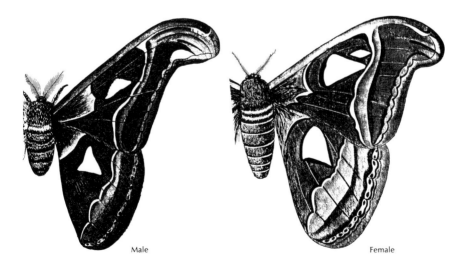

Male

Female

House rules for silk-workers

These rules were for silk-workers at special silk-reeling factories in the Cévennes. The management of the factory paid transport expenses. Hours of work in 1904 were 6 a.m. to 8 a.m., 9 a.m. to 1 p.m. and 2 p.m. to 6 p.m.

1. Silk-workers must obey those responsible for supervising them, both in their lodging house and in the silk-reeling room.
2. At the first sound of the siren at 5.30 a.m., all silk-workers must get up, wash and arrive at the place of work by five minutes before the 6 a.m. work time.
3. It is expressly forbidden to eat or keep food in the dormitory which must be kept absolutely clean. Every week two girls will be nominated in turn by the supervisor to sweep the floor and empty the dirty water.
4. The windows of the dormitory will be kept open during the day and the beds will be kept turned back to permit the straw mattresses to be aired until 8 a.m.
5. During the morning rest period between 8 a.m. and 9 a.m. each worker will make her bed, and carefully shake the sheets and blankets.
6. During the rest period workers are allowed to walk and amuse themselves in the courtyard adjacent to their lodging. They may only go into town to make purchases which are absolutely necessary, having obtained permission from the supervisor.
7. It is absolutely forbidden to go into the town for any pretext whatsoever {sic}. The street door will be locked at 6 p.m. in the evening in winter and 9 p.m. in summer, and the courtyard door will be locked at 8 p.m. in the winter and 9 p.m. in summer. Girls who go into town outside of the permitted hours without authorization from the director will be dismissed and lose their rights to a return journey.
8. With reference to rule 7, workers who draw attention to themselves because of their unsuitable dress or conduct will also be dismissed.
9. After 9 p.m. the lights will be put out, both in the dorm and refectory when silk-workers must be in bed and keep quiet.
10. Silk-workers must go to church on Sundays and feast days.
11. Any infringement of these rules will be severely dealt with either by fine or dismissal or extra duties.

Working in the filature was almost exclusively women's occupation, though men were required to regulate some of the heavier mechanical equipment. Here a rather important *madame* appears to be in charge

PROCESSING THE SILK

Unreeling silk from cocoons was labour-intensive and done in purpose-built factories. Invariably the buildings were long to house the complicated equipment, and were sited next to flowing water, the source of energy to turn the machinery.

In the Cévennes many of these long filature buildings still stand along the major rivers. One of the most impressive is the ruinous filature factory at Laroque near Ganges, which dominates the little village. A huge barrage across the Hèrault harnessed the water to one side, so that it drove the many wheels and cogs needed for the mechanical extraction of silk threads. Another three filatures stand further upstream on the Hèrault, one at Ganges, a small one towards the Pont d'Hèrault, and the third at Peyregrosse. Yet another with a magnificent double sweep of steps is the Filature de Pont de Salindres (between Anduze and Saint Jean du Gard) on the River Gardon.

Filature was a job for women and young girls, their nimble fingers being able to master the fine threads and connect them to machinery. It was a hard life; ten hours' work each day, except Sunday.

From Silkworms to Silk

A group of workers photographed in 1922 at the Château de Mareilles (Le Vigan) pulling the cocoons from the broom 'tents' (décoconage)

Work inside the noisy mechanical filature was regulated into a variety of sequential activities designed to unreel the silk from the cocoon, collect it up and prepare it ready for shipment, dyeing or preparation into silk materials.

First of all the incoming cocoons had to be cleaned up ready for processing and picked over for pieces of leaf and twig tangled in the silk fibres. This process was called *décoconet*. Then the cocoons were steamed (*étouffage*) for three minutes to stifle the chrysalis inside, and submerged in boiling water. This helped to loosen up the sericin – a glue laid down by the caterpillar to bind all its silk threads together. Without the sericin loosened the continuous thread of silk could not be unwound mechanically. Ladies who were involved with this 'baptism' in water process were called the *bateuses* and often this particular job was for old ladies, who had hardened hands used to dipping into the hot water. One can imagine the organic smell which emanated from these pots through the decomposition of warm chrysalids. The cocoons would at this stage be dehydrated and dried in a chamber so that they could be stored for future use.

If the cocoons were to be unreeled immediately, they were put in hot water where rotating brushes would collect the silk threads which by now would be coming off the cocoons. This process was called *purgeage*.

A young lady, a *fileuse*, would collect several of these threads with their bobbing cocoons on the end, and pass them behind her to *attacheurs*. Their job was to attach each silk thread to the machinery which would then proceed to pull the continuous thread from the cocoon until there was nothing left (*dévidage*, *enroulage* or *unreeling*). The raw silk at this stage is

67

Workers at the Lullingstone Silk Farm, Kent reel the silk threads from the silk cocoons after they have been immersed in hot water. The machine continues to unwind the threads after they have been attached to the machines.

called *soie grège* and is normally 20–22 denier by weight. If it is doubled or twisted with a similar sized strand of silk one or more times (throwing) on the machines, it becomes 40-44 or 60-66 denier. This tensioning process is called *moulinage* and *assemblage*.

What was left after these processes was the remains of the chrysalis, which would be thrown away. The thread of another cocoon would then be placed on the machine as soon as possible so as to maintain the silk at a uniform denier. Of the quality of the silk cocoons coming to the filature, there were sometimes poor cocoons, known as *peau*, which were small or malformed. These had to be used up, so it was customary to twist three threads from good cocoons with one bad thread.

From Silkworms to Silk

ABOVE: Here the ladies of the filature – an all-woman work-force – sort the cocoons ready for processing. Laying the cocoons in the sun would have kept them dry and stopped any bad chrysalis rotting inside the silk. Photographed at Maison Rouge, St Jean du Gard, Gard

BELOW: This weighing machine sorted out male from female cocoons according to their different weight. It is calibrated to weigh male cocoons, which are lighter than the females so that they do not depress the arm. When a female cocoon is placed on the arm its heavier weight causes the arm to touch the table. It was essential to keep a selection of male and female cocoons over to the next year so that an adequate supply of eggs was maintained. This machine obviated the need to dissect the cocoon and sex the chrysalis

From Silkworms to Silk

The typical all-women workforce in a filature stop work for a moment to face the camera, illuminated by the light of the big side and end windows

It was in the boiling water of the cauldron that most silkworms met their death. The hot water also served to loosen the sericin glue which binds the silk fibres together. Without loosening it, the silk could not be wound off. The cocoons would be submerged for a few minutes only

ABOVE: Threads from two or more bobbins of raw silk are twisted together to make a thicker silk thread. Here the *attacheurs* are connecting the threads together

BELOW: A working loom makes a lot of noise, with the shuttle shooting across between the warp (carried on the hanging sections) and the weft, which is drawn along the axis of the machine

From Silkworms to Silk

Octogenarian Madame Marie-Louise Ducros of Cabanevieille, St Martial, photographed in August 1989, used to work in one of the filatures at Sumene. She recalls the hard work and the chapped hands from working all day with cocoons in boiling water. Her son, Rolland, and his wife, Georgette, all used to rear silkworms at Cabanevieille up to the 1950s

The silk was collected on to large circular reels, and then transferred to bobbins. The whole filature was a pretty sight when up and running, especially if the natural yellow of the cocoon fibres was showing through. Perhaps the most disliked job was being a *fileuse*, since their hands had to be in and out of the boiling water. Hands had to be treated overnight with a home-made *pomade* to get them ready for the next day's work.

NOTES

1. Richard Kane of the University of Philadelphia has kindly drawn my attention to this precise kind of detail which has been repeated in Muriel Spark's novel *The Hothouse by the East River*, London, Viking (1970), in which the woman also incubates silkworm eggs in her bosom.
2. Sir Cyril Clarke of Liverpool University has examined the 200 year old eggs in the Hunterian Museum housed in the Royal College of Surgeons in London and has found them to be simply collapsed eggs. It does not appear that Hunter was successful; cf. 'Lepidopteran Genetics' in *Antenna*, Vol. 13, No. 4, p. 179.
3. M. Tweedie, *Insect Life* (1977).
4. Robert Goodden, personal communication.

CHAPTER 4

Mulberry Trees

To Master Nicholas Gesse
The tree acquainted with the British soyle,
And the true use unto our people taught,
Shall trebble ten times recompence the toil,
(From forraine parts) of him it hither brought.

From a poem by Michael Drayton (1563-1631)
in William Stallenge's book of 1609

I t is a common myth that silkworms (i.e. *Bombyx mori*) will eat all sorts of plants other than mulberry, and Henry Barham's comments in his *An Essay Upon The Silkworm* (1719) are typical:

> The silkworm will feed on occasion upon the leaves of elm, poplar, oak, apple-tree, crab tree, cherry tree and plumb-tree, bramble leaves, dandelyon and lettice and sundry other trees, shrubs and leaves.

Through evolution *Bombyx* silkworms have become inextricably linked with the mulberry tree which belongs to the mulberry family (*Moraceae*) and they are now entirely dependent upon it for their sustenance. In fact the caterpillars probably derived some sort of chemical defence from the secondary plant substances in the leaves which are subsequently stored in their bodies.[1] Quite what the natural predators of silkworms and silkmoths were in the wild, other than birds, is impossible to say, since the silkmoth now only occurs in the domestic environment; it is extinct in the wild. This close coevolution between a moth and a tree, not unusual within the world of insects, has to be admired for its intricacy and uniqueness.

The *Moraceae* is a fairly large plant family with up to 1,850 species

Mulberry Trees

worldwide. Members are mostly tropical and subtropical; relatively few are temperate species. There are some interesting and surprising relatives however, such as the fig (*Ficus carica*), whose young leaves may be mistaken for the mulberrry, and the Osage orange (*Maclura pomifera*). The fig shares two characteristics with its fellow mulberries: it has a sprawling nature and its newly unfurled leaves can look like the lower and much-indented leaves often sported by the mulberry. In maturity, however, the leaves of the fig bear little resemblance to those of normal mulberry leaves.

The flowers of mulberry trees are generally small and unisexual, and each sex is carried on the stem as a separate spike. Mulberry leaves are arranged alternately along the stem and the fruits are closely packed drupes (fleshy with a kernel), in many cases edible. When leaves or stems are broken a white latex is sometimes liberated. Curiously, the *Morus* genus of mulberry trees defy the attentions of many leaf-eating insects, other than the silkworm, and are rarely eaten by any natural pest – undoubtedly due to the deterrent nature of the leaves.

In Europe there are two similar-looking species: the white and the black mulberry. The black is found predominantly in Britain, the white in the rest of Europe. The only other common mulberry species to be found in Europe is the paper mulberry (*Broussonetia papyrifera*) which today makes a useful street and shade tree by itself or grafted onto false acacia (*Robinia pseudoacacia*) root-stock. In the USA both the black and the white mulberry tree are naturalized, having originally been introduced, and there are a further two species of native mulberry tree, the red mulberry and the Texan mulberry.

THE BLACK (OR PERSIAN) MULBERRY, *MORUS NIGRA*

Identification

The leaves of the black mulberry typically have lobes at their base, and it is this feature which distinguishes them from the white mulberry. The margin is weakly serrated and the lamina relatively large. Some leaves of the black mulberry can be immense, more than 22 cm (9 in) long. There is a curious highly lobed and indented form of the leaf which is found on some trees, the form of which departs greatly from the normal mulberry leaf. This variety was described as the 'Lesser Black Mulberry' by Philip Miller writing in 1731. This leaf formation is also seen in the white mulberry and bears a striking resemblance to the emerging leaves of figs as described earlier.

ABOVE: Black Mulberry. The heart-shaped leaves are an important characteristic in the identification of this species. The base of the leaf is straight across in the white mulberry

BELOW: Black Mulberry. Both black and white mulberry trees often have heavily lobed leaves low down near the base of the tree. In this respect they both show their close evolutionary proximity to figs which have a similar leaf. It is difficult to separate the leaves of black and white if only these peculiar leaves are chosen for comparison

Mulberry Trees

Heavily-lobed leaves like this are usually seen at the base of the tree, where very small shoots originate from the bole, but occasionally may be seen at the apex of young trees, twenty to thirty years old. Some trees show a propensity for this leaf formation, others not at all.

The floral parts of each sex are borne as separate structures on the stems, such as the catkins in the male. In some specimens the catkins can be 3 cm long. Tiny female flowers are borne over the drupe which becomes the fruit.

The black mulberry is named after its fruits, but their black nature is not always obvious. The fruits are actually red most of the time, but just prior to being really ripe they take on a deeper red hue which verges on black. It is in this condition that the fruits fall from the tree and collapse with all their juices on impact.

Black mulberries have a long fruiting period, in Britain at least, from late July to September when birds such as blackbirds feast on the fruits. The red fruits seem to be in the trees for several weeks over the summer before they become excessively ripe and fall, and some fruits do not fall at all but remain in the tree into early winter, becoming covered in a growth of white fungus.

The profile of the black mulberry is most distinctive. It has a spreading nature – sometimes as far as 25 m (82 ft) on a single span; trees are always wider than they are tall. This frequently causes collapse of a heavy limb and if the conditions are right the fallen branch will root and produce a new tree. There is a fine example of this in the East Sussex parish of Rodmell, near Lewes, where there is a grove of what appears to be about thirty mulberry trees. In fact it is one tree that has collapsed, grown further on its 'knuckles', collapsed again and grown yet more 'trees'. The effect is quite extraordinary and possibly unique in Britain. It has, however, been known in the past since one such spreading tree was engraved for Loudon in 1838.[2] By virtue of a humid climate one mulberry can obviously produce a small grove of related trees.

Black mulberry trees grow fast and furious. They appear to age quickly, contrary to popular belief. Scores of venerable specimens are propped with wood, bound up and supported in chains. One gigantic specimen which required special treatment is described at a Ministry of Defence establishment in Essex. It was:

repaired with the enthusiastic help of the Garrison Engineer. It absorbed 6 cwt of steel bars, 1½ cu yd of concrete, 14 lb of bituminous paint, 28 lb of bituminous sealing compound, 56 lb of fertilizer, and 15,000 gallons of water. It is still, ten years later, making vigorous growth.[3]

Mulberry Trees

The spreading nature of black mulberries can be exploited through espaliering; David Stuart[4] reported that there were two large espaliered nineteenth-century mulberries at Holkham Hall in Norfolk – now they are recumbent and it is thought the 200-year-old kitchen garden walls were built around the existing trees.

Apart from their spreading nature mulberries can be recognized in winter by the great proliferation of shoots and twigs at the extremities of their branches. It is as if there has been furious growth at the tips of the limbs, in some cases approaching the concentrated growth of 'witches broom' fungus galls on silver birch (*Betula pendula*) trees caused by an invading fungus. This curious concentrated twig effect erroneously suggests longevity, but indeed the noted tree expert Alan Mitchell recalls how he carefully calculated someone's massive mulberry tree from its girth and general appearance to be in the order of three hundred years old, only to be told it was planted fifty years earlier![5]

The autumn colour of mulberry trees is quite distinctive and the lemon-yellow hue of the leaves could only possibly be confused with lilac (*Syringa* spp.) which turns the same colour in late September to mid-October. The rich orange glow of the gnarled bark in winter is more easily confused with that of the sycamore (*Acer pseudoplatanus*) and the limbs of sycamore can also look a little gnarled and twisted like those of the mulberry.

The mulberry is one of the last to relinquish its autumn leaves. Equally, the leaves of the black mulberry are the last to come out in Britain, safely after the last damaging spring frosts. This was the time that John Evelyn recommended bringing potted plants out of the orangery:

> Never expose your Oranges, Limons, and like tender trees, whatever the season flatter, 'til the Mulberry puts forth its leafe, then bring them boldly out of the Greene-house; but for a fortnight, let them stand in the shade of an hedge, where the sun may glimmer onely upon them.[6]

Heights of black mulberries rarely reach beyond 9 m (29 ft) because of their spreading nature. This may be useful for distinguishing black from white mulberries since white are usually taller. If height cannot be used then there is very little which distinguishes the two species in their leafless condition. Curiously there are no known varieties or cultivars of the black mulberry; a surprising feature since its relation, the white mulberry, has an enormous number.

Mulberry Trees

The English plantsman Christopher Lloyd[7] recommends the black mulberry for gardens. His own garden, Great Dixter (Kent), had two mulberries either side of a series of curved steps planted by the famous designer Edwin Lutyens. Sadly, one tree was blown down in the 1950s, and the remaining one became a casualty of the Great Storm of October 1987. The moral for mulberries in gardens is to allow them plenty of space and plant them in the lee of the house. Never put a mulberry in a kitchen garden, as William Cobbett said,[8] for it takes up too much room.

Origin and distribution

Most authorities agree that the black mulberry came from Persia. Curiously it has never been found growing as a true wild species.

In Britain the black mulberry is the most abundant mulberry species, and some people never see a white one; in France, the opposite is true. In Piedmont (Italy) and in Provence (France) black mulberry trees used to be grown during the last century for their luscious fruit rather than for silkworm food, for their leaves were thought to be poisonous to the silkworms. But as British silkworm-rearers can vouch, the black is avidly eaten by caterpillars. The black mulberry was also grown occasionally in high mountain areas as it was thought that it was hardier than the white.

In contrast to this, during the cold winter of 1984–5 my young white mulberries survived and the black mulberries were apparently killed. Although I waited until the customary Midsummer Day (21 June) for any sign of life, the black finally sprouted at the base but died a few days later.

Both the black and the white mulberry were introduced to Europe, but when? Very early English accounts mention mulberries but neither the colour nor species. However, it is clear that the Romans cultivated mulberry trees in orchards, since Pliny the Naturalist (c. 23–79 AD) describes them at his coastal villa near Rome. Although there is no documentary evidence that mulberries were brought to Britain or elsewhere in northern Europe by the Romans, the noted gardening chronicler, Miles Hadfield (1903–82) mentioned that 'possibly they [the Romans] brought the black mulberry to Britain'.[9] More substantial information comes from John Harris[10] who states from archaeological evidence that the mulberry (species not stated), as well as the fig, peach and medlar, were certainly introduced to England in Roman times. Support for this is seen in the existence of Anglo-Saxon and Old German names for the mulberry. In West Germany the mulberry was

Mulberry Trees

This black mulberry tree in a private garden at Rodmell, south of Lewes in East Sussex, has extended itself many times over by means of its collapsed limbs which have taken root at the 'knuckles'. There is now, on the site of the original mulberry, what appears to be a grove of mulberry trees, where in fact there is only one. John Claudius Loudon published an engraving of an extraordinary spreading mulberry tree in his 1838 book *Arboretum et Fruticetum Britanicum*

documented as early as the twelfth century in lists belonging to the Abbess Hildegard of Bingen (SW of Frankfurt). In France John de Garlande's garden in Paris in 1220 also had mulberries.

The English monk and chronicler Gervais of Canterbury (d. *c.* 1210) wrote that the knights who murdered Thomas à Becket at Canterbury in 1170 threw off their cloaks and gowns under a branching mulberry tree.[11]

There are other early references to mulberries in York in the thirteenth century; the prebendal house and gardens called *Mulberiahalle* and *Mulberihawe* were named after mulberries in 1276 and 1361 respectively. There still exists a black mulberry at Ribston in Yorkshire, once a stronghold of the Templar and Hospitallers, and it is thought that the returning Crusaders brought back the mulberry as well as the oriental plane tree. This must have happened before 1312 when the order was suppressed.

From the accounts of Henry III (1216–77) we learn that his fruiterer, one 'John The Fruiter of London' supplied cherries, mulberries, medlars and peaches for the king's table. These must have been local, for mulberries do not travel. No details of colour or species are given. There are also documents which record that the clerk to the king paid 6s. 8d. for mulberry and raspberry drinks in 1241. In 1382, at St Albans (Hertfordshire), a monk refers to mulberries in his catalogue of garden plants.

Anne Boleyn (1507–36), wife of Henry VIII (1491–1547), is said, according to Muller,[12] to have planted a mulberry at Sheerness (Isle of Sheppey, north Kent) when she visited the islands before marrying Henry in

ABOVE: The mulberry trees at Hatfield House are reputed to have been planted by James I. Some have been lost and have been replaced. This is a veritable survivor with a huge bole. The short stature is due to it having been pollarded many times; branches of the black mulberry typically grow horizontally, sprawl and often need propping. One of the last tree species to come out in leaf in the spring, the mulberry is also one of the last to shed its leaves

BELOW: It was during the reign of Queen Victoria that the mulberry avenue at Windsor Castle was laid out in the queen's private garden at Home Park. The avenue is comprised of seven pairs of black mulberry, though some have now been replaced. As far as is known, the avenue is unique in Britain, though another once existed at Rye (Kent)

This white mulberry tree at Mt Vernon, Virginia, was planted by President George Washington in 1785. It has grown fast, as white mulberry trees do in North America, and in 1989 was about 3.3 m in circumference at 1 m from the ground. It stands near the entrance to the grounds next to a white gazebo. George Washington, like Thomas Jefferson, had at least a passing interest in the silk industry and perhaps this stimulated both of them to plant mulberry trees

Mulberry Trees

Mulberry tart made
from the squashy
fruits of the black
mulberry makes a
delicious dessert

1533. Was she planting mulberries to help support a silk industry, and did she plant any in the grounds of her Tudor house at Hever (Kent)? There is only a 40-year-old black mulberry there today. The herbalist John Gerard (1545–1612) mentions in his celebrated *Herbal* that mulberries were growing in various English gardens in 1597.

These early accounts of mulberries in England are very interesting since it is generally assumed that mulberries, black ones at least, were introduced during the reign of Henry VII, towards the end of the fifteenth century, along with other useful fruits such as apricots.

It is also sometimes erroneously stated that the mulberries at Syon Park (Middlesex) were the original trees introduced to England. These were planted in *c.* 1548 and may well be some of the oldest mulberry trees in Britain. Gerald Howe[13] agrees that the Syon mulberries 'were amongst the first introduced to England' and quotes Dugdale (a leading botanical authority) that one old mulberry tree there bore the label '1546'. Hilliers[14] repeats the often misquoted information that they are said to have been first grown in England in the sixteenth century.

By the early seventeenth century James I had, of course, introduced masses of black mulberry trees in his great adventure and Parkinson, as admitted in *Paradius Terrestris* of 1629, knew of three types of mulberry in England – the

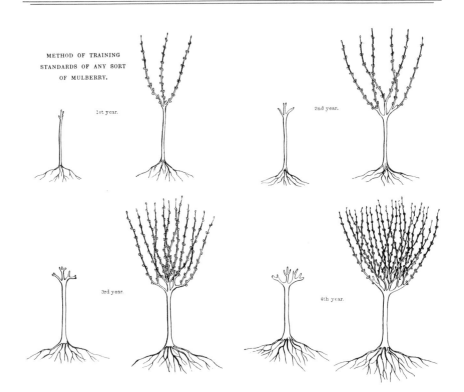

METHOD OF TRAINING
STANDARDS OF ANY SORT
OF MULBERRY.

1st year.

2nd year.

3rd year.

4th year.

How to train
mulberry trees or
bushes so that they
will produce large
yields of leaves was
depicted in Mrs
Whitby's 1848 book,
*A Manual for Rearing
Silkworms in England*

white, black and Red Virginian. The Red Virginian was the New World *Morus rubra* from a land where the younger John Tradescant had been collecting specimens for his father at Lambeth. A century later an unsuccessful attempt to establish mulberry trees in Hertfordshire was made by a certain Thomas Andrew Knight, and from this it was concluded that it was 'far too north' and that the trees weren't happy growing there.

One of the last of the more recent attempts to establish mulberry trees in Britain was reported in the *Morning Herald* of 9 July 1835 when The Norfolk Co. had been set up to produce silkworms. The company planted 100,000 trees and 'already had 120,000 insects'. What became of these trees we do not know; Norfolk Museum Services cannot find any documentary trace of them nor of any silkworm production in Norfolk.

Her Majesty the Queen presently looks after what is probably the only surviving mulberry avenue in Britain. This is in the private gardens of Home Farm on the Windsor Castle Estate. The seven pairs of black mulberry trees were planted around the time of Queen Victoria, though the exact date is not known; some of the trees are recumbent, while all are very fructiferous.

Mulberry Trees

There used to be another avenue of black mulberries behind the High Street of the old smuggling (and Huguenot) town of Rye in East Sussex but this has disappeared, leaving a legacy of just a few trees in the town.

THE WHITE (OR SILKWORM OR RUSSIAN) MULBERRY,

MORUS ALBA

Identification

The most useful characteristic which distinguishes *alba* from *nigra* is the shape of the leaf. M. *alba* does not have the extended lobes at the base. The *alba* leaves are very slightly hairy on the undersides and the leaf stalk may also be hairy. In some lights the fine hairs appear as a grey-white bloom, completely absent on the leaves of the black mulberry. Both species of mulberry may have the multi-lobed leaves so often found around the base of the trees – the 'lesser black mulberry' effect of Philip Miller.

The fruits are distinct. They are always opaque and whitish, sometimes faintly yellowish or pink, never pure white. As they mature they become suffused with pink and the remains of the floral parts wither, giving the fruit a blackish look. At this stage they taste extremely sweet, almost too much so, and have none of the acidic-sour taste or juiciness of black mulberry fruits. Confusion cannot occur between the fruits of the white and black mulberries since they are quite different. The mature fruits of the white are not as large as those of the black mulberry which become lush and engorged with deep-red juice just before falling.

During the winter months it may be difficult to identify an *alba* from a *nigra* since their barks are very similar. Generally the white mulberry grows taller and is less spreading than its relative, but of course this will not be so if the mulberry in question has been pollarded, which is frequently the case.

Varieties

Unlike the black mulberry, the white mulberry has many varieties. The French recognize far more varieties and forms than the English, since working with silkworms and mulberry trees was a way of life for many generations of people and they have noted subtle differences in form.

ABOVE: White
Mulberry. Note how
the base of the leaf
blade is straight
across, and this
distinguishes it from
the black mulberry

BELOW: White Mulberry.
The irregular leaves
are incredibly similar
to the equivalent
leaves of the black
mulberry and it is
difficult, almost
impossible, to
distinguish the
species using these
leaves alone

Mulberry Trees

The most impressive is the weeping mulberry (cultivar (cv.) *Pendula*) a resplendent variety which cascades from about 3 m (9.8 ft).[15] Other varieties include a pigmy white mulberry, cv. *Fegyvernekiana*; one with deeply-lobed leaves, cv. *Lacinata*; and a very large leaved variety with leaves up to 28 cm (11 in) long, cv. *Macrophylla*.

There is another cultivar of the white mulberry which has received some attention in the past, cv. *Multicaulis*, which as the name implies has several stems rather than one main trunk. A fine example, planted in 1905, stands in the Edinburgh Botanic Gardens. This variety was originally introduced to France from the Phillipines by Perrotet in 1821. In fact it is sometimes called the Philippines mulberry.

In her delightful 1848 book on silkworms Mrs Whitby mentions that she imported one hundred standard and one thousand small plants of *Morus multicaulis* in 1836. These established themselves very successfully in her grounds at Newlands, near Lymington, Hampshire. The cultivar thrived and as she says 'one acre of land, planted with 2,400 *Morus multicaulis*, will at the end of two years' growth yield from 20,000 to 24,000 cuttings, sufficient, when rooted, for another acre.' Mrs Whitby mentions nurserymen in England and France from whom this stock can be obtained. She also mentions some silk production being carried out near Truro, Cornwall, by a Mr John Hodson.

Presenting her sylvicultural results to the Royal Agricultural Society of England, Mrs Whitby was very proud of the fact that she had succeeded with this particular mulberry. She had had the inspiration after visiting northern Italy in 1834 after learning that an English gentleman had set up a silk manufacturing establishment near Milan and had doubled his capital in three years. The British climate was ideal for this particular mulberry; she had travelled extensively and found that Britain did not have the north-east winds of Lombardy which blew mulberry trees down, the thirty-three day fog of Milan or the snow and 'iron-bound' frosty land, or the uncertain weather of Florence!

Multicaulis also made its way to the USA in 1829 when it was introduced by a Dr Felix Pascalis of New York. It was then used widely and had the advantage that two crops of silk could be produced each year, since leaves will regrow quickly. The efficaciousness of this cultivar was verified by Madame Parmentier at her horticultural establishment on Long Island, New York State.

Other white mulberry varieties include cv. *Pyramidalis* which has a conical profile, another with small leaves, cv. *Tatarica*, and one with yellow veins on the leaves, cv. *Venosa*. There is also a dwarf 'Nana' form.

Mulberry Trees

In 1944 Lady Hart Dyke acquired several thousand cuttings of a interesting variety of the white mulberry called 'Osigian'. This variety was developed by a Dr Vartan K. Osigian in Venezuela especially for the long leaves, up to 22 in long. 'Osigian' proved to be successful for Lady Hart Dyke. Two thousand cuttings were later made from a handful of her plants at Ayot St Lawrence after she died, and now form the basis of the mulberry plantation at Worldwide Butterflies & Lullingstone Silk Farm in Dorset. This variety produces enormous leaves up to 30 cm across, even bigger if grown in plastic tunnels. The 'Osigian' variety is believed to be a distinct mulberry species rather than a variety of the *M. alba*, according to Robert Goodden who is the only person in England who has grown it regularly in quantity.

Less scientific, but showing a greater eye for detail, the French had their own names for the varieties of the white mulberry. Constant du Castelet, in his book on the white mulberry and its varieties published in 1760, noted those listed below growing in Provence. This part of southern France saw so much activity and experimentation in breeding silkworms and finding suitable food plants that it is hardly surprising that so many varieties were known. It is interesting that he describes a female tree, since dioecious mulberry trees – those that bear male and female floral parts on separate trees – had never been recorded before. Individual male and female parts occur separately on the same tree and it is easy to miss the male tassel-like catkins in a surfeit of luscious fruit. The varieties he describes are sorted according to the shape of leaf or colour and taste of mulberries. The first four are what he calls 'wild species' which give little seed; the rest are all grafted and produce much better stock.

Mûrier feuille-rose (rounded leaves, small insipid white fruits)
This was also called 'The Rose-leaved mulberry' by other authorities, as it has round leaves like roses. Presumably this means the 'leaflets' which make up the compound leaves of roses.

Mûrier feuille-dorée (long shiny leaves, small purple fruits)
This was perhaps the 'Small Queen' variety noted by others.

Mûrier feuille-batarde (leaves twice as large as *feuille-rose*, irregular along its long axis, black fruits)
This was perhaps the 'Roman leaf' noted by others.

Mûrier femelle (spiny tree, fruits appear before the trilobed leaves appear)

Mulberry Trees

ABOVE: Old mulberry trees, probably fifty years old, are closely clipped for fuel and forage, their knobbly heads making an attractive sight on a Cévennes hillside in winter

BELOW: In the spring, shoots carry large numbers of leaves which, in the Cévennes, are used for goats rather than silkworms

Mulberry Trees

Mûrier reine à feuille luisantes (much larger tree than all preceeding, ash-coloured fruits)

Mûrier grosse-reine (dark green leaves, black fruits)

Mûrier feuille de phlox (dark green leaves resembling the last variety but not as long, scented stems; numerous fruits which never reach maturity)

Mûrier feuille d'Espagne (very large thick leaves, with a matt surface and long white fruits)

Monsieur Boitard, in his 1828 *Traite de la Culture de Mûrier*, recalls that in Syria the best and most widely grown variety was called *le calmoung* and that *le harutin* was the next best. Another, *le merselly*, had large 'milky' leaves (they dripped a white sap) which had to be left in the shade to dry for twelve hours before giving them to the silkworms – a great disadvantage. Cooling the leaves after harvesting in warm weather generates another problem which could have been confused here.

In 1956 new varieties of the white mulberry from Japan were introduced for field trials at the Centre Agronomique de St Christol les Alès in support of the revival of the silk industry of the Cévennes which had lain dormant for over fifty years. The best cultivar tested for suitability to the rigorous climate of the mountainous Cévennes was one called *Kokuso*. This is a robust bush species which has large leaves and can be grown twenty thousand to the hectare.

Currently over thirty varieties of white mulberry are grown in the old silk road area of the southern USSR, Azerbaijan. These include triploid varieties (with three times their chromosome number) such as 'Tadjik seedless' and 'Khazar toot' and tetraploid varieties (four times) such as 'Uzbeksky'. The Russians are keen on inter-cropping with alternate rows of vegetables between their mulberry bushes.

American varieties of *alba* include a useful non-bearing (fruitless) form most suitable for gardens and municipal parks where mess from spoiled fruits is a potential problem. *M. alba* grows well as beach plantings in California and is a useful shade plant in drought areas. 'Tea's Weeping' is low growing and strongly weeping. 'Chaparral' is weeping and non-fruiting. Other modern varieties include 'Fan-San', 'Fruitless', 'Kingano' and 'Stribling' – a maple-leaf variety.

The amazing variety of the white mulberry can be appreciated in India

Mulberry Trees

where the Central Sericultural Research and Training Institute in Mysore, has catalogued no less than four hundred accessions including 185 indigenous, 114 exotic and 101 elite F1 mulberry hybrids. Their K2 variety produces 42,245 kg (93,132 lb) of leaves per ha under irrigated conditions.

Origin

Unlike the black mulberry which has a mysterious origin, the white mulberry came from China. When it arrived in Europe is not recorded but no doubt it travelled via the shipping and silk routes, perhaps as contraband seeds with silkworm eggs.

White mulberry trees have been in Europe from earliest times, though the year given for France is about 1424, and for England, 1596. One of the earliest plantations of mulberries (presumed to be white) in Europe is from the fifteenth century. It was recorded that Lorenzo the Magnificent (1449–92), of the famous Medici family, had an extensive plantation of mulberries (species not mentioned) at his prestigious villa at Poggio, 16 km (10 miles) from Florence. We presume this was the white mulberry since Europe has a traditional base for this species.

The white mulberry was introduced to south-eastern America, probably during the early seventeenth century during the early years of the Virginia Co. There were many English and French working in the silk industry in America who would have been familiar with the species and who may have imported it. Today the white mulberry has spread 'like weeds' in American cities and the berries litter the sidewalks.

Like the black mulberry, the white mulberry is now widespread in Europe. However, although it is exceedingly common in France, one would have to travel well south of Paris, even south of Lyon before white mulberry trees are seen, and then they are usually pollarded. In Britain the tree is rare.

This odd reversal of species is entirely due to the mix-up of species that James I's sylviculturist succumbed to in the seventeenth century, promoting black mulberries in Britain instead of white ones.

In France and England at the end of the sixteenth century, William Stallenge (see his book of 1609) was employed to establish mulberry plantations. At a council meeting in Paris in 1589 he gave an address on 'The Gathering of the Silke' in which he said: 'Amongst the pleasant places of the void fields of Paris, I have marked Madril, and Vicenes Wood royal manfions, and very capable to receive and nourish 300,000 mulberries . . .'

Mulberry Trees

By 1594 the King of France had resolved to have white mulberries grown in all the gardens of his houses. The following year he went on a journey to Savoy, Provence, Languedoc and Vivares, presumably to see silk production in the south. Then in 1601 Stallenge was commanded to set up the French royal mulberry plantations and the General Surveyor of the Royal Gardens, Monsieur de Burdeaux, Baron of Colences, asked Stallenge to propagate and look after the trees. This was confirmed, authorized and ratified in letters of patent on the 14 October and 3 December 1602. The trees were to be planted in four *généralités*: 'Paris, Orleans, Toures, Lion'. Tens of thousands of trees were involved, and seed too had to be distributed. The king had already built a large house for silk-rearing and reeling silk at the end of his Tuileries garden, where several hundred mulberries were planted. It is not specified whether these trees planted by Stallenge in France were white or black mulberries, but it is clear that the black mulberry was being used in the profitable areas to the south of France since he mentions these following places with respect to the black species: 'Lombardie, Anduze, Alès and towards Sevenes of Languedoc'. This is curious since the area is now a traditional *white* stronghold. One suspects that Stallenge perhaps mis-identified the species. This is lent support since he says: 'My purpose is, and I will to project, that within five years to furnish England with 10 millions of white mulberry trees.'

Somewhere along the way, Stallenge managed to get the black mulberry established in England, not the white. It might have been a mistake of identification, but there is no evidence of this to support the popular belief that he did.

At about the same time, silk production was in progress in the Low Countries. Stallenge mentions that 'the Noble Ducheffe of Afcot' was getting good silk from her silk-rearing endeavours in Leiden (Holland), and that she had made silk garments that even her 'gentlewomen' wore. That was in 1593–5. It was this success which was perhaps used to sell the French king the idea for silk production in France.

In the eighteenth century the region around Tours became an important silk producing region, most probably due to the enthusiasm of the king. Thanks to some recent research of old manuscripts (Maillet, 1971), a great deal is known of white mulberry plantations and sericulture between the years 1760 and 1780. The area planted up can be found within the area enclosed by the following towns: to the north Cigogne and Orbigny, Montresor and Chatillon to the east, Le Bridore, Paulmy, Liguel to the south and Ligueil à Cigogne par Tauxigny to the west. The town of Loches profited

Mulberry Trees

from this venture into silk production. Good years for silk production were 1766, 1768 and 1769; bad years 1667 and 1772.

This silk enterprise was all by royal command. There was a certain Monsieur Aubry who was *L'Inspecteur des Manufactures et pepinières royales de mûriers blancs de la Généralité de Tours*. Eggs to start off the venture came from Avignon, some from Spain. Researchers are not sure where the actual magnanerie was sited, but details indicate that it would have been about 39 m (128 ft) long and covered 77 sq m (252 sq ft). It was planned to handle 3,400 'ballets' of silk and to produce thirty-six books of silk. Three thousand silk cocoons made up a 'book', thirty-two cocoons one 'ballet'.

There were some years when the weather was not in their favour. Late frosts were often to blame, shrivelling the leaves on the trees and thus starving the silkworms. In 1767 it was frost, followed by hail, followed by continuous rain which destroyed their labours – a familiar story even today! It was then accompanied by attacks of the dreaded muscardine, a fungus which kills caterpillars in humid conditions. Some years supplies of leaves would run out and emergency supplies, of white or black, would be obtained from far and wide.

The region around Tours and Loches was an important contributor to the silk effort, but it was not the epicentre of France's silk productivity. The real mulberry country, where it was almost exclusively 'white' was in the south. In particular the *département* of Gard had an estimated four million trees (see Table, page 90). The census returns show how the declining number of mulberry trees reflected the decreasing importance of silk, because of increased silk imports and the introduction of artificial fibres.

Plantations of the new Japanese *Kokuso* cultivars of white mulberry can be seen in the small French village of Monoblet, north of St Hippolyte du Fort in Gard. Today, 'St Hippo' is the centre of the rejuvenated Cévennes silk industry.

Some of this *Kokuso* stock has now been taken by the French to the Azores in an attempt to re-establish silk production in those volcanic islands. About thirty years ago the Azorians planted white mulberry trees extensively, particularly on the islands of St Miquel (the major island) and Pico, where today broken avenues of them can be seen along miles of country roads. The University of Azores in Ponta del Garda (St Miquel) boasts probably the longest avenue of white mulberries in the world with over a hundred pairs of trees.

In England, Zoë, Lady Hart Dyke, established a large plantation of white mulberry trees at her Lullingstone Silk Farm in Kent. Sadly all these trees

Mulberry Trees

Mulberry Census in France

(Source: Association pour le Dévelopement de la Sériculture en Cévennes, 1978)

Départements	1853	1929	1940
Gard	4,000,000	800,000	504,760
Drome	3,000,000	497,300	230,210
Lozère	2,600,000	79,000	20,590
Vaucluse	2,500,000	55,000	46,610
Ardeche	2,000,000	699,900	261,030
Isere	1,500,000	85,900	19,000
Var	300,000	112,000	74,200

have been grubbed out. I have walked over the grassy meadows with her heirs, where once a mulberry orchard flourished. In the 1940s Lady Hart Dyke sent a hundred white mulberry trees to Jealott's Hill Research Station, Berkshire for a study of plant productivity. Today none of these original white mulberries can be traced on the Jealott's Hill Estate.[16]

Today's specimens of mature white mulberries in Britain can almost be counted on the fingers of one hand. However, there are nurseries which sell 'whips' (small two-year-old trees) of white mulberry at very modest cost so there are now quite a lot in general distribution in Britain. They are easy to propagate and double their size each year, like *nigra*. Notable specimens occur in the Edinburgh Botanic Garden, the Oxford Botanic Garden and in Shrublands Park, Ipswich. A young white mulberry grows close to a black mulberry at the famous Sissinghurst Castle Gardens, Kent.

The Japanese have perfected high quality leaf production from white mulberry bushes by attending to fine details of planting and irrigation. Planting density is 20,000–23,000 bushes per ha. The result of the excellent leaves is that the cocoons are of superior quality, up to 700 kg (1,543 lb) of cocoons per ha of mulberry trees. By comparison, India often has a far greater planting density, in the order of 35,000 per ha, yet the quality of the leaves and thus the cocoons is less: they achieve only 300 kg (661 lb) of cocoons per ha.

Inferior 'English mulberries' were noted in Australia by Johns and Stevenson[17] with small, hard fruit. They thought that the species was *M. alba* but the climate was really too hot and dry for successful develop-

Mulberry Trees

The Kokuso variety of the white mulberry tree from Japan was originally selected from hundreds of cultivars and was found to be suitable for the harsh climate of the mountainous Cévennes. It bushes out, produces enormous leaves, and never develops into a tree. Ladders are no longer required to gather leaves, making it safer and more productive. The origin of the nursery rhyme 'Here we go round the mulberry bush' is mysterious and not cited in the Opies' exhaustive treatment of nursery rhyme origins

ment of the tree. It is quite likely that emigrating English parson-naturalists took with them mulberry cuttings or seeds, as they did with numerous other plants.

Propagation

Mulberries of the genus *Morus* have several similarities and can be discussed together for the purposes of propagation.

Taking autumn or winter cuttings from trees and bushes and striking these in the ground is a well established way of increase for the mulberry. The size of the cutting can be as small as 1.5 cm using softwood, but large branches of hardwood, called 'truncheons', with a diameter of about 0.5 cm or so are said to strike in the ground after a year to eighteen months. However, I have had no success with this. Propagation can also be done by taking root grafts. A new system of air-layering is used in Taiwan today. This involves growing cuttings in a bolus of nutrient-rich soil under controlled conditions.

Mulberry can be grown from seed very readily but it does not have commercial application since it does not pass on identical characteristics as with cuttings or grafting. The mixing of genes from different trees which occurs during sexual reproduction and seed production causes too much variety in form. At least with grafting the characters you wish for in a mulberry are replicated identically and quickly.

Mass production of mulberry is now achieved in laboratories by tissue and organ culture under controlled conditions. Mulberry improvement programmes are now being implemented by tissue culture and micropropagation. This results in clones of mulberry with desired characteristics, such as leaf size and productivity, being mass-produced on the laboratory bench.

Mulberry wood

The wood of the mulberry has always been highly regarded, and has been used in both the Old and the New World. It is compact, pliant, hard, water-resistant and receives a good polish. It was favoured by upholsterers, turners, carvers, joiners and boat-builders. William Stallenge (1609) went to great lengths to discuss the usefulness of making linen cloth from the bark of white mulberry. He insisted that it was only a profitable exercise if one had 2,000–3,000 trees. Each year 250–300 trees would be stripped of their bark and this would make 300–400 'burthens' of wood. The bark was taken when the sap was rising and laid in water for four days. It was then laid out in a meadow for up to twelve days, covered up in the heat of the day, then allowed to soak up the night's dew.

RED (OR MORAL (USA)) MULBERRY, *MORUS RUBRA*

The red mulberry is native to eastern and central America where it was known to the early English colonists. It was certainly recommended that its leaves should be used for feeding silkworms during the early part of the seventeenth century at the height of James I's campaign to get members of the Virginia Co. interested in money-making ventures.

The presence of so many wild red mulberry trees growing around Colonial Williamsburg in 1619 encouraged the burgesses to decree that everyone should plant and look after six mulberry trees a year for seven years. There were penalties for not planting mulberry trees and there were incentives of tobacco offered in exchange for raw silk produced.[18]

Mulberry Trees

The red mulberry is a native of the eastern United States and is a prolific grower. Once used by the early settlers as a ready source of food for silkworms, it is now widely found in the countryside

It was probably these red mulberries that the Mendoza-Lopez expedition to the Jumanos in 1684 saw near the San Clemente River (Colorado): 'The bottom lands of the river are luxuriant with plants bearing nuts, grapes, mulberries, and many groves of plums.' These are mentioned in Juan Dominquez de Mendoza's manuscripts now in Mexico City. A hundred years later Nicolas de la Fora noted in his diaries of the 1766–7 expedition into the Spanish province of Texas that 'there are immense numbers of walnut, mulberry, plum, chestnut and medlar trees which offer a supply of wild fruit to travelers'. The Choctaw Indians used to weave cloaks from the fibrous inner bark of young trees. The timber was good for agricultural instruments, fenceposts and furniture. In Le Page du Pratz's *History of Louisiana* it is mentioned that many of the Choctaw Indian women wear cloaks of the bark of mulberry trees.

In the southern states the red mulberry is still planted today as a source of fallen food for pigs and poultry. There is a mature specimen in the Dallas Arboretum (Texas) with a circumference of 274 cm (108 in), its bole looking identical to that of a *M. nigra* in maturity. The red mulberry differs from both the black and white mulberries in having leaves whose undersides are much more downy and the leaves are also extremely pointed. The tree can reach 19 m (62 ft). There is also a dwarf form called 'Nana'.

The red mulberry was originally introduced to England in 1629 and has been grown at Kew Gardens. It does not grow very well in Britain, probably because of the climate, but can grow as tall as the white species.

THE TEXAS (OR MEXICAN OR MOUNTAIN MULBERRY), *MORUS MICROPHYLLA*

This is a much smaller species up to 6 m (19.7 ft) tall in maturity, with a tendency to form clumps. Male and female flowers are born on separate trees. It is a native of southern Oklahoma and Texas and may be found west to Arizona and south to New Mexico. The fruit was eaten, and the species introduced to the Grand Canyon, by the Havasupai Indians. The leaves of the Texas mulberry are tiny compared to those of *M. rubra*.

It is not known whether this species was used for rearing silkworms in America, though there were several attempts in Texas to establish a silk industry. Introduced to England in 1926, this American mulberry species is scarce and rarely used for silkworm-rearing.

OTHER *MORUS* MULBERRY SPECIES

There are four other species of *Morus*, all introduced to England by the collector Ernest Wilson (1876–1930) from his travels in China and Japan. These are *Morus australis*, native to China, Japan, the Ryukyu Islands, Formosa and Korea; *Morus cathayana* Hemsl., from central China; *Morus bombycis* (formerly *Morus kagayamae*), from Japan and the small islands of Hachijo and Miyake of the Izu-No-Shichito chain, where Wilson reported that the leaves were much used by the natives for feeding to silkworms; and *Morus mongolica*, from China and Korea. *M. bombycis* is a large shrub with ovate, toothed leaves up to 20 cm (7.9 in) long. From the East there is another mulberry species, *M. cathagensis*, which grows to 14 m (46 ft). Many of these other mulberry species, scarce in Europe, would be suitable for feeding to silkworms, but they have rarely been tried out.

Mulberry Trees

THE PAPER MULBERRY, *BROUSSONETIA PAPYRIFERA*

The paper mulberry was brought to France from Japan as an alternative food plant for silkworms. It was named after the French naturalist T.N.V. Broussonet (1761–1807) who lived in Montpellier, a centre of active silk production.

In England, Lady Hart Dyke ran into trouble with Customs and Excise because she imported so many mulberry trees into Britain. The customs repeatedly demanded their 33 per cent tax, but eventually relented in October 1937 and issued a rule stating that no more tax had to be levied on paper mulberries or plants grafted on it as a rootstock. Today, however, the paper mulberry is extremely rare in Britain, even rarer than the white mulberry.

The paper mulberry was brought to France from Japan as an alternative food plant for silkworms. It was named after the French naturalist T.N.V. Broussonet (1761–1807) who lived in Montpellier, a centre of active silk production.

There are two species of *Broussonetia*: *B. kazinoki* and *B. papyrifera*, both of

T
H
E
.
S
T
O
R
Y
.
O
F
.
S
I
L
K

A garland of paper mulberry demonstrates the different features which set it apart from the genus *Morus*. It has red pom-pom like fruits and much smaller simple leaves.

which belong to the mulberry family. There is a third species known in Japan, *B. kaempferi*, but it is now botanically recognized as being the same species as *B. kazinoki*. *B. kazinoki*, known as *kazinoki* or *kozo* in Japan, is the smaller of the two species, from 2 m (6.6 ft) to 5 m (16.4 ft) tall while *B. papyrifera* is 8 m (26.2 ft) to 10 m (32.8 ft) tall. Both are much less woody than white and red mulberry trees and have male and female flowers borne on the same stalk. Catkins of *kazinoki* are the longest of the two species, a useful identification feature. The leaves of *kazinoki* are deeply lobed, pointed, serrated and covered in silky hairs on both sides. Those of *B. papyrifera* are three- or five-lobed when young but become oval when the tree is mature.

The flowers and fruits of the paper mulberry are fascinating structures and appear in mid-August. They are sweet and tasty too, on the outside, but not suitable for eating because of their large green pithy centre. Each inflorescence arises as a green drupe, a marble-like ball which looks like the fruit of plane (*Platanus*) on a short 1 cm stalk. After a few days tiny pink seeds emerge from the green pile and progressively extrude up to 8 mm from the surface of the ball, the whole drupe then looking red, with each extrusion containing a single red-brown seed enclosed in one plane at the tip. At this stage the ripe fruits drop to the ground where they litter the pavements like any black mulberry.

The origins of these trees is a little obscure. *B. kazinoki* is regarded to be indigenous to Japan, though may have been introduced in ancient times from Taiwan or other places in the South Seas. *B. kazinoki* is a native of Burma, China, Korea, Thailand and Polynesia. Precisely when paper mulberry made its appearance in Europe is not known, but it is an important tropical tree once used extensively for paper-making (and still used today in Japan). It is likely the species would have been transported around the world on-board ship by enthusiastic traders. Today it is commonly seen in southern Europe and in parts of the southern states of the USA.

TREES FOR OTHER SILKWORMS

While silk production from *B. mori* silkworms is the norm, other silkworm species are often tried out for their effectiveness for silk. If, for any reason, the *B. mori* strain runs into problems with disease, alternative species are often used. This was the situation in southern France at the end of the last century.

Mulberry Trees

Serious attempts were made in France to grow plantations of the tree of Heaven (*arbre du ciel*) (*Ailanthus altissima*: Simarubaceae) for the caterpillars of an attractive silkmoth species, the American Robin moth (*Hylophora cecropia*). The moth was originally introduced to Europe from Louisiana *c.* 1840.

The tree of heaven is a Chinese species which is now quite widespread in western Europe. It was originally introduced into England in 1751 from a mixture of different seeds which were sent to the Royal Society in London. Some were later sent over to the Jardin des Plantes in Paris in 1757. The tree is now naturalized in urban areas and may be seen along such habitats as railway embankments, on waste ground and in untended city gardens. There are many town gardens and parks where it is used as an ornamental species. Its distinguishing features are its pinnate leaves and masses of reddish fruits. In the Mediterranean it grows freely on river beds and reaches a considerable height.

Between 1861 and 1867 several hundred trees of heaven were planted in the Parc de Flamboin, south-east of Paris between Fontainbleau and Troyes, once a very important industrial centre for silk production. Napolean III (1848–73) had his Royal Farm at Vincennes planted with the species and at the same time a society was founded to seriously exploit silk production, using the Robin moth and the tree of heaven. Vincennes was a thirteenth-century château in the heart of Paris. To the east of Paris four other plantations were established: one at Gray in Haute-Saône (near Dijon and Juras), one at Champlitte (between Gray and Chalindregm, north-west of Gray, one at Troyes (Aube) and one at Barbery, north of Troyes (Aube).

The Eri or Ailanthus silkmoth, *Philosamia cynthia* (*Le Croissant* or *Le Bombyx de l'ailante*), is also, as one of its French names suggests, a feeder on the tree of heaven, *Ailanthus altissima*. In its native Asia it feeds on *A. altissima* and castor oil, *Ricinus communis*, but its catholic tastes allow it also to be reared on ash (*Fraxinus excelsior*), blackthorn (*Prunus spinosa*), privet (*Ligustrum*), Lilac (*Syringa*) and, very rarely, on sycamore, as well as Ailanthus species.

The Tusseh silkmoth, *Antheraea mylitta*, the species from which Tusseh silk is made, is Asian in origin and was introduced to France (L'Ile de France) from Bengal in 1829 by Monsieur Lamare-Piguot. In Europe the caterpillars eat common oak (*Quercus robur*) but will also eat holm oak (*Quercus ilex*).

Mulberry Trees

PESTS

Mulberry trees appear to be fairly resistant to many pathogenic organisms and defoliating insect pests. Very occasionally they may play host to the semi-parasite mistletoe (*Viscum alba*), but they are not harmed by the association. Surprisingly there are very few insects which feed on mulberry leaves. This may be due to their comparatively recent introduction into Europe, since the native insect species consequently lack any adaptation to the species. Alternatively, the leaves contain a chemical or suite of chemicals which acts as a feeding deterrent.[19]

However, one mulberry moth, also called the North American Weaver Tiger-Moth (*Hyphantria cunea*), which was introduced into Europe from North America after the Second World War, is a known pest. Each female moth lays between five hundred and a thousand eggs and the caterpillars are gregarious. They may cause a lot of damage to mulberry trees as well as other fruit trees. Over one hundred species of deciduous tree are recorded in America as food plants of the caterpillars, including *Ailanthus*. So far the moth has not been recorded in Britain but it is increasing its range in the region near Bordeaux and in the Landes district of eastern France.

Mulberry pests appear to be more of a problem in the USA than in Europe. It is cited by Johnson and Lynon[20] that a variety of invertebrates attack mulberry including the Californian red scale, *Aonidiella aurantii*, which is believed to be the most important citrus pest in the world. The Texas root knot nematode may find resistant mulberry species in the USA, but in India it is a problem and is controlled by application of 'Furadon', 'Rugby 10G' and 'Pongamia' or 'Neen'.

NOTES

1. J.B. Harborne, *Introduction to Ecological Biochemistry* (1977) believes that two compounds, morin and isoquercetrin, are the important leaf attractants for the silkworm as they are dietary requirements. Morin is almost exclusively found in mulberry leaves. Secondary plant substances, such as morin, by definition are compounds which are secondary to substances such as chlorophyll and which serve a variety of purposes.

2. G. Wilkinson, *Epitaph for the Elm* (1978).

3. E. Hyams & A.A. Jackson, *The Orchard and Fruit Book* (1961).

4. D. Stuart, *The Kitchen Garden Book* (1984).

5. A. Mitchell, 'Facts about black mulberries', in *The Garden*, December 1984, Vol. 109 (12), pp. 514–15.

6. G. Keynes (ed.), *Direction for the Gardiner at Says-Court* (1932).

7. C. Lloyd, *The Well-tempered Garden* (1970).

8. W. Cobbett, *Rural Rides* (1911).

9. M. Hadfield, *A History of British Gardening* (1960).

10. J. Harris, *Mediaeval Gardens* (1981).

11. It was actually described from the Old English as a large *Sycomor* but, as Harris points out, a sycamore at this time was in fact a mulberry. There are various fifteenth-century manuscripts which describe mulberries as sycamores, such as *Sicomorus*, *fructus celsi* and *vel mori*.

12. F. Muller, *Trees of the British Isles in History and Legend* (1922).

13. G. Howe, *The Garden Book of Sir Thomas Hanmer* (1933).

14. Hillier, *Manual of Trees* (1984).

15. A most impressive mature weeping mulberry stands on the lawn outside the Victorian Wightwick Manor (National Trust) in Wolverhampton, West Midlands.

16. This is now part of the Plant Protection Division of Imperial Chemical Industries (ICI).

17. L. Johns and V. Stevenson, *The Complete Book of Fruit* (1979).

18. J.P. Dutton, *Plants of Colonial Williamsburg* (1979).

19. There has been a recent suggestion that the chemical constituents of mulberries have been useful in treating Aids.

20. W.T. Johnson and H.H. Lyon, *Insects that Feed on Trees and Shrubs* (1976).

CHAPTER 5

Mulberries, Monasteries and Gardens

Mulberries at Clevedon

I stood upon a lawn whose greensward spread
   Smooth-levell'd by the scythe; two mulberry trees
Beyond it stretch'd their old and foliated areas;
   Th'acacia quiver'd in the wind....

(by kind permission of Lady Elton of Clevedon, Somerset)

MONASTERY AND CATHEDRAL GARDENS

There is considerable evidence to support my original hunch that 'men of the cloth' were in fact 'men of the silk cloth'. To me it was more than just coincidence that mulberry trees were all too frequently found in cathedral precincts, priories, churchyards, rectories, vicarages and abbeys.

What were the connections, if any, between these mulberries and the industrious monks, who still look after their Augustinian, Capuchin, Franciscan and Carthusian monasteries? The last group can be ruled out immediately since the Carthusians have always shown a marked tendency to select mountain sites, and therefore were not likely to have had mulberry trees to establish a silk industry. Yet they have never experimented with

Monasteries and Gardens

vines either, which *is* surprising for monks who normally know how to profit from the land.

There are two complementary theories why mulberries are associated with ecclesiastical dwellings. First, for wholesome food, in this case the juicy fruits full of vitamin C – or was it for wine? Second, as a source of food plant for silkworms. It would have made sense for monks to look after silkworms and to furnish silken garments for the clergy. In any case emissaries of the clergy travelled in the East and must have wondered how to corner a market in this wonderful material.

As early as the seventh century the Venerable Bede mentions that an Abbot Bishop, called Benedict (628–690), brought back two cloaks from his fifth voyage to Rome. They were of finest silk and of incomparable workmanship so it is not surprising to find that King Alfred paid an estate of three hides on the south bank of the River Ware especially for them. It was in the court that representatives of both the Church and Crown were best suited to display their finest silks.

Fragments of figured silks have been found in tombs in Durham, Canterbury (the tomb of Archbishop Hubert Walter) and in Westminster Abbey in the shrine of Edward the Confessor. There are also numerous references to figured silks in the inventories of Durham, York, Exeter and Lincoln.

At Durham Cathedral there is the remarkable silk-embroidered stole belonging to St Cuthbert. The famous garment was made to the order of Queen Aethelflaed, the daughter-in-law of Alfred The Great, for Frithstan, Bishop of Winchester, at the end of the tenth century. The royal family had close association with the city of Winchester, since this was the old capital of Wessex and Frithstan was bishop there from 909 to 931. The stole was probably made in Winchester and it is edged with tablet-woven braids of silk and gold thread. Many details of the design of the stole are paralleled in Winchester manuscripts and wall-paintings. Alfred's widow, Ealswith, had founded a nunnery (the 'Nunnaminster') in Winchester, so there was a house under royal patronage there, where embroidery was practiced. After Frithstan's death, the embroideries reverted to royal ownership for Aethelstan to present them to St Cuthbert's shrine.

It is well known too that English ecclesiastical embroideries in silk, collectively called *Opus Anglicanum*, were found throughout Europe. They are mentioned in papal inventories at the end of the thirteenth century, in particular vestments and robes from the tenth century onwards. English silks were also found on the effigies of the late-twelfth and early-thirteenth century English kings and queens.

Mulberries,

The black mulberry tree within the precincts of Canterbury Cathedral was finally dispatched by the storm of 16 October 1987, despite its wooden supports and props. It has now been replaced with a very vigorous black mulberry sapling

There is evidence discussed by Dale (1933) which shows that there were silkwomen at the beginning of the reign of Edward III (1327–77). It was not until the fifteenth century that the London silkwomen established their art in London, a century later than those in Paris. They organized themselves into a guild in all but name and were very much under the wing of the powerful Mercers' Company.[1] They worked at home often as widows or women trading as *femmes sole* independently. One such woman, Alice Claver, made

Vicarages, Rectories, Churchyards and Religious Colleges with Mulberries

East Sussex
Alfriston, The Old Clergy House
Hastings, St Clement's, Old Hastings
Icklesham, vicarage garden
Rottingdean, churchyard

Gloucestershire
Bitton, Canon Ellacombe's church garden

Kent
Birchington
Brasted, The Old Vicarage (blown down October 1987)
Canterbury, Christ College, former Abbey Garden
Canterbury, St Lawrence Priory Chapel at Sutton at Home
Dartford, Garden of St John of Jerusalem
East Malling
Kemsing, garden close to church
Hucking
Hythe
Kingsworth, The Old Rectory
Margate, St John's Vicarage
West Malling, Church House and Aldon Old Rectory

Leicestershire
Narborough, The Old Vicarage

Lincolnshire
Gainsborough

London (Metropolitan)
Bromley College
Camberwell, St George's Vicarage
Chelsea, The Old Rectory and College of St Mark and St John
Lesnes Abbey

Somerset
Porlock, vicarage

Suffolk
Stowmarket, The Old Vicarage

Surrey
Limpsfield, St Peter's Church
Glebefield, behind rectory

Warwickshire
Warwick, St Mary's Collegiate Church
Warwick, St Nicholas's Church, nr castle

West Sussex
Nuthurst, nr Horsham, grounds of old vicarage garden
Slaugham, The Old Rectory

Mulberries,

mantles and laces for Richard III and Queen Anne. By 1455 these members of the 'Sylkewymmen and Throwsterres of the Craftes and occupation of Silkewerk' had petitioned parliament for protection from the cheap silk imports. Many girls from the the shires such as Buckinghamshire, Warwickshire, Lincolnshire, Yorkshire and from Norfolk and Bristol, came to make a living as silkwomen in London. They were apprenticed to London silkwomen and prepared much of their silk from imported materials from Italy, Genoa in particular. The prepared silk was not liked by noble households and knights.

Silken garments would not always have been in favour in the Church, particularly in the sixteenth century. The Protestantism of Henry VIII consisted of a deep hatred of any Catholic pomp and monastic expertise, so we might not expect any mulberry plantations and silk industry to have survived during this period. Some of the skills of the craft may have gone underground. During the persecutions of the English Civil War a bland Puritan type of attire was favoured, hardly befitting silk and circumstance.

Yet, in a curious turn of events, it is said that the Roman cardinals in Rome had to get their special red hats from Wandsworth in south-east London, made by the same Huguenot dyers who fled from Roman Catholic persecution on the Continent.

Men of the cloth were therefore 'men of the silk cloth', and mulberry trees may have carried some religious symbolism, the juicy fruits of black mulberry looking just like blood. However, no hard evidence has been unearthed to support this. According to the Doctrine of Signatures theory of Nicholas Culpeper in the sixteenth century, plants which were red, exuded a blood-like fluid or changed green oil (e.g. olive) to red oil, would have been regarded with considerable religious respect. Mulberry does not seem to fit easily into this particular symbolism, unlike St John's wort, *Hypericum perforatum* (whose yellow flowers turn oil red), or the red Apothecary's rose, *Rosa officinalis*. However, we should not forget the significance of Thisbe finding Pyramus covered in splashes of blood (see plate 1).

There is no lack of evidence of mulberry trees in English cathedral gardens and precincts from an early date. It would be nice to think that these cathedral trees once supported a local silk industry but it has been difficult to find hard evidence. It is quite likely that the clergy led the way in the introduction of mulberries; they would have represented some of the more intellectual members of society, eager to be involved in new projects, the trees being used for production of food or silk. Supporting this fact, we find that some of the largest and most venerable of mulberry trees in

Monasteries and Gardens

England are in the environs of cathedrals, if not in the precinct gardens themselves, then in the deanery gardens, for we know that mulberry trees were in the monastic gardens around Canterbury Cathedral from the twelfth century and in York in the thirteenth century.[2] Cathedrals with mulberry trees include Canterbury, Ely, Lichfield, Norwich, Rochester and St Paul's in London. Chester precinct used to sport a mulberry tree. Mulberry trees diminish in numbers the further one progresses northwards in Britain, to the degree that they are scarce in Scotland. The reason for this is probably due to lack of enthusiasm in planting and a reflection of the limits of Huguenot distribution, rather than a climatic one, since mulberry trees do grow well in Scotland.

During the sixteenth century the clerics at Norwich may have been dabbling in silk production, for we understand from Grigor's *Eastern Arboretum* (1841) that the Bishop's Garden at Norwich had a mulberry tree which he thought was 250 years old, thus placing it in the 1590s:

> In the palace garden there is a very old mulberry which measures
> three feet and a half in diameter a foot from the ground. The
> vicissitudes of some centuries have left us with a wreck of what this
> tree has been, its top robbed of some of its largest boughs,
> presenting but a meagre, dilapidated appearance.

However, we now know that mulberry ages quickly and deceives attempts to age it, so this 'old' tree may not have been quite so old.

In England other bishops' gardens excel around the country. There is a 7 m (23 ft) girth living mulberry stump in the Bishop's Garden at Chichester, with others in the Deanery Garden and Treasury Garden. Rochester also has a specimen which may well be the largest in the county, in the Archdeaconry Garden. There are three more around Rochester's castle and Precinct Gardens. At Ely the Bishop's House (formerly the Deanery), the Old Bishop's Palace and two other fine houses close by also have mulberry trees.

Another ecclesiastical connection with silk, this time from the Continent, can be read in the diaries of John Evelyn. While in France on ambassadorial duties he visited the Archbishop's Palace at St Gatian, not far from Tours in the Loire Valley, as well as other churches, chapels and monasteries. The visit took place on 18 May 1644 where he saw fine silks. Evelyn also visited the Convent of the Capuchins (a branch of the Franciscans) where he witnessed silk production:

Mulberries,

One of the original mulberry trees still stands in the *place* at Monoblet, a reminder of the 'cocoon markets' held here every year. This tree also figures in the photograph on page 54

. . . for in this town they drive a very considerable trade with silk-worms, their pressing and watering the grograms and camlets, with weights of an extraordinary poise, put into a rolling engine.

Evelyn must have stayed a while at St Gatian since on 25 May it was their Fête Dieu and 'the whole streets hung with their best tapestries, and their most precious moveables exposed, silks, damasks, velvets'.

MULBERRY TREES IN ENGLISH GARDENS

The mulberry has played an important part in the English garden ever since the twelfth century. It was a useful fruit tree, grown alongside other trees such as the walnut, quince and medlar. On other occasions it was planted for

Monasteries and Gardens

its usefulness in the production of home-produced silk. It is surprising how many well-established gardens have these four species still growing in them. Older plants are often propagated from cuttings, with the ancestry of some fine trees passed on in the same kitchen garden or walled garden for many generations.

There are some gardens which are said to have mulberry trees originally planted by James I on his instructions. A typical example is at Charlton House, Greenwich, where James's son was tutored and where he had a thriving silk industry. The tree there bears a label stating it is a genuine James I mulberry tree. Another such tree is at Romsey in the New Forest. In London, it is said that James I planted mulberries in St James's Park, and today a small one, perhaps a cutting from one of the originals, still stands by one of the walks, shedding its 'bloody' fruits onto the tarmac each year.

In the case of the Buckingham Palace mulberry trees, these are claimed to be remnants of the former mulberry orchard established on the site by James I, and to which John Evelyn later referred. One of James I's residences was Hatfield House, a typical Jacobean building. Today there is a venerable

There are numerous mulberry trees associated with Shakespeare, and many cuttings from Shakespeare's tree have been cultivated in various parts of England

Mulberries,

mulberry tree in the garden, thought to be one of the original specimens. Other, much younger, replacement mulberry trees have been planted to replace older ones. According to Miles Hadfield[2] the grounds of Hatfield were laid out lavishly and mulberry trees were imported from the Continent.

John Tradescant the Elder (1570–1638) was Royal Gardener to Charles I (son to James I) and had his own gardens just across the Thames from the Houses of Parliament, at Lambeth Palace. He was also charged with looking after silkworms as part of his garden remit. Charles I appointed him in charge of 'His Majesties Garden, Vines and Silkworms' in 1630. Earlier, in 1615, Tradescant had been to Canterbury to create new gardens for Lord Wooton at St Augustine's Palace which was built by Henry VIII. The formal gardens were planted with exotics like mulberry, mandrake, melon and pomegranate – 'the faire gardens and orchards, sweet walks, Labyrinth-like wildernesses and groves, rare mounts and fountaines, all which together take up the encompassing space and circuit of neere twenty or thirty acres.'

Some mulberry trees have also played a part in history, and there are famous examples connected with Shakespeare, Milton, and Garrick for instance. Of Shakespeare's mulberry trees at Stratford-upon-Avon, we know quite a lot. In the Great Garden of New Place there is an ancient mulberry tree which, according to tradition, is a direct descendant of the mulberry tree said to have been planted by Shakespeare himself. Not far away there is a cutting, struck in 1969. Another tree which is an offspring of the original Shakespeare tree stands near to the Knot Garden in the area occupied by the foundations of the New Place alongside Nash's house.

There are also mulberry trees at Hall's Croft, the home of Shakespeare's daughter Susanna and Dr John Hall, situated in the Old Town, while in the garden of Shakespeare's birthplace in Henley Street, there are two other specimens.

Shakespeare was a very knowledgeable amateur naturalist and to draw attention to this point the Shakespeare Tree Garden was created. It is close to Anne Hathaway's house. Inaugurated on 19 April 1985, Her Majesty Queen Elizabeth the Queen Mother planted a mulberry to complement the whole range of trees planted there which are mentioned in Shakespeare's plays.

There were probably numerous cuttings of Shakespeare's original mulberry tree which were carried all over England. A notable one is in Tamarisk Yard, Old Hastings where the famous Shakespearean actor David Garrick presented his friend Edward Capel (a noted Shakespearean scholar) with a cutting. That was in the 1770s. Now the large tree occupies most of the tiny courtyard, sheltered from the sea winds.

Monasteries and Gardens

The kind of English garden where one might expect to find a mulberry tree growing today is typically a vicarage or rectory garden. Fortunately a plan of the eighteenth century vicarage garden belonging to the famous Bishop Henry Ellacombe of Bitton (Gloucester) is still in existence and today we can see mulberries growing in his garden filled with other exotic trees, such as false acacia, *Robinia pseudoacacia*, American wellingtonias, *Sesquoiadendron giganteum*, tulip trees, *Liriodendron tulipifera* and Indian bean tree, *Catalpa bignoniodes*, all from the USA. Ellacombe was a Shakespearean scholar and his choice of mulberry next to the vicarage may have been influenced by this.

The Milton Mulberry at Christ Church, Cambridge is the one under which Milton is said to have written *Paradise Lost*. In the nineteenth century it was a site of pilgrimage for Milton enthusiasts. It is said that Milton also planted a mulberry in the garden of the Old Vicarage, Stowmarket, Suffolk when he stayed there with his tutor, Dr Young.

Rudyard Kipling's two homes, one at Rottingdean, the other at Bateman's, both in East Sussex, have mulberry trees. It is not known whether Kipling was particularly keen on mulberries, but he was certainly in contact with William Robinson, the garden-writer and father of wild flower gardening, who lived at Gravetye Manor, near East Grinstead. Robinson had a mulberry, still growing beside the walled kitchen garden.

In Chelsea it is said that Sir Thomas More planted the mulberry which still stands in the garden of his Beaufort Street house, which he bought in 1524.

CITY SILKS AND MULBERRY TREES

There is a great tradition of silks within the City of London, from the silks imported by the Vikings, through to the Worshipful Companies of Mercers and Lombards, to members of the Queen's Court 'taking the silks'. Today mulberry trees can still be found in the City.

Imported silks were brought into London and other trading centres such as Derby, Leicester, Lincoln, Stamford and York, as early as the tenth century by the Danish Vikings. They traded up the Dnieper and the Volga with the Islamic Empire and acquired gold and silver jewellery as well as silks and dyestuffs.

By the time of the 'Domesday Book' in the eleventh century we know that

Mulberries,

Two black mulberry trees stand in the gardens around St Paul's Cathedral in London. The tradition of mulberry trees in precincts is perpetuated here, with an enormous one not far away in Amen Court

ABOVE: The red colour of the indigo flowers belies the dark blue colour of indigo the dye. There are several members of the *Indigofera* genus and many have been cultivated for the dye which is present in largest amounts in the leaves. It was a major source of income, for instance in the eastern states of America during the nineteenth century. This species, *I. heterantha*, a native of north-west Himalaya, makes a beautiful shrub for the herbaceous border

BELOW: Dyeing has always been a secretive and competitive business for various sects such as the Jews. Little was written down and a lot of techniques were confined to memory and passed from generation to generation. The use of natural ingredients was a necessity until the introduction of synthetic dyes. Making the colours fast posed other constraints

Detail from
*Butterflies and
Spring Grasses*. This
was painted by a
follower of
Maruyama Okyo
(1733–95) during the
late Edo period. It is
painted as ink and
colour on silk,
54½ × 38½ inches as
a hanging scroll or
karemono, and is in
a private collection.
The details of the
butterflies are so
good that it is
possible to identify
the species. This
'naturalistic'
approach was a
characteristic of the
Maruyama school

Monasteries and Gardens

at St Paul's Cathedral there were people making and mending ecclesiastical robes, presumably embroidering them with fine silks bought on the open market. In the thirteenth century gloves, perhaps of silk, were being sold on London Bridge. The demand for silk from the clergy would have been great since there were ninety-nine churches within London's city walls.

It was not until the reign of Henry VI (1422–71), however, that the grand companies of London were taking shape and the mercers became exclusive dealers in silks and velvets. They may have been importing their silks from the Lombards.[3] Later, in the sixteenth century, the chief sellers of Italian silks lived in Cheapside, St Lawrence Jewry and Old Jewry. Like most master traders they had grand houses, four to five storeys high. In Elizabeth I's reign the mercers were summoned before the Queen's Council for selling velvets, satins and damasks at too high a price.

John Evelyn's diaries give us a little clue to silk work in the City of London. It is quaint to see that the nuns of St Catherine's 'monastery' sent him silk-work flowers on his birthday, 31 October. In 1652, we learn that Evelyn went to a factory belonging to a Monsieur La Dorees in Moorfields to see how silk and grograms were camletted. On another occasion he was presented with 'a Turkish bridle woven with silk and very curiously embossed with other silk trappings'.[4] A factory for wool and silk fringes operated out of the Choir of St Bartholomew's Hospital in the early nineteenth century and by 1833 the Lady's Chapel was also being used.

The Huguenot silk-workers were largely responsible for planting mulberries in London from the seventeenth century onwards. Since then the fortunes of the mulberry in London, particularly in the City, have dwindled as the need for space becomes ever more demanding. Some mulberries have survived through the centuries, perhaps as cuttings from mulberries which were planted on or close to the original site that one can find them on now. There are survivors though. Completely out of sight to the general public, there are mulberry trees growing in the private areas of the Bank of England. Here, there are four young specimens, planted in about 1940. They probably replaced an original mulberry tree planted by Sir John Houblon, a Huguenot, who founded the Bank in 1694, and it is interesting to speculate whether Houblon was persuaded by his fellow Huguenot silk-weaver friends to plant mulberry trees at his work-place.

The precincts of St Paul's Cathedral have two young mulberry trees, but even more impressive is the magnificent specimen in Amen Court, the Deanery of St Paul's. The trees' huge limbs are supported on sawn-off telegraph poles and the enormous quantities of fruit are eaten by city

Mulberries,

blackbirds every year. Just outside the original City limits is a little grove of mulberries in the garden of the Charterhouse.

No mulberry trees are found in the Old Bailey or the courtyards behind, though QCs still 'take the silks' and discreetly receive payments in the silken pouches sewn into their cloaks at the nape of the neck. The Court still courts silks and, as if to emphasize the point, four mulberries stand in the private gardens of the 'Honorable Society of Lincoln Inns' – the centre of the legal profession in England.

NOTES

1. Thanks to Dr Caroline M. Barron of Royal Holloway and New Bedford College, for drawing my attention to the silkwomen of London (see Dale, 1933 and Sutton, 1980).
2. Miles Hadfield, *The Education of a Gardener* (1983).
3. William Caxton was a member of the mercers for thirty years before he took up printing.
4. John Evelyn, *Diaries of John Evelyn* (Dent, 1972, 1973)

CHAPTER 6

Natural Dyes

Dark is the rising tide the berries grew,
And, white no longer, took a sable hue;
But brighter crimson, springing from the root,
Shot through the black and purpled o'er the fruit.

G.S. Boulger *Familiar Trees* 1906

The natural colour of silk straight from the cocoon varies from pure white to a strong yellow. This is determined genetically and the cocoon colour is therefore a characteristic of certain races of silkworms. What makes natural silk coloured are the carotenoid pigments, obtained by the caterpillar from the mulberry leaves and stored in the silk as a protection against sunlight. Over several months carotenoids break down in light and a yellowish cocoon will eventually become white.

Dyers like to start with a uniformly coloured silk, so raw silks were often treated to make them white. Dyeing silk with animal and vegetable dyes was the only resource available thousands of years ago for people who wanted to colour their precious silks. The regal masters of the dyers demanded 'status' colours such as purple and red.

Today, synthetic dyes are regularly used but there is an increasing interest in natural dyes for a number of reasons. Having gone to the trouble of producing silk – a natural fibre – it is more fitting to dye it with a natural dye. Some dye plants grow in abundance in the wild (or used to) and are easy and cheap to harvest, while others can be grown at home from bought seed. But the most important feature of natural dyes is that they produce the most subtle colour tones, tones that cannot be reproduced by modern dyes; this overrides the disadvantage that natural dyes are not consistent, batch by batch, and that some colours fade quicker than modern synthetic equivalents.

This fugitive or non-fast nature can be alleviated somewhat by adding an extra substance to the dyebath to make the natural fibre accept the colour.

Natural Dyes

This is called mordanting. One of the favourite mordants was alum which produced brightness in the silk, while tin had the same effect but was expensive. Both chrome and iron produce a dullness in silk fibres but have the disadvantage of damaging the material in the long-term with their oxides.

As a modern-day craft, using natural dyes recreates the artistry and traditional crafts of the silk-dyers who developed the skill thousands of years ago. It is a challenge to rediscover some of the more complicated methods that the early dyers employed to colour silks and cloths. To a certain extent what was a good dye for wool was also good for silk, though there are some exceptions, and the bulk of world literature on dyeing concerns wool. The wool fibre is much thicker and whiskery compared to the silk fibre, however, and is slightly easier to dye.

There was limited scope for colouring silks in earlier times. It depended upon who you were, where you lived and whether you had access to a supply of essential dyeing material. For people living around the Mediterranean one of the first colours to be used was purple, acquired from shellfish, while reds were often derived from tiny insects living on certain oak trees.

So much of the history of dyeing is unwritten, with secrets being passed from father to son, and kept within communities or religious groups such as the Jews, as a specialized trade. Dyeing was such an exact craft that the English often left all the dyeing, except the blues, entirely to 'foreigners'. This was especially true at Norwich in 1567 where the Huguenots were the expert dyers, under the leadership of master dyer Anthonye de Pottier.

In England the technique of printing did not get started until the second half of the seventeenth century. Beautiful printed silks had been arriving in London on boats of the East India Co. and the techniques, particularly of mordanting, were quickly learnt. By the end of the century there were a dozen master printers in London.

Water was needed for powering machinery such as washing stocks, squeezes and calenders, and consequently silk and cotton factories became established along three of London's rivers, the Lea from Waltham Abbey to Bow, the Wandle from Croydon to Wandsworth and the Cray at Crayford and Dartford. One of these companies still trades on the Cray at Crayford: David Evans & Co., established early in the eighteenth century. There was another reason for these out-of-town sites; the centre of London was too polluted, and the soft waters of the River Cray were just what was required. Silks, felts and other fabrics were traditionally dyed in the Wandle up to the period of William Morris in the nineteenth century. Liberty's was based here too.

Natural Dyes

PURPLE

One of the first recorded natural dyes used on silk in western Europe is purple. This has always been, and still is, favoured today as a regal colour. The Egyptians were the first people documented as producing purples and using mordants; their famous dye industry flourished from 1,500 BC to AD 638, when it was destroyed by invading armies. The industry was centred on the coastal port of Tyre, now in Lebanon. This 'purple of Tyre' was made from various seashells found in Italy and throughout the Mediterranean. There were at least three species involved; two are now called Linnaeus shells, *Murex trunculus* and *M. brandaris*, while a third was *Purpura lapilla*. Other species known to produce the dye are the common whelk *Buccinum undatum* and a Nicaraguan species, *Purpura patula*.

The art of dyeing passed via the Phoenician traders to the Roman Empire; Julius Caesar wore purple clothes and had purple curtains draped in his rooms. Present English royalty frequently use purple at State occasions and it is a popular colour with members of the clergy. Purple had been the colour of kings and queens for thousands of years, but 'mauve' caused quite a stir when it came into fashion and changed the course of dyeing history. The sensation occurred in 1862 when Queen Victoria appeared at the Great Exhibition wearing a mauve dress, which soon became a talking point. The mauve had been made from aniline, an organic chemical extracted from coal-tar. A certain William Perkin had accidentally discovered in 1856 that a lavender dye could be extracted from coal-tar. This spelt the end for natural dyes and paved the way for artificial replacements.

BLUE

One of the oldest blue dyes for silk is from the legendary woad, *Isatis tinctoria*, a member of the cabbage family. It is the dye associated with early Britons especially Boudicca who, in AD 61, fought against the Romans, themselves users of this natural dye. The Victorian authority on silk, Sir Thomas Wardle, possessed a piece of blue and red silk used on one of Richard I's (1189-99) deeds. He used this as demonstration material at his lectures and ascertained, probably correctly, that the blue was from woad, and the red from insects on the Kermes oak.

Woad is a tall-growing, yellow-flowered biennial plant that belies its

Natural Dyes

blues; the colour is due to oxidation of chemicals released from the plant brew. Fresh green leaves allowed to stand in boiling water release some of their colour which is further assisted with a strong alkali. Into this brew, silks or wool can be dropped and, when withdrawn very slowly without allowing any drips, they become blue on exposure to air. There are several different methods.

In England woad was introduced at some early time from central and southern Europe and was cultivated in Somerset and East Anglia during the eighteenth century. Woad mills coped with the trade. It was also grown in Ireland as well as Yorkshire and Hampshire.

While woad supported the livelihoods of so many people in England there was another plant which eventually took more and more of the market despite a lot of protest and denigration of what was in fact a superior product. This was indigo, *Indigofera tinctoria*, a member of the pea family (Leguminoseae) native to the Himalayas. England, France and Germany tried to suppress indigo entering their markets by banning its import, but this was unsuccessful and indigo dyes became dominant. There are a number of *Indigofera* species used in dyeing and much indigo was grown in America.

It is interesting to note that the mid-Atlantic islands of the Azores (Portugal) were originally settled by Flemish immigrants who brought woad with them. A small export of woad dye followed but was curtailed when indigo arrived from Brazil in about 1840. Such was the demand for indigo that the world was using around 5,000 tons of it in about 1900 and places like India were working hard to supply the demand. However, all this was short-lived since synthetic indigo was produced from 1907 and put paid to indigo itself as a natural dye.

In Latin America the Aztecs were good dyers and they had their own indigo species, *I. suffruticosa*. This know-how was eventually brought back to Spain and known as 'azul de anil' or 'anil'. The Aztecs also knew how to make purple dye from the local sea clam, *Jatropha curcas*. The word indigo was loosely applied and even referred to as the dye from woad. In China it was extracted from Chinese indigo, *Polygonum tinctorium*. Indigo (and cotton) production in the southern states of the USA (the Carolinas and Georgia especially) far outstripped the importance of silk and was responsible, in part, for the demise of the silk industry there.

Synthetic dyestuffs were created from 1856 onwards, particularly one called alizarin made from anthracene, a coal-tar product. This is identical to the chemical in madder which provides the orange colour.

Natural Dyes

RED

The obvious source of red dye was the fruit of the black mulberry itself when in season. There have been some occasions when it was used, but better sources were available, meaning that mulberry has not been widely used. Red pigments have been traditionally prepared from plants, especially the madder, and from scale-like insects.

Independently, on both sides of the Atlantic tiny 'cochineal' insects have been exploited as sources of red dyes for silk, probably for at least two thousand years. In London one of the wealthiest of Huguenot silk merchants, Etienne Seignoret,[1] was fined an amazing £10,000 in 1695–6 for illegally importing cochineal (and silks) from France worth £7,000. During the eighteenth and nineteenth centuries cochineal and the plant madder, *Rubia tinctoria*, were the most important red dyestuffs available. French soldiers' red trousers, like those of the English, were always dyed red from madder to hide the colour of blood.

Reds were also extracted from brazilwood, *Caesalpinia sappan*, while wild plants such as alkanet, *Anchusa tinctoria*, and the two North American species, safflower, *Carthamus tinctoria* and pokeberries, *Phytolacca sp.* were also used. President Thomas Jefferson had a personal interest in madder production, importing seeds from France, and encouraging its cultivation. It was grown extensively in Virginia.

Madder was used in different ways, sometimes fresh, sometimes dried and prepared into a paste, then kept for up to three years. The source of the madder and how it was processed was therefore crucial, and determined colour shades and commanded different prices. Jefferson believed that three-year-old roots, freshly ground, produced a red colour twice as good as madder processed in the ordinary way on the Continent. Such was the demand for madder in England that in about 1806 the annual import from Holland alone was worth £180,000. By 1886, 70,000 tons of madder were produced worldwide.

Traditionally madder roots were oven-dried, ground and the husk removed. This provided the first extract, but a third-quality product. A second pounding produced a second grade product and the final grinding produced the most coveted extract or prime quality. This was called 'Kor-Kraps'. It was such 'kraps' that the Jewish dyers of Uzbekistan imported especially from India to prepare their dyes for their suzanis and ikats. They also used 'Kyrmisi', a red dye extracted from the kermes oak.

Natural Dyes

Madder (*Bayak* to the Jews) is native to India and also westwards towards the north of the Mediterranean. Genuine madder silks are still produced today by David Evans & Co. at Crayford.

The use of insects for red dyes had thus been known, independently from both the New and the Old Worlds for a long time. In Mediterranean Europe the kermes oak, *Quercus coccifera*, harbours small sap-sucking insects related to aphids and cicadas called *Kermes ilicis*, which were traditionally collected from wild trees, especially in southern France and Spain and used to make a red dye. Only the females were used. Kermes oaks, with their tiny but fiercely spiky leaves, used to grow on much of the rugged mountains round the Mediterranean, but have since declined. Today they are quite a rare species, at least in France. The red dyestuff *granum tinctorium* has been used from time immemorial. However, the red colour is not as bright as that from the cochineal insects of South America.

The more widely known of the cochineal insects is *Dactylopius coccus*, a relative of the European species, and it sucks the sap of various species of cacti. Of importance is the prickly pear, *Opuntia ficus-indica*, on which it breeds readily and which is still used today for commercial rearing in parts of North Africa and Central America.

When the Spaniards invaded Mexico in 1518 they noted the natives dyeing clothes with what they mistook for seeds. As soon as the Spaniards knew the truth they were quick to cash in on the production and harvesting of these native cochineal insects which were then sent back to Europe, particularly from Mexico and Guatemala. Towards the end of the eighteenth century colonists in America were complaining about having to pay extortionate prices for cochineal which had to be routed from South America (just on their own doorstep) via England, and then across the Atlantic to Virginia at great cost. At one stage in 1763 it was proposed to make a commercial venture of producing cochineal in Georgia and South Carolina but it never succeeded, even though a prize of £40 was offered for the largest amount exported in any one year.

Commercial production of cochineal relied upon one acre of prickly pear producing about 113–36 kg (250–300 lb) of cochineal per annum, with about seventy thousand dried insects representing each pound. It must have been quite an arduous task collecting them! 'Silver cochineal' was the name given to the silvery-looking mass of insects dried in a stove, while the normal method was to sun-dry the insects immediately after collection from the cacti bushes and kill them in hot water. Insects collected from the wild cacti bushes instead of cultivated ones only yielded about a fourth of the strength of the red

Natural Dyes

pigment. Cochineal was most used for producing crimsons, pinks and scarlets for both wool and silk, especially when mordanted with tin or alum.

Naturally-occurring lichens from the Mediterranean coast have also been used since earliest times to produce shades between red and blue. The dyestuff extracted from the lichens is called orchil and it was members of the *Rocella* genus which were collected (e.g. *R. tinctoria*). Other sources were the Canaries and Cape Verde Islands.

In the mountainous Auvergne of France a lichen species, *Ochrolechia parella*, produced very similar colours to orchil. The technique was to stew the lichens in a broth of fermented urine or slaked lime (anything alkali) for several weeks, let it redden up and then use it for dyeing silks. Slight changes in the alkali determined the hue of blue or red.

YELLOW, ORANGE, GOLD

Yellow, of course, was generally available throughout Europe from the Saffron Crocus *Crocus sativus*, much cultivated and traded throughout the Continent. Places like Saffron Walden in Essex, Safronbolu in Turkey and Krokos in Greece all allude to the importance of this dye plant. It was the yellow male anthers which were the source of the pigment. There were severe penalties for adulterating saffron; people were even burnt alive for their troubles.

It is not mulberry wood which everyone thinks of today as a suitable natural source of yellow dye for silk, but other common plants like nettles, *Urtica dioica*, and ragwort, *Senecio jacobeae*, or the bark of alder, *Alnus glutinosa*, which can do the same job. But for three hundred years an important tropical mulberry species, dyer's mulberry, had been used as a dye. This was the fustic of the seventeenth century that every dyer relied upon.

Dyer's mulberry, *Morus tinctoria*, is a tropical member of the mulberry family (Moraceae) and grows in Africa and South America. It was traded widely and greatly esteemed for dyeing silk, wool and cotton. With this invaluable yellow dye other colours could be produced to make compound hues, such as yellow and blue to make green. Other colours like snuffs, drabs, oranges and red oranges could also be produced. In colonial America fustic was in great demand and the inventory of one dyer in Boston (Massachusetts) in 1695 records 104 kg (230 lb).

It was the splintered wood of dyer's mulberry which was used for dyeing.

Natural Dyes

Roots and gnarled trunks were the best pieces, especially if the wood glowed a bright yellow with an orange tinge when cut. The wood splintered easily. Soaked in water for two days to extract plenty of dye the bagged chips of wood would be immersed in the dyeing vat ready for use together with alum as the mordant.

Dyer's rocket or weld, *Reseda luteola*, was another important dye plant for silk and was much respected by the Romans. It is a native throughout much of western Europe and was eventually introduced to North America. Silk dyed with different mordants produces a subtle range of yellowish shades; with alum a primrose-yellow, chrome a slightly deeper colour, iron a dull fawn and tin a warm yellow.

At the Lewisham Silk Mills in south-east London in the nineteenth century, where military garments were made in enormous quantities, incoming undyed silks were always dyed a uniform gold colour; all other incoming silk skeins had been previously dyed. Upstairs in the attic, according to the historical researchers of this now defunct mill, there used to be a man whose only job was to dye the silks, and his arms and legs were permanently yellow from this work. Though the method of dyeing is not described, or the plants involved, it is probable that bark of alder was used in a large vat. Alder bark, when peeled from the trunk, glows with a fiery orange and it is not hard to see that this species would be ideal for producing various shades of yellow and orange. The gold colours were most appropriate for the military garments, many of which were exported for overseas troops, since it was made for regimental stripes, lapels and shoulder decorations.

For 'sulphur-yellows' another plant, which is a familiar garden plant of the herbaceous border, was used, at least in Uzbekistan (Soviet Union). This was larkspur, *Consolida ambigua*, a relation of the delphinium. It was called *Isparak*. The Jewish dyers, for this was their trade in Uzbekistan, also obtained a yellowish-green dye from *Turkhmak*, a fungus of the Mulberry tree.

In the eastern USA safflower or Dyer's Thistle, *Carthamus tinctorius*, was employed to dye silks yellow. Silks were simmered in safflower blossoms for an hour, then mordanted with alum. African marigolds, *Tagetes sp.*, were used as an alternative substitute dye plant.

GREEN

Greens were usually made from combinations of dyestuffs. Thus the Jewish dyers of Uzbekistan made green by combining indigo dyes with *Turkhmak*,

Natural Dyes

the dye from the mulberry fungus. Turmeric, *Curcuma longa*, was widely used in the eighteenth and nineteenth centuries with other dyes to make various shades of browns and olive greens. By itself it produced one of the finest yellows and it didn't need a mordant. However, it faded badly. In Malaya fast greens were produced using the young leaves of rambutan, *Nephelium lappaceum*, an edible relative of the lichi-nut, in combination with turmeric. Yellow-greens could be made from *Sapium indicum*. The famous madder green was made from a combination of the fast yellow colour, extracted from an oriental berry, and typical indigo dye.

BROWN

Lichens figure strongly in the production of browns. Most notable among fabrics were the Harris tweeds which acquired their brown, tan and gold colours from a stew of one particular common lichen called crottle, or *Parmelia saxatilis*. There are several different types of lichen which can be used for dyeing silks, and brown colours are not necessarily the outcome. Depending on how the lichen is processed, or the state or season in which it is picked, colours can range from yellow, through brown to orange, red, purple and blue.

In the tropics the bark of one species of mangrove, *Rhizophora mangle*, was almost certainly used as a dye source to make silk tan-coloured. It had the advantage that no mordant was required. In the Bahamas, mangrove dyes were actively employed.

BLACK

Black silks were prepared either from a compound mixture of colours or from the chipped heartwood of logwood, *Haematoxylon campechianum*, which contains the pigment haematoxylin. This is a Latin American tree which enjoyed a lucrative trade across the Atlantic from British and Spanish traders. The usefulness of logwood was recognized as early as the sixteenth century but it is a fugitive dye (i.e. the colour fades quickly) and regulations were brought out in Elizabeth I's reign banning its use because of this flaw. Once mordanting techniques had improved a hundred years later, the regulations were lifted. Mention of 'Spanish Black' in London probably refers to logwood imported and traded by the Spanish, whereas 'London Black' may have been another trade secret. Dyes from logwood also produced a 'faded purple' colour.

Two other black dyes were known to the Jewish dyers of Uzbekistan. These were the peel of pomegranate fruit, *Punica granatum*, and *Abuzgunta*, a gall nut from the pistachio tree, *Pistacia vera*. The peel of pomegranate was sometimes mixed with iron oxide which, in the long term, produced corrosion of silk fibres, a major problem in present-day conservation of old silk materials.

In south-east Asia, in Malaysia, Kalimantan, Sumatra and other places in Indonesia, black silks were produced from a Malaysian tree called a gambier, *Uncaria gambir*. Its leaves and twigs released a black dye on boiling. Rambutan fruits also produce a black colour on silk which has previously been dyed red.

Grey hues were made in England from using two common plants, bramble, *Rubus sp.*, and bracken, *Pteridium aquilinum*, for which 0.5 kg of bramble or bracken shoots would be required for dyeing. In Victorian England clients often wanted their black silks to hang or drape a little heavier than normal silks. The ingenious craft of weighting silks with the tannin expressed from plant galls, such as the oak apple, was therefore developed. The silks were often introduced to the dye-baths together with iron salts to give extra body to the material.

NOTE

1. Etienne Seignoret is sometimes referred to as Stephen Seignoret, in an anglicized form.

CHAPTER 7

Uses of Silk

Here we go round the mulberry bush,
The mulberry bush, the mulberry bush,
Here we go round the mulberry bush,
On a cold and frosty morning.

*T*he major use of silk is, of course, for clothing. However, there are numerous other uses, some very sophisticated. They all rely upon the unique nature of silk as a natural product. Silk's chemical and physical characteristics are the key to its exclusive usage.

Silk is a natural fibre made by caterpillars of all butterflies and moths, spiders, some Latin American ichneumon flies and some aquatic crustaceans. The two moth families which produce more silk than any other group are the Saturniidae (silkmoths) and the Bombycidae (true silkmoths), to which the *Bombyx* silkmoth belongs.

There are scores of other 'wild silkmoths' which occur throughout the world, particularly in India and across to China, and these also produce silk. Although their silk shares some of the properties of *Bombyx* silk, it tends not to be as fine and smooth a natural fibre as that of *Bombyx*. The use of other invertebrate silks is limited, but that of the spider is regarded as being a little more resilient that than of *Bombyx*, but it does not lend itself to commercial production. The qualities of silk are a reflection of its physical and chemical attributes.

PHYSICAL CHARACTERISTICS

Toughness and resilience

Silk has a high tensile strength, in fact it is said to be stronger than

Uses of Silk

a filament of steel of equivalent dimensions.[1] This means that the silk threads do not yield to breaking and are even tougher if twisted round each other.

Elasticity

Silk threads can be readily expanded to 20–25 per cent of their natural length. This is usefully employed in stockings and socks, the silk material expanding to meet demand. Providing silk is not stretched to more than 2 per cent of its length, it will revert to its former shape immediately; greater than 2 per cent of its length and it will take a little longer. The use of silk as guy-ropes has been extensive through the ages, due to this elasticity.

Draping

One hundred per cent silk garments hang very delicately and give materials an extra appeal over other fibres. They can be made to hang less delicately and more firmly by the inclusion of various metal salts. This was sometimes produced deliberately for clients.

Size

Bundled or folded up silk reduces to extraordinary degrees. A normal sized silk scarf can always be pulled very easily through a finger ring. Its chemical composition allows it to bounce back again very quickly. An example of the use of this characteristic is in secret silk maps which were concealed in clothing during the Second World War.

Weight

Silk is one of the lightest of all natural fibres, thus enhancing its use in dresses, saris, shirts and kimonos ('ki'=silk). The national costume of the Philippines, the Barong Tagolog, is traditionally made of silk.

Uses of Silk

Warmth

Silk clothes have a 'warm' feel to them (when you can actually feel them on you!). This happens both with loose-fitting garments such as dresses and shirts and with close-fitting socks, which enhances this feature. Silk is more heat resistant than wood and, if deliberately burnt, will decompose at 340 °F, 171 °C.

Combustibility

Pure silk is actually very difficult to burn since it stifles itself quickly with accumulated carbon. Silk that has been adulterated with any other additional component burns more easily.

CHEMICAL CHARACTERISTICS

Hydroscopic nature and insulation

The amino-acids of silk allow it to absorb considerable quantities of water before the material feels damp. Various authorities claim that from one-third to three times the silk's weight of water can be absorbed. The advantages in the tropics are obvious: silk keeps you cool and is light to wear. When the amino-acids take on water vapour they hydrate and give off a small amount of heat. This helps in the cooling process. The advantage in cold environments is that silks offer a useful insulation layer. Silk padding is used in some military clothing, and in many ski clothes.

Dye affinity

Silks have a great affinity to dyes and produce more permanent (fast) and richer colours than other materials. By comparison other materials can produce very disagreeable colours, known by some as foggy or *brouillard* shades.

Uses of Silk

ABOVE: Genuine
French silk dresses
re-appeared in the
Cévennes in the late
1970s. They were
expensive then at
£250 each (£500 at
1990 prices). But the
demand was there.
Parisian women were
prepared to pay that
amount on holiday.
Since then, the
Cévennes silk
industry has gained
government backing

Silk scarves
and cravats are now
marketed to tourists
in the museums of
southern France

THE · STORY · OF · SILK

An example of
Jacquard woven silk
produced by
Cartwright and
Sheldon of Paradise
Mill, Macclesfield,
Cheshire for the
British Empire
Exhibition at
Wembley, London in
1924

The Jacquard loom with its punched cards was the forerunner of the computer, and of the fairground organ and pianola. It was first exhibited in Paris in 1801. The warp had to be prepared on a horizontal warping machine prior to being woven on the Jacquard loom. It would take two men five days to make up the warp which would eventually comprise anything between nine thousand and sixteen thousand threads. The warp had to be made up in sections on the warping machine using 450 spindles and bobbins at a time. Each thread had to be fed through an eyelet, correctly tensioned, no two touching each other and no threads crossing. The two men worked as a team, one pushing the threads through the eyelets, the other drawing it through. All this was unpaid work since the weaver was only

Jacquard Silk Weaving
on hand looms at
Paradise Mill Macclesfield

Silk handloom weaving began in Macclesfield in the 1750's The firm of Cartwright & Sheldon, established in 1912, was the last in the town to practise the tradition. Their handloom operation closed in 1981 and is now a working museum.

Weaving silk by hand is a skilled craft involving 3 basic actions: *shedding*—parting the warp threads to allow the shuttle to pass between, *picking*—placing the weft or 'pick' into the warp, and *beating up*—packing the pick into the cloth. The efficiency of handloom weaving has been improved by two inventions: the *Jacquard* and the *Flying Shuttle*.

The Jacquard, a French invention of 1804, is a shedding device for selecting and raising patterns of warp threads. This enables complex figured fabrics to be woven.

Joseph Marie Jacquard was born in Lyons in 1752. His machine replaced the drawboy who worked the warp threads by hand. It was first exhibited in Paris in 1801. Although Napoleon recognized its worth and praised Jacquard for his efforts, it caused unrest among the silk weavers who burned the new machines in 1804. The Jacquard was a forerunner of the computer and is still used today to weave patterned fabrics.

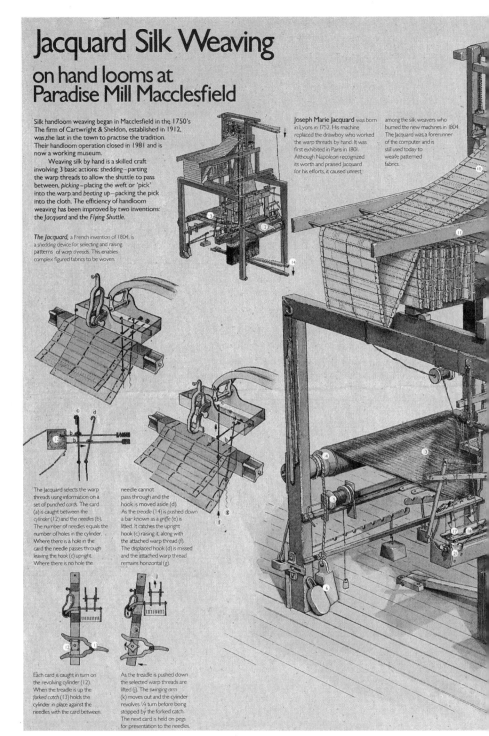

The Jacquard selects the warp threads using information on a set of *punched cards*. The card (a) is caught between the cylinder (12) and the needles (b). The number of needles equals the number of holes in the cylinder. Where there is a hole in the card the needle passes through leaving the hook (c) upright. Where there is no hole the needle cannot pass through and the hook is moved aside (d). As the *treadle* (14) is pushed down a bar known as a *griffe* (e) is lifted. It catches the upright hook (c) raising it, along with the attached warp thread (f). The displaced hook (d) is missed and the attached warp thread remains horizontal (g).

Each card is caught in turn on the revolving cylinder (12). When the treadle is up the *forked catch* (13) holds the cylinder in place against the needles with the card between.

As the treadle is pushed down the selected warp threads are lifted (j). The swinging arm (k) moves out and the cylinder revolves ¼ turn before being stopped by the forked catch. The next card is held on pegs for presentation to the needles.

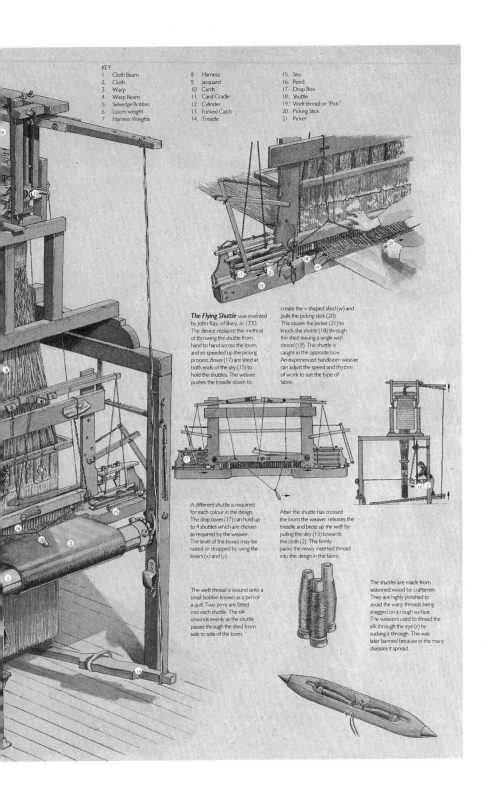

KEY
1. Cloth Beam
2. Cloth
3. Warp
4. Warp Beam
5. Selvedge Bobbin
6. Loom weight
7. Harness Weights
8. Harness
9. Jacquard
10. Cards
11. Card Cradle
12. Cylinder
13. Forked Catch
14. Treadle
15. Sley
16. Reed
17. Drop Box
18. Shuttle
19. Weft thread or "Pick"
20. Picking Stick
21. Picker

The Flying Shuttle was invented by John Kay, of Bury, in 1733. The device replaced the method of throwing the shuttle from hand to hand across the loom, and so speeded up the *picking* process. *Boxes* (17) are sited at both ends of the *sley* (15) to hold the shuttles. The weaver pushes the treadle down to create the v-shaped shed (w) and pulls the picking stick (20). This causes the *picker* (21) to knock the *shuttle* (18) through the shed leaving a single *weft thread* (19). The shuttle is caught in the opposite box. An experienced handloom weaver can adjust the speed and rhythm of work to suit the type of fabric.

A different shuttle is required for each colour in the design. The *drop boxes* (17) can hold up to 4 shuttles which are chosen as required by the weaver. The level of the boxes may be raised or dropped by using the levers (x) and (y).

After the shuttle has crossed the loom the weaver releases the treadle and *beats up the weft* by pulling the *sley* (15) towards the cloth (2). This firmly packs the newly inserted thread into the design in the fabric.

The weft thread is wound onto a small bobbin known as a *pirn* or a *quill*. Two pirns are fitted into each shuttle. The silk unwinds evenly as the shuttle passes through the shed from side to side of the loom.

The *shuttles* are made from seasoned wood by craftsmen. They are highly polished to avoid the warp threads being snagged on a rough surface. The weavers used to thread the silk through the eye (r) by sucking it through. This was later banned because of the many diseases it spread.

paid for the length of material he wove. Once made up, the warp could be woven in two ways, either 'flat woven' for dresses, scarves or handkerchiefs or, 'figure-woven' where patterns were incorporated into the material.

Figure weaving depends on either the warp or weft threads showing on the face of the cloth. If the warp threads are to be shown, the loom harness picks up the warp, so that the weft threads go underneath; if the weft threads are to show, the harness keeps the warp down so that the weft can go over the top. This is all worked and controlled by the strings of the harness which go up into the jacquard cards – or 'brains' of the machine – one card for every weft thread in the pattern. The cards hang together in an endless roll.

A fine dress made in
Spitalfields from
Spitalfields silk in
about 1740–50. Today
dresses like this are
of great historical
importance as well
as being collectable
antiques

Uses of Silk

ABOVE: The Cévennes probably made more silk underwear than anywhere else on earth. After synthetics were introduced earlier this century, local factories changed quickly to other materials such as cotton synthetics and denim. Tradition has it that the word denim comes from Nîmes, i.e. *de Nîmes*

BELOW: Multi-coloured silk threads are available in the Cévennes, dyed with synthetic rather than natural dyes

Uses of Silk

Hygienic silk – its imputrescible nature

Silk, as a natural product, does not rot. This attribute is advantageous when silk is used as stitching material by surgeons.

PRACTICAL USES

Banners

At an important Chinese archaeological site called Tun-huang, the German archaeologist Marc Aurel Stein found long silken banners which he supposed were to be draped from the tops of cliffs. They had lain wrapped for thousands of years and were compressed into fragile packets which would eventually take the British Museum seven years to unravel. Others to use silk banners were the Romans and Henry VIII.

Carpets and Embroidery

Silk, beaten or pressed with wool, used to be made into carpets in China in the T'ang Dynasty (AD 618–907), and specimens exist from that period today. Silk is still worked with wool in Britain today.

Making-up and embroidering with silk can be very time-consuming. Some of the distinguished silk houses in France in particular may take several years to complete an important commission. This is nothing new. On a much smaller scale, a Chinese family of twelve people may take five years to complete an intricate silk robe of fine stitching and couching.

Wrapping corpses

The wrapping of bodies in silk was a common practice in ancient China, as Stein found out when he robbed the tombs in the great cemetery of Astana in the Turfan region. From there he took away forty-five camel-loads of frescoes and other treasures, unwrapping the silk garments from the corpses. He noted that the silks bore a variety of motifs representing a mixture of Chinese and Middle Eastern patterns.

It is probable that bodies of royalty in both China and Egypt were

Uses of Silk

wrapped in silks, often the finest silk garments worn when the deceased was alive. According to Egyptology scholars, silks became more common in Egypt from the fourth century onwards. The silks did not necessarily come from the *Bombyx* silkworm, since a silk funerary fabric found at Qustul was of a wild silk, probably from the Tusseh silkmoth. (To an expert the fibres are different, coarser in a wild silk.) Another silk garment found in Egypt dated from the Roman period and was dyed red and blue.

Silkscreen printing

This is a development of the traditional stencil printing used in the past. Fijian islanders made some of the earliest stencils for printing textiles. They cut holes in leaves and put vegetable dyes through them onto bark and cloth. The Japanese made four- and five-colour stencils.

Stencils were often used for religious pictures and illuminated manuscripts in the sixteenth century. Then in the seventeenth century, they were used to produce the ever-popular flocked wallpapers in England.

In 1907 Samuel Simon of Manchester was granted a patent for a silkscreen

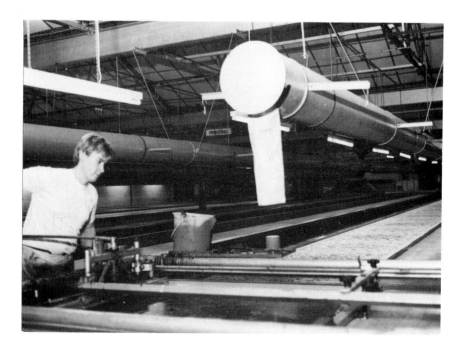

Dry hand-block printing as it is done at David Evans & Co., Dartford, Kent. Note how the silk is stretched out along the table and the apparatus is drawn over the fabric at the exact spot so that the pattern can be stamped down

Air-drying silkscreen
prints at David Evans
& Co., a process
which has since
been superseded

process and is usually considered the first to use silk fabric as a screen or ground. By 1914, American John Pilsworth had developed a multi-colour method of stencil printing.

The silk fabric is stretched over a frame and ink is forced through it on to the paper or textile that is placed underneath. The picture or design is produced by making the silk screen into a stencil. This is done by preventing the ink from being squeezed through some areas. This 'blocking' or masking can be achieved in various ways; for example, painting the screen with gum arabic or a more modern filler, sticking on hand-cut paper stencils or coating the screen with photo-sensitive emulsion, exposing the design and developing it to leave a blocked image.

Multi-coloured images are achieved by reprinting the screen with different colours or, more usually, printing from several screens to achieve a compound image or design.

Because of its fineness, silk was for many years considered the best mesh, but it has now largely been superseded by terylene and nylon.

The virtues of silkscreen printing were extolled by that connoisseur of silk fabrics William Morris (1834–96). Patterns were transferred on to fabrics such as wallpaper, curtains and general household furnishings, using silk as a medium. Morris carried out much of his silk printing at Merton in Surrey at

Late nineteenth-century examples of Tusseh silk printed with an old Indian design and over-worked with Tusseh silk embroidery; a form of needlework developed by Mrs Wardle of the Leek school employing subtle shades of Tusseh silks. From Thomas Wardle's 1881 book

Uses of Silk

his own establishment next to the River Wandle. The water was particularly good here for the washing of silks, and his factory was eventually taken over by Liberty of London. Also, there used to be a much smaller silk printing works on the banks of the River Hogswill in Worcester Park, but this disappeared earlier this century.

Silkscreen printing is brilliantly executed by the house of Hermès in Lyon. It turns out 300,000 scarves a year, screenprinted on 90 cm (35 in) squares of silk from rows of 100 m (328 ft) long print tables. It takes two years to convert the bale of raw Chinese silk into a Hermès silk scarf which has a distinctive heavyweight twill of 75 gm, selling for £110 each. Hermès has an archive of over eight hundred designs, and a shade catalogue of over two thousand colours from which to choose.

Gloves

Silk was made into gloves, just as much as lingerie, shirts and ties. But to make a pair of silk gloves from other animal's silk verges on the bizarre and the ridiculous. It *is* possible with incredible patience to collect sufficient spider's silk to spin a pair of gloves. This was done in Montpellier (France) in the last century. The Victorian naturalist Francis Buckland recounted how he had seen a pair of ladies gloves made from the 'tow' or silk secretion (scientifically called the byssus) which pinna shells (*Pinna spp.*) use to anchor their shells to rocks.

Paintings

The earliest Chinese silk painting so far discovered dates to the late Chou and Western Han (*c*. 206–220 AD) periods. Silks had to be sized first with alum or animal glue so that the inks and colour dyes would not run. Silk was better than paper for it allowed fine control over grading ink and colour washes.

Paper-making

Silk was one of several natural products used in ancient China in the first century AD for making paper. Bamboo and wood, especially the bark from

Uses of Silk

mulberry trees (*Morus* as well as *Broussonetia*) were used, in contrast to the *Papyrus* reeds used extensively in ancient Egypt.

Quilts

Silk-padded jackets are made today by a cottage industry in Britain out of imported silk 'bells' from China. A bell-shaped cap of silk (usually about 500 gm) is made from the silk of twenty-five cocoons from which the moths have escaped, each layer of silk being placed on top of the other to form a bell. These particular cocoons are the ones from which the specially selected 'queen' adults have been allowed to hatch so that they can mate and lay eggs for the next generation. Normally the old cocoons are discarded since on exit the moth dissolves his or her way out by secreting a substance which breaks down all the silk fibres blocking its path; but marketing the bells like this has provided another Chinese export. The bells can be put to many uses. For instance there is sufficient silk to make two padded jackets, if each layer of silk is peeled off and spread over material, or, if spun, it is sufficient to make three blouses.

RAF parachutes and maps

Silk is an ideal fabric for parachutes and secret maps since it is lightweight and can be folded to such a small size. When the Second World War was declared, Zoë, Lady Hart Dyke of the Lullingstone Silk Farm (then in north-west Kent), immediately volunteered her silk output to the Ministry of Supply – but it had to measure up to their high ministry standards. Fortunately the tensile strength of Zoë's Kentish silk passed the test of being greater than 18 kg (40 lb) per sq in. However, Lady Hart Dyke's efforts only went a tiny way towards helping the war effort since her total output was only sufficient for two hundred parachutes. Ironically the ministry had refused her permission in 1939 to boost her output.

In Macclesfield the mills were turned to parachute production during the war, making eight hundred a week. All silks had been requisitioned by the Silk & Rayon Control Centre, but this was the advent of the artificial fibres, nylon and rayon. The new nylon parachutes were only used for bomber crews since the bulky artificial materials were found to be too big for the Spitfire and Hurricane crews.

Zoë, Lady Hart Dyke
photographed in
about 1946 at
Lullingstone Castle,
Kent

Uses of Silk

During and after the war parachute silk was eagerly sought by the general public, since there were no fine materials available in the haberdashery shops for making clothes. People had to make do with whatever they could find. Parachutes were meant to have been handed in, if found, but many got on to the black market and enterprising housewives turned their skills to making all sorts of clothes. So covetously were ex-RAF silks regarded that, forty years later, there are still people who keep pieces of precious silk and use them for such niceties as lining the pockets of their menfolk. There was a colour code for parachutes which identified them when dropped behind enemy lines as being for food, equipment or men, and these different coloured silks and other materials clandestinely changed hands.

On the Continent British soldiers were instructed to burn parachutes after landing, but the French people also liked silk parachute material for their lingerie. Unfortunately, the wearing of silks that could not otherwise be explained by the French made it clear that they were collaborators, or were harbouring British parachutists.

Silk was also put to incredibly good use by the RAF as part of the emergency kit of personnel flying over the Continent. Fine silk squares about two feet square were overprinted with the map of Europe. The maps of France, Germany and Switzerland were so detailed that all major roads and town names were included. Francophiles motoring in France today could easily find their way around using these maps, since all the main arterial roads are included; though not, of course, the new auto-route system. The square folded down to such a small size that it would easily fit into a matchbox, or could be slipped into a lining, or other secret place.

PHYSICAL USES

Electricity and physics

Silk is a great insulator and has been used for the insulation of electric wires. The American statesman, Benjamin Franklin (1706-90), was fascinated by electricity, and also used silk in the manufacture of his kites.

In the classic physics experiment to demonstrate static electricity, pith balls are rubbed on silk to charge them up. The result is attraction.

Uses of Silk

Surgery

Following an ancient art of the Romans for tying up blood vessels with silk, the Chinese have today extended the use to vascular surgery, replacing vital veins and arteries with fine silk 'straws'. It was reported[1] that Surgeon Dr Feng Youxian of the Zhongshan Hospital in Shanghai actually used a piece of his own silk shirt for an operation.

Silk is still used widely, in Britain at least, for surgery. As a natural product which is not likely to degrade within the body, it is sometimes used for internal stitching. For stitching up skin two colours are available commercially: black and white. The black silk threads (they are made up of several silk threads twisted together) are used on white-skinned people, and the white silk threads are used on black-skinned people, the contrasting colours of the silk against the skin making it easier to see.

The Musée de Soie at St Hippolyte du Fort exhibits long fibrous strands of another silk material, as tough and as thick as spaghetti. They call it *Crin de Florence* and it is extracted silk from *Bombyx* caterpillars taken out of them when live or freshly killed. It is said that *crin* was used in surgery, but it also had a supplementary role for making fishermen's nets.

HIGH-TENSILE STRENGTH USES

Armour

Even the brave Japanese Samurai warriors of the sixteenth century used silk to fasten their series of protective metal plates together as used in their armour. Good examples, for instance, can be seen at the Smithsonian Art Museum in Springfield, Massachusetts.

Clock pendulums

Connoisseurs of antique clocks all know that a genuine eighteenth-century French bracket clock has its pendulum hung on a short piece of pure silk. English ones do not. The silk is made up of several threads coarsely twisted to form a tough 1 cm long loop. In the eyes of the clockmaker, pure silk presumably conferred qualities of durability and damped any tensions.

Uses of Silk

Genetic engineering

The high-tensile strength of silk, particularly spider's silk, has been used as a model by genetic engineers for the proposed manufacture of bullet-proof jackets and flak jackets. Special bacteria are fed with genetic information so that they can make artificial high-tensile silk.

Guy ropes

As early as the time of the Roman Empire there are reports of silk being used to make ropes, but silk would have been used much earlier in China.

However, in China in the thirteenth century, for the Kublai Khan to have the guy ropes of his portable bamboo hunting palace made of silk was hardly an extravagant use, for he ruled over a country which produced millions of tons of silk each year. The use of silk for guy ropes was presumably because it helps to absorb changes in strain.

Kublai Khan's servants also wore silk masks when serving at the table, to keep germs off the food. It was the travel-writer Marco Polo who has given us this insight into royal China of the thirteenth century.

Musical instruments

In Europe, the Levant and Africa strings for instruments have traditionally been made of gut (animal intestine, usually sheep, not cat!) and also of metal-wire, when the technology was developed in about the thirteenth century. In the East, however, silk was the usual material for making strings, wound or plaited.

As might be expected, the earliest records of its use are from China. An ode dated *c.* 1,100 BC, refers to a long zither with seven silk strings, called a *ch'in* which was used as a solo instrument and in the Confucian ceremonial orchestra. All the strings are of equal length, but their thicknesses vary, being composed, at least in theory, of 48, 54, 64, 72, 81, 96 and 108 strands. It is still played today and has led to a wide variety of zithers throughout the Far East. In China, the other main ones are the 25-stringed *sho* and the 14-stringed *cheng*. Japanese instruments derive largely from the Chinese, but often preserve more archaic forms and have a greater variety of strings. The *koto* is perhaps the most important and nowadays has thirteen

Uses of Silk

strings, although formerly it had twenty-five. It is also worth mentioning the Korean *komunko* and the Burmese *mi gyuan* which has the form of a crocodile.

The other main group of instruments to use silk strings are lutes. The *p'ip'a* was introduced in China about two thousand years ago and present-day forms have not changed greatly. It has four silk strings. It is called a *biwa* in Japan and had already become very large in the tenth century.

The number and variety of eastern zither- and lute-derived instruments is great and the use of silk strings remains the norm.

Telescopes

Another interesting contribution that Lady Hart Dyke made to the war effort was to provide silk cocoons to the Royal Greenwich Observatory. The silk was used in two ways. Single strands were used as cross-wires in low-powered telescopes and magnets were suspended on silk.

Between 1840 and 1910 the Royal Greenwich Observatory measured the strength and direction of the Earth's magnetic field with 0.91 kg (2 lb) magnets suspended on eight to twelve strands of unspun silk about 20–23 cm (8–9 in) long. The advantage of silk over other materials was that it was effectively tortionless. Today, with much smaller and lighter instruments, quartz fibres have replaced silk. Nylon thread replaced silk in the low-powered telescopes.

In higher magnification telescopes spider's silk is used since it has much greater strength, durability and fineness than silk. Spider's silk is still in use today in Royal Greenwich Observatory telescopes and in some cases has remained unchanged for up to twenty years. Provided that someone does not accidentally poke their fingers through fine silk cross-wires (which has happened) the silk is good for many decades.

The technique used by astronomers for relieving the ordinary garden spider (*Araneus diadematus*) of its valuable silk was to suspend it on a two-pronged wire fork and persuade it to hang downwards. By winding the silk as the spider spins downward, the first few centimetres are discarded because it is not uniform (and presumably blobby) and the remaining silk is kept. Like this it will keep for years.

Great consternation occurred at the Royal Observatory in Herstmonceux (East Sussex) in 1987, however, when an errant fly got inside a 66 cm (26 in) diameter telescope and broke the optical cross-wires. Considerable correspondence in the local papers and the *Daily Telegraph* ensued, with suggestions about how, and with what, the silk wires should be replaced. It was suggested that small spiders make fine silk and that their threads can be collected off a pencil. And the captive spider would have to be very calm, otherwise the silk thread would be too blobby. One correspondent suggested that a species of South American spider with yellow silk produced the best quality. There was also the observation that only special garden spiders from York made the best silk, and that these used to be collected on Strensall Common by apprentices of the Vickers Instruments factory. The raw spider's silk was 0.0003 in thick, far too thick for precision instuments, so a Vickers expert would patiently tease out a single thread from the mix of silk produced from the battery of spider spinnerets. Unfortunately these cooperative spiders have been superseded by advanced fibre technology.

Cyclists and jockeys

The light weight and elasticity characteristics of silk are employed by both cyclists and jockeys; French cyclists prefer silk tyres which give amazing traction and a smooth ride, and jockeys dress resplendently in bright silks which both help to advertise the owner's colours and are extremely light.

GLAMOROUS SILKS

Ladies' make-up

The use of macerated silk is widespread in the preparation of ladies' make-up. Helena Rubinstein, for instance, advertises that its products contain 1 per cent hydrolysed silk to give the make-up a suspicion of sparkle. In the East, living silkmoth pupae are pressed to make 'pupa oil' which is incorporated into face creams and soap.

QCs and the Houses of Parliament

To 'take the silk' is a traditional custom undertaken by members of the Queen's Counsel, the highest appointment for Her Majesty's lawyers in Britain, whereby they exchange their ordinary stuff gown for a silk one.

Uses of Silk

Thereafter the lawyers are called 'Silks'. There is an even more interesting aspect to this ancient practice, since the lawyers' silk gowns have a tiny silk pouch attached near the nape of the neck. Into this is placed money for services given – when the lawyer is facing the other way – since it would be exceedingly improper to deal with it directly.

The origin of QCs taking silk appears to be entirely lost in antiquity. Ede & Ravenscroft Ltd of Chancery Lane, London, who have been 'Robe Makers and Tailors since the Reign of William and Mary in the year 1689', believe the custom started after the Restoration and coincided with the wearing of wigs. It is not surprising that QCs still maintain their silk tradition since it is wholly appropriate for them to wear silks in the company they keep with fellow members of the court and royalty.

It is interesting that it is also a tradition in the Houses of Parliament for the Speaker of the House to wear ceremonial silk stockings. The current incumbent of the title even wears silk tights for the honorable gentlemen he serves, thus preserving this old custom, steeped in centuries of tradition.

NOTE

1. N. Hyde, *National Geographic* (January 1984), pp. 12–48.

CHAPTER 8

Royal Silks

So spins the silk-worm, small its slender store,
And labours till it clouds itself all o'er.

Alexander Pope

DRESS AND FURNISHINGS

I n the past five thousand years, the rich commodity of silk has been zealously acquired by kings, queens, princesses, emperors and empresses. In its time silk has commanded prices equal to gold, set nation against nation, and the secret of its production has been strictly controlled. British royalty continue the trend of having silk wedding dresses, preferably made from pure English silk, a tradition which dates back to earliest times.

The Church, Crown and court are inextricably linked and we find many early examples of silks being used in ecclesiastical situations (Chapter 5). For example the daughter-in-law of Alfred The Great commissioned famous silk and gold embroidered vestments which are still in Durham Cathedral.

There was no lack of silk available to the Romans. Julius Caesar (100?–44 BC) wore purple silk every time he appeared in public and had silk curtains made up for his rooms. His choice of clothing may have been influenced by his lover Cleopatra, who used to flaunt herself in fine silks, as the writer Lucan records:

her white breasts resplendent through the Sidonian fabric, which, wrought in close texture by the skill of the Seres, the needle of the workman of the Nile has separated, and has loosened the warp by stretching out the web.

Silk commanded a price equal to gold in the Roman Empire and it was used for such diverse things as tying up blood vessels in surgery and making ropes.

Purple was a popular colour with the wealthy Romans, a tradition continued to this day by royalty especially among the British – the Queen and Queen Mother often wear purple. This 'royal' colour originally designated status since the dye was acquired only from certain types of Mediterranean shellfish. The Phoenicians had originally been adept at producing purple and blue dyes from shellfish, but it was an expensive process, and therefore limited only to the resources of the rich.

The Greeks and Romans adorned themselves richly in silk but restrictions had to be made since some silks were so transparent as to be almost indecent; especially the fine silks from the Greek island of Kos which caused the Roman poet Horace (65–8 BC) to remark, 'As if unclothed she stands confessed, in a transparent Coan vest.' Plutarch (AD 46–120) tried to dissuade his prudent wife from wearing silk, yet it was the Roman child emperor, Elagabalus (AD 218–22) who was apparently the first Roman to wear a 'holosericum' or robe of silk. He was by all accounts very beautiful, and he played upon this during his magnificent ceremonies, achieving enormous popularity. In spite of this Elagabalus was not at all sure about his destiny and he kept a silken rope of purple and scarlet to hang himself should this be necessary. He never used it as he was murdered by his troops. He was also, incidentally, a transvestite who used to dress up as a female prostitute, perhaps in his silks, and go down to Ostia to pick up sailors. On several occasions he was beaten up by disappointed men, so the apocryphal story goes. Pliny the Elder (AD 23–79) described how his villa at Ostia, near Rome, overlooked mulberry orchards, and one wonders whether he wore home-produced silk clothes.

Another emperor, Lucius Aurelian (AD 270–5) forbade his wife to buy a silk shawl because it was as expensive as gold, weight for weight. The emperor Gaius Diocletian (AD 284–305) gave notice in his Edict of Diocletian (AD 305) that the following maximum prices could be charged for tailoring silk clothes:

To the tailor for silk lining a fine vest . . . 6 denarii. To the same for an opening and edging of silk 50 denarii . . . To the same for an opening and edging with stuff made of a mixed tissue of silk and flax . . . 30 denarii.

Anyone who exceeded these prices was punished by death or deportation.

Lady Diana Spencer's
wedding dress was
made of silken paper
taffeta tulle, with a
train 7.6 m long
trimmed in old lace.
Designed by David
and Elizabeth
Emanuel, it carried a
silk tulle petticoat
lavishly trimmed with
frills, bows and
hand-made flowers.
It also incorporated
English silk from the
Lullingstone Silk
Farm in Dorset

The gold and silver
brocade from the
King's bedchamber
at Versailles, on the
loom at Prelle et Cie,
Lyon

Royal Silks

These prohibitions and prejudices of the Roman Empire suggested to some signs of corruption and effeminacy. Silk was becoming so widespread that novelist Lynn Linton wrote in *The Queen* in the middle of last century: 'The material an emperor refused to his empress, the vagrant and the pauper toss on to the dust-heap when they have done with it.'

Persia had a tradition of sericulture, and had strict rules regarding the wearing of silk; in fact it was forbidden in the Koran for men to wear silk. In London imported silks had been worked since the fourteenth century by silkwomen, and according to Dale (1933) men as well as women were selling silk fringe and other silks by the pound for the 'great wardrobes' of Edward III (1327–77) and Richard II (1377–99). There was much trouble from imported worked Italian silks which dampened the English market for silks, and an Italian who set up a silk-weaving business in Westminster during the reign of Edward IV (1461–83) did not succeed. Later Henry VII (1485–1509) issued an Act which forbade anyone bringing in silk worked anywhere out of the realm; this included laces, girdles and corsets. Both Henry VIII and Elizabeth I promoted silks especially for themselves, not for the general public.

The royal regulation of silk continued, for Queen Mary (1553–58), daughter of Henry VIII, made a law forbidding people of lower rank than 'magistrates of corporations' from wearing silk, and 'that whoever shall wear silk in or upon his or her hat, bonnet, or girdle scabbard, hose, shoes, or spur leather, shall be imprisoned during three months, and forfeit 10 pounds'. This was quite a stiff penalty at the time.

Yet for many centuries the only silk garments available to royalty in western Europe were silk stockings which were flaunted at Court and in public. As if to emphasize the status of wearing silk stockings, various contemporary authors wrote about what they saw, but to the ordinary public these commodities were totally unavailable.

In England the first documented royal user of silk stockings appears to be Henry II (1154–89), who wore them below his breeches, for this was the usual royal dress of the time. Henry VIII (1509–47), with all his extravagance, could not get enough pairs of silk stockings and apparently wore imported Spanish ones. His agent in the Low Countries, Sir Thomas Gresham (1519–79), was presumably well placed to arrange consignments of stockings – he was also a member of the Mercers' Company, which dealt in cloth – for it is on record that Gresham presented Elizabeth I's brother Edward VI (1547–53) with a pair of long Spanish silk stockings.

Henry VIII, in his flamboyant style, enjoyed the luxury of silk. Fine clothes embroidered in silks were the prerogative of royalty, and laws banned the common people from wearing it

Royal Silks

The restrictive practice governing silk continued with Elizabeth I (1558–1603) who clearly knew its value. In 1560 her silkwoman, Mrs Montague, provided her with a pair of knitted black stockings with which 'she was so impressed she never wore any cloth garments again'. Henry Dewhurst in his 1839 book on the silkworm records,

> that she [Elizabeth I] might be desirous that the more becoming silken testure should remain a regal priveledge and while she displayed her own ankles in the delicate knit, was, perhaps, well pleased that her maids of honour should conceal theirs under the clumsy and inelegant cloth hose, lest, haply, among these some might have been found rather more beautiful than her own.

In Hatfield House (Hertfordshire) there is a pair of silk stockings which belonged to Elizabeth I, 'believed to be the first pair worn in England', as the plaque says on the cabinet. They are of a most delicate nature, with a diamond design throughout the length with a plain white top. Perhaps they were the first pair of *all-English* silk stockings made from English silkworms worn in England, since those of Henry VIII would have almost certainly been imported from Italy or Spain.

Elizabeth I is reputed to have refused to grant a patent of monopoly to the inventor of the first stocking machine in 1589 because the stockings produced were comparatively coarse, unlike those imported from Spain which were finer and made of silk. The inventor was the Revd Lee of Calverton (Nottinghamshire).

Later, James VI of Scotland is said to have borrowed a pair of silk stockings from the Earl of Mar so that he could appear before the English ambassador, enforcing his cogent appeal with, 'For ye would not, sure, that your King should appear as a scrub before strangers'.[1] This was presumably before James had his own silk production in full swing.

Silk stockings became regular attire for royalty and for dress around the Court. In France, the Marquise de Pompadour (1721–64) set the fashion for the rest of the world, such was her delight in silk finery. Hose was fashionable for men until the end of the nineteenth century. Silk hose then became more widely available. In 1814 a skilled silk-worker in the Macclesfield area could produce one pair of stockings in a day.

Royal Silks

AT COURT AND IN BATTLE

The King of Norway, Sigurd I Jorsalafar (the Crusader) (1103–30) is said to have used silk-trimmed sails when he set out for Constantinople (Istanbul) in 1110. He was called 'the Crusader' after his visit to Jerusalem. It was customary in the twelfth century for returning Crusaders of the Knights of St John of Jerusalem to be given a silk cloak after their tour of duty. Four hundred years later silk was being lavishly used by Pope Julius II (1503–13) who apparently gave his entire Swiss regiment heavy silk banners. Not content to live in Rome he travelled extensively in Europe and led his men in many battles. This is not the first time that featherlight silks were used to good effect; Roman emperors used to be borne on a litter or in a carriage with flanks of guards dressed in gilt or silver armour, each with silk banners designed to float deftly in the air in the shape of dragons.

King John of England must have had an extravagant taste in fine silk clothes since an inventory taken after his death in 1216 at his favourite castle, Corfe Castle, Dorset, shows he had no less than 185 silk shirts and numerous other silken garments.

Henry V (1413–22) spent much of his time on the Continent and after his stunning victory at the Battle of Agincourt (1415) is said to have had his moveable headquarters draped in a purple silk cloth. Of course he used the silk as a status symbol to impress his followers rather than for any aesthetic appreciation of the fine material.

Another hundred years later Francis I put on a 'silk extravaganza' for his royal cousin Henry VIII at the Field of the Cloth of Gold (7 June, 1520). The impromptu palace and grounds which Francis had erected between Guines and Ardres in northern France covered 1,672 sq m (2,000 sq yd). A painting in Versailles' Musée du Chateau shows the jamboree-like event, and the enormous golden marquee, big enough to hold a hundred people. No expense appears to have been spared on the spectacle. The silk-workers, *brodeurs* and *passementiers* were all asked to contribute and, incredibly, sixteen thousand 'books' of silk were used to make the tents; each book was 0.9 kg (2 lb).

Henry and Catherine of Aragon were attended by five thousand followers decked out in the most sumptuous velvet, satin and cloth of gold. The Master of Ceremonies was Cardinal Wolsey who was escorted by two hundred crimson velvet-clad gentlemen and two hundred crimson dressed archers.

It is said that Francis wore the first pair of silk stockings in France, but

Royal Silks

Properties with Exhibited Silks

National Trust

Arlington Court, Devon	Collection of ladies dresses
Beningborough Hall, N. Yorkshire	Silks on William and Mary bed
Blickling Hall, Norfolk	Tapestries and damasks
Castle Coole, Co. Fermanagh	Crimson silk upholstery
Clandon Park, Surrey	Silk *petit point* pictures
Coughton Court, Warwickshire	Embroideries
Erddig, Clwyd	Spitalfield velvet
Gawthorpe Hall, Lancashire	Embroideries
Ham House, Surrey	Sumptuous damasks and velvets
Hardwick Hall, Derbyshire	Elizabethan embroideries
Knole, Kent	Silks for James II's bed
Oxburgh Hall, Norfolk	Mary Queen of Scots embroidery
Packwood House, Warwickshire	Italian embroideries
Salton House, Devon	Velvet wall hangings
Standen, Sussex	Wall hangings
Tatton Park, Cheshire	Patterned red silk wall hangings
Wightwick Manor, West Midlands	Morris silk tapestries
The Vyne, Hampshire	Red damask from Italy

Other Major Properties

Belton House, Lincolnshire	Chinese silks
Castle Howard, Yorkshire	Yellow silk wall hangings
Hatfield House, Hertfordshire	Silk stockings
Holkham Hall, Norfolk	Genoan velvet
Syon House, Middlesex	Spitalfield silks
Quex Park, Kent	Chinese silks

this was perhaps the first pair made entirely from genuinely French-produced silk, instead of that imported from Italy or Spain. Francis lived at Château Chambord in the Loire Valley, not far from the Tours silk mills.

Henry VIII's rich and flamboyant style of dress was itself a powerful

Royal Silks

advertisement for silk. A Venetian ambassador wrote in 1511 that 'his fingers were one mass of jewelled rings, and around his neck he wore a gold collar from which hung a diamond as big as a walnut'. His sumptuous clothes were of silks, satins, sarcenets and cloth of gold. Some of these were obviously carried to his death bed, for it is recalled[2] that the procession of eight black horses which bore the coffin of Henry VIII to Windsor each had a child on horseback carrying one of the king's silken banners flowing in the wind. There were so many banners at the ceremony that trees were felled along the route to Windsor so that none of them would be spoilt.

Royal households contained many silk items and it is fortunate that details of two silk cushions have been recorded. One of Henry VIII's inventories records his having a purple velvet cushion with needlework of gold and silk as 'cloth-of-gold tissue'. James I (1603–25) is also reputed to have had an embroidered silk cushion, which shows mulberry fruits, leaves and silkworm caterpillars set around his coat of arms.

Not long after this, Celia Fiennes[3] visited Windsor Castle during one of her several journeys around Britain and described the rich décor inside:

> next is the Queen's Chamber of State all Indian Embroidery on
> white sattin [sic] being presented to her by the Company [East India
> Co.] on it is great plumes of white feathers.

In northern India wild silkmoths provided a valuable source of silk for Himalayan kings; the Mohammedan marauders who invaded Assam in 1527 stayed on and the Ahom kings are said to have used muga silk for all their Court and ceremonial dresses. It is customary for a caste of coolies to tend the silk caterpillars in the forest and protect them from predators.

In Britain the royal beds too were decorated in silk. A fine example is the bed believed to be the nuptial bed at the marriage of James II (then Duke of York) and Mary of Modena in 1673. It is now at Knole House, Kent and was thought to have arrived there with other of the king's effects in 1701.[4] In 1988, after thirteen years of painstaking restoration, the bed shows all its silky magnificence. The outer bed curtains are made from cream and yellow silk warp with gold and silver weft. This produces a 'Cloth of Gold' appearance. Old dyeing methods produce problems in restoration; for instance, oxidation of wools and silks to powder was inevitable with the use of iron as a mordant. During restoration, polyester thread is artificially dyed to match the original colours. Stitching two pieces of fabric together required 8,000–9,000 volunteer hours.

Royal Silks

Completely restored in 1988 by the National Trust this fine four-poster, believed to have been the nuptial bed of James II, is exhibited at Knole House, Kent. It took volunteers over nine thousand hours, over thirteen years to complete the restoration

Other important silks and tapestries have been restored by the National Trust at Blickling Hall (Norfolk) and Clandon Park (Surrey).

REGAL ROBES AND WEDDING DRESSES

Silk has been used in wedding dresses since at least the twelfth century. Perhaps the most extravagant display of silks by royalty and nobility was seen at the wedding of Henry III's (1216–72) daughter Margaret to Alexander III of Scotland in 1251. According to records 'a thousand knights appeared in *cointises*[5] of silk on the nuptial day'. On the following day they were clad in another set of equally gorgeous and splendid robes. These robes were certainly made from imported silks, probably from Italy – or Spain – since there is no evidence that England had a silk industry as early as this. Presumably the bride also wore silk on this occasion, but she is overlooked in the records. It would be another four hundred years before English silk re-appeared.

Mary Queen of Scots (1542–87) was noted for her silk embroidery, developed during her sixteen years of house arrest split between Tutbury Castle, Sheffield Castle, and Chatsworth as well as Buxton and Wingfield. Some of her fine work can be seen at Hardwick Hall (Derbyshire), but of outstanding note there is the collection of silk embroideries of Elizabeth, Countess of Shrewsbury, Bess of Hardwick (1547–1608). The collection is better than anything else in the museums of Britain or United States and depicts in vivid colours, as bright as the day they were made, country scenes full of wildlife, from grasshoppers and beetles to birds, frogs and snakes. Some of her wall hangings were made up from old silk garments and it is very revealing that she acquired second-hand velvets and silks, some of fifteenth- and sixteenth-century origin, from the dissolution of various religious houses. Sir William Cavendish bought old copes (ceremonial religious cloaks) from the dissolved religious house at Lilleshall in 1557.

The English royal tradition to be wed in a silk dress, made from silk produced by English-reared silkworms, seems to have originated with James I's wife, Queen Anne of Denmark. She went along with all of James's plans to promote a silk industry and wore an all-English silk taffeta dress on James's birthday, 19 June 1566. The silk probably came from the Charlton Estate where James had already established mulberry orchards and employed a couple to make Greenwich silk.

Royal Silks

A detail from the silk embroidery worked by Mary Queen of Scots and exhibited at Hardwick Hall in Derbyshire

Meanwhile, in America silk was being produced in Virginia by entre-preneurs and sent back to England for royal use. According to Leggett (1949) Virginia silk was used in the royal robes of both Charles I (1625–49) and Charles II (1660–85) who 'found the silk of Virginia to their likings'. The period costume for ladies in Virginia at this time was white silk dresses with a coloured floral design.

John Evelyn (1620–1706), the diarist, gives a fair insight into the use of expensive materials in the royal Court with his description of the coronation of James II at Westminster Abbey in 1685. 'There were 136 esquires to the Knight of the Bath – this magnificent train on horseback, as rich as embroidery, velvet, cloth of gold and silver, and jewels – horses hung with rich tapestry.' The following year on 9 June 1686 he was at Hampton Court: 'The Queen's bed was an embroidery of silver on crimson velvet, and cost 8,000l., being a present made by the States of Holland when his Majesty returned.'

Evelyn could not help seeing other magnificent silk garments on his travels as a roving ambassador moving in diplomatic circles. He describes the ordinary clothes that eastern diplomats wore in London. In 1681 he was with the Moroccan ambassador and his entourage and they were 'all clad in the Moorish habit, cassocks of coloured cloth, or silk, with buttons and loops, over this an *alhaga*, or white woollen mantle . . . and large calico sleeved shirts'. He describes the garments of the Bantam, East Indian ambassadors, as 'rich Indian silks, flowered with gold, viz, a close waistcoat to their knees, drawers, naked legs, and on their head a cap made like fruit-baskets'.

More silk from the new colonies of America was sent back to England in the eighteenth century and made into dresses for Court and the queen. In 1755 a Mrs Pinckney brought back enough silk from Charleston, South Carolina, which she had raised from silkworms and spun herself, and from which she made three dresses. One of these she presented to the Princess Dowager of Wales. Sir Thomas Lombe had attested in his 1741 book that the quality of silk from South Carolina was as good as that from Italy. A little later in 1770 a Mrs Susanna Wright of Columbia, Pennsylvania, made a 'mantua' 54.8 m (60 yd) long from her own home-produced cocoons, and this was afterwards worn as a Court dress by the Queen of Great Britain.[6] Martha Washington is said to have worn a dress made of silk produced, reeled and woven exclusively in Virginia on the occasion of her husband, George, being inaugurated as President of America in 1789.

When Queen Victoria married Prince Albert in 1840, she wore a white Spitalfield's silk satin wedding dress, thus upholding the English tradition of having an all-English silk dress. All her bridesmaids had identical robes, with head-dresses of orange blossom. At the Royal Jubilee Exhibition in Manchester in 1887, Queen Victoria's wedding dress and train was displayed. It was made at the old mill in Portland Street by Louis Schwabe, who described it in a letter to the British Association:

The dress executed by the gracious command of Her Majesty in 1839 is by far the most costly work ever done at my establishment, and thereby Her Majesty's distinguished patronage given me the opportunity of producing a specimen which may be considered unique of its kind.

The marriage of Princess Alexandra of Denmark to the Prince of Wales in 1863 attracted the displeasure of the British silk industry for not buying British, and she had to abandon her first choice of having Brussels lace, in favour of a Victorian crinoline festooned with orange blossom. The dress was corseted and trimmed with flowers. When Princess Mary of Teck, later Queen Mary (1867–1953), married Prince George in 1893, her flowing

Royal Silks

wedding dress was of typical Edwardian style with lace trimmings. The present Queen Mother (formerly Lady Elizabeth Bowes-Lyon) had a very straight styled twenties look about her ivory chiffon dress when she married in 1922.

In 1936 Queen Mary, as patron of the Silk Association of Great Britain and Ireland, paid a visit to the new Lullingstone Silk Farm near Sevenoaks (Kent) to inspect the industrious work of Zoë, Lady Hart Dyke. Soon Lady Hart Dyke received an order to supply silk for Queen Elizabeth's white satin coronation dress and for 'the little Princesses, Elizabeth and Margaret Rose'.

The queen's coronation dress was ivory-tinted satin and the train was purple velvet six yards long. It was designed by Madame Handley-Seymour and incorporated all the floral emblems of the British Isles, the Dominions overseas and India including the rose, thistle, shamrock, leek, maple, wattle, lotus, protea and fern fronds. In the silk were worked golden threads and lamés, tiny gold beads, diamantes and sequins.

It has been a custom this century for all the coronation robes to be made by the Royal School of Needlework. It was founded in 1872 and has always enjoyed close royal patronage. The present Duchess of Gloucester is the president of the school, but Queen Mary and Princess Alice were accomplished needlewomen too, as the duchess is today. The school has a few coveted royal silk possessions such as Queen Anne's silk love-letter bag, unfortunately without its contents. The Royal School of Needlework is a very young society compared to the Cologne Guild of Embroiderers who manufactured silk vestments as early as the fifteenth century.

Coincidentally, Queen Anne used to visit Lullingstone Castle regularly when she was a child (it was to become a centre for English silks three hundred years later) and accidentally left a toy doll made of wood, but with a satin dress, the folds of which distinctly show, 'the flawless rose-coloured silk gleaming as softly as it did the day it was woven and dyed over 200 years ago'.[7]

The tradition of having all-English silk incorporated into the wedding dress continued. Some Lullingstone silk was incorporated into the train of Princess Elizabeth's wedding dress in 1947, though most of the silk for the dress came from China, not from the rival silk-producing countries of Italy and Japan. Zoë, Lady Hart Dyke had silkworm eggs flown in from Cyprus (a British Crown colony), and the silkworms were farmed out to local people with mulberry trees, fed on English mulberry leaves and the cocoons reeled on English reeling machines.

Lullingstone silk,
from the silk farm at
Lullingstone in Kent,
was incorporated
into the train of HRH
Princess Elizabeth at
her wedding in 1947

Royal Silks

The wedding dress was white satin *crêpe-de-chine* designed by Norman Hartnell, and was trimmed with symbols of the Crown and Commonwealth. Princess Margaret married in a stunningly simple white silk organza dress in 1960. Princess Anne's wedding dress of 1973 was designed by Maureen Baker and had a high-standing collar stitched with pearls.

When Lady Diana Spencer married Prince Charles in 1981 her silk wedding dress stunned the world with its extravagance of silken paper taffeta tulle. It was carried over a silk tulle petticoat lavishly trimmed with frills, bows and hand-made flowers. Silk from the Lullingstone Silk Farm was incorporated, but by this time the equipment from Lady Hart Dyke's exploits at Lullingstone had been bought and set up at Worldwide Butterflies in Dorset and English silk was being reeled by Robert Goodden. The dress had a train 7.6 m (24.9 ft) long trimmed in old lace and was designed by David and Elizabeth Emanuel.

Princess Diana's slippers were of the same ivory lace, spangled with pearls, with a large frilled, heart-shaped rosette of embroidered and sequined lace on each shoe. A pale coral-pink tussore silk dress designed by Belleville Sassoon was her going-away dress. At the wedding many other silks were in evidence. The queen wore aquamarine silk *crêpe-de-chine*, the Queen Mother wore the palest sea-green silk georgette and the Princess Royal wore a white silk *façonne* decorated with sprays of yellow and green flowers. A year later, at the christening of Prince William of Wales on 4 August 1982, the traditional royal christening robe of Honiton lace and white satin was used, in which the Prince of Wales, the Queen and the Queen Mother had also been christened.

Sarah Ferguson's marriage to Prince Andrew in 1986 departed from tradition in using Italian silks for the wedding dress. Designed by Lindka Cierach, the dress had over 5 m (16.4 ft) of train. Bees and thistles were embroidered and beaded into the bodice of the dress and train as well as into the satin Louis-heeled shoes. The bridesmaids all wore peach taffeta pinnies. There was no lack of silk hats and dresses on display to millions of viewers worldwide. Sarah Ferguson's mother, Mrs Barrantes, sported a buttercup-yellow Marocain silk hat, the Queen had a delphinium-blue hat of stitched crêpe, the Duchess of Kent had a blue on cream embroidered hat of silk faille and Princess Margaret wore a brilliant turquoise silk dress.

Royal Silks

NOTES

1. W. Kirby and W. Spence, *An Introduction to Entomology; or, Elements of the Natural History of Insects* (1858).

2. G.E. Bates, *And So Make A City Here* (1948).

3. The seventeenth-century forebear of Sir Ranulph Fiennes who circumnavigated the globe by both poles in 1983: C. Morris, *The Illustrated Journeys of Celia Fiennes, 1685–1712* (1982).

4. The National Trust, *Magazine*, Autumn 1987, No. 52.

5. 'Cointises' were very elaborate costumes.

6. 'Mantua' is a gown made of silk, after the Italian town of Mantua; a corruption being mantua-maker (one who makes mantuas), thus manteau.

7. So wrote Zoë, Lady Hart Dyke in her book *So Spins the Silkworm*.

CHAPTER 9

🦋

Huguenots and the Silk Tradition

La Marche des Canuts

'Voila les p'tits canuts qui se la coulent dou-ce D'St Just a la Croix Rousse.
Partout ils sont connus
Et bis-tan-cla-que pan! La navette et l'battant R'gardez
Comme ils sont ch'nuts
Voila les p'tits......

Marching song of the Lyon silk workers who, in the (18th, protested their rights.

The Huguenots[1] played a central role in the history of silk and textiles in Europe from the sixteenth century. Like the Jews, they have been the subject of repeated religious persecution through the ages. Followers of John Calvin (1509–64), they copied the Genevan Church in having meetings. Their popularity gained momentum until it was challenged by the Roman Catholic Church, with catastrophic results. During the repeated persecutions a guerilla movement was set up and members of this underground organization were called 'camisards'. They derived this named from their habit of wearing a sort of smock over their clothing in the evening.

Survivors of the horrendous persecutions in France during the seventeenth and eighteenth centuries took refuge in at least ten other countries, crossing the north and south Atlantic, English Channel and Irish Sea to escape their Catholic persecutors. Their ordered society allowed them to integrate quickly into the fabric of their host countries, becoming bankers, goldsmiths and master silk merchants; their practical skills were put to good use as silk throwsters, spinners and weavers.

Wherever the Huguenots sought refuge their skills as silk-weavers were much in demand; indirectly the persecutions played a great part in the history of silk in Europe, particularly in Protestant England which offered a safe refuge.

However, in Lyon, long regarded as the silk capital of France, the Huguenots were not allowed to practice their silk skills, and so a few of the Huguenots who settled in London were from this city. Others came from Amsterdam or via Canterbury before settling in London.

For over four hundred years before the Huguenots arrived, Great Britain had been a welcome refuge for spinners and weavers. England, the great wool-producing country, played host to Flemish weavers as early as the fourteenth century. They were encouraged to settle in London when the Flemish princess Philipa of Hainault married Edward III (1327–77).

Persecution of the Protestants in France started as early as 1520 when the Huguenots began to flee to safer countries. The Low Countries were an attractive proposition since there were plenty of weavers and traders in cloth living there. Belgium's commercial centre was Antwerp, which had been a more prosperous town than Venice. It was reported that five hundred ships a day would use the port and two thousand carts would arrive in the town each week; Antwerp would do the kind of trade in a fortnight that Venice would do in a year. But towards the end of the sixteenth century disaster struck. In 1576 religious strife manifested itself in 'The Spanish Fury', during which Spanish soldiers killed six thousand people and burned eight hundred houses. The strife spread over much of Belgium. A few years later, in 1585, the Duke of Parma, Governor of the Spanish Netherlands, broke the siege of the town and sent all the Protestants into exile. Many of these skilled weavers came to England and, it is thought, a third of all the silk artisans and merchants of Flanders and Brabant also fled across the Channel.

There were two major exoduses of Huguenots out of France, separated by about hundred years, the first towards the end of the sixteenth century with the Massacre of St Bartholomew, and the second, at the end of the seventeenth century, with the Revocation of the Edict of Nantes. Both were stimulated by religious persecution. Huguenots arrived in England not only from France but also from the Low Countries. Most of the immigrants arrived in south-east England, particularly at Canterbury and east London. From there they branched out and established Huguenot communities in the midlands and south-west England.

and the Silk Tradition

MASSACRE OF ST BARTHOLOMEW

The Massacre of St Bartholomew was a bloody affair which terrified all the Protestants in France. It started on St Bartholomew's Day, 24 August 1572, when Catherine de Medici, with the approval of the king, tried to have all the Huguenot leaders killed. In Paris, Catholics started to attack Protestants and the uncontrolled carnage continued unabated until 17 September. Some Huguenots sought refuge in the British Embassy and eventually made their way to England. The persecution of the Protestants spread to the provinces but some regions such as Normandy did not sanction the killings. The north coast of France may have been a safer haven for persecuted Huguenots and allowed them the chance of fleeing to England.

To get out of France many refugees followed secret escape routes across the country. Some fled via La Rochelle on the north coast, while others were hidden in crates and transported via harbours and frontiers. It is estimated that about fifty thousand Protestants were killed throughout France during this persecution. Pope Gregory XIII was so pleased with Catherine de Medici that he had a medal struck in her honour.

The largest movement of Huguenots occurred during the reign of Elizabeth I (1558–1603) who, being a fervent Protestant, welcomed the immigrants with open arms. Many of the refugees would have been skilled weavers and Elizabeth, keen on silks herself, encouraged them to establish their trades in south-east England.

Times got a little better over the next few years for Protestants in France and the French king, Henry IV of Navarre eventually gave concessions under the Edict of Nantes in April 1598. Protestants could hold services and have full civil liberties again. When Elizabeth I died in 1603 and James I took office, Huguenots were well established in the fabric of British society with still more French refugees coming across the English Channel.

For the next few decades silks were being produced by the Huguenots but the British public soon developed a liking for imported French silks. By 1668 silk was becoming widely worn by all classes of people and feeling was running high that it had been devalued: 'The women's hats were turned into hoods made of French silk, whereby every maid-servant became a standing revenue to the French king of one half of her wages.'

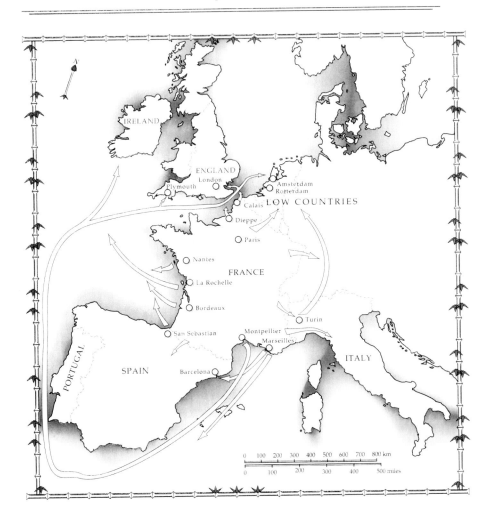

Huguenots went to extraordinary lengths to flee France, travelling from the south and west coasts by boat to other places in western Europe or farther afield across the Atlantic. Many fled to the north into the Low Countries, some eventually settling in England. Other groups went direct to south-east England ports, others to Eire then England – Spitalfields in particular

REVOCATION OF THE EDICT OF NANTES

All was reasonably well for the Huguenots in France for about a hundred years, then the terror and animosity erupted again. On 18 October 1685, Louis XIV revoked the edict. Carnage occurred, Huguenot blood was let, and thousands joined the exodus out of France. Somewhere between 200,000 and 250,000 left France for other countries, and 700,000 stayed and renounced their religion.

The largest flow to England was in 1680 and various authorities give the number of Huguenots arriving in England between 1670 and 1690 as about

and the Silk Tradition

40,000–50,000 refugees. This was at a time when the total population of England was only 5½ million. The entry of Huguenots to England was not necessarily a drain on England's revenue, for it was estimated that each family came with £100 per head, amounting to some £4–5 million.

By 1700 about five per cent of Londoners were Huguenot weavers. Large numbers (about 50,000–60,000) also went to the Low Countries, 25,000–30,000 went to Germany and ten thousand each to both Ireland and America. About 2,200 went to Switzerland, two thousand to Denmark and north-east Europe and a group of about four hundred went as far as the Cape of Good Hope.

Today a museum at St Jean du Gard (the Musée du Desert) in southern France relives the persecution of the Huguenots and camisards. It tells of the systematic genocide of all intellectuals, magistrates, teachers, businessmen and people from the army and navy, of a well organized Huguenot society in which silk production was at its height.

HUGUENOT SETTLEMENTS

Many Huguenots settled in the port towns in southern England where they arrived, such as Sandwich, Rye and Winchelsea. Others moved on straight away to newly-formed Huguenot strongholds inland. At Winchelsea (just west of Rye) there is still a 'Frenchman's field' where the Huguenots gathered before dispersal. Spitalfields became the centre of the Huguenot tradition in Great Britain, with a French hospital and a church built there. Some Huguenots moved from Spitalfields to the north, later establishing a silk-weaving industry in Macclesfield (Cheshire), while other Huguenots joined their compatriots from Ireland at Spitalfields much later on.

At first the new Huguenot immigrants were regarded with a little suspicion since they kept very much to themselves and maintained their customs, but this changed to jealousy as they excelled in trade. At Canterbury the new arrivals became so prosperous they started to employ local workers; they contributed to taxes, looked after the poor and some became magistrates. They had strict puritan laws and did not allow mixed marriages. The only restriction placed on them by authority was that they were not allowed to make cloth or kersies of the English type. They were, however, at liberty to make their own 'Flanders Cloth'.

Further movement of Huguenots continued in the eighteenth century.

Huguenots

Thirty families arrived at the south-east Ireland town of Innishannon (near Cork) in 1760. Today, half the Protestants there are reckoned to be descended from these immigrants. In the town of Innishannon there is a hill called 'Colony Hill' on which some of the Huguenot refugees built their houses and a 'mulberry field' where perhaps they tried to establish orchards to support the silk industry. None of these houses remain in Innishannon today, but the Huguenots are remembered there by their French or Dutch Huguenot names: Ducros, Herriot, Batman (originally Betman, from the Dutch Betjeman), Hornibrook, Mullard, Perrott, Perrier and Travers.

HUGUENOT FAMILIES

The Huguenots contributed to the tradition of the silk industry through their practical skill and shrewdness, and their complex and intricate patterns woven on silk, some of which they brought over as trade secrets from France or the Low Countries. These they masterfully reproduced in England, gaining the respect of the English business community. They were strongly loyal to Britain, but also looked after their own family and religious links. Secrets were passed from family to family, through inter-Huguenot family marriages.

One of the most famous Huguenot families to become established in England was the Courtaulds. They fled France in the 1680s, fearing persecution from Louis XIV, and became rich silk weavers. A later descendant, Samuel Courtauld developed the new synthetic silk called rayon in about 1910. This, combined with cheaper Italian imports, led to thousands of country folk in southern France permanently losing most of their family income, since the market for silkworm cocoons fell catastrophically. The household name of Courtaulds remains associated today with textiles and some of the wealth derived from Samuel Courtauld's inventive work is seen in the magnificent collection of Impressionist and Post-Impressionist paintings which he collected and which are at the Courtauld Institute Galleries in London.

Curiously, Samuel Courtauld's work with rayon had been foreseen over two hundred years earlier. The English scientist, Robert Hooke (1635–1703), discussed the possibility of making an artificial fibre in his *Micrographia* published in 1664; so too did the French scientist, René A.F. de Reaumur (1683–1758) in 1734. Mechanical spinning of rayon and other

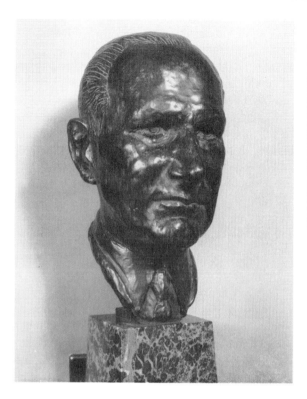

Samuel Courtauld (1876–1947). The English Courtaulds were originally Huguenot refugees from the region of La Rochelle in France. Samuel Courtauld became the general manager of the textile mills in Essex in 1908 and chairman from 1921 to 1946. His company was a highly-respected industrial giant in the artificial silk industry which developed between 1898 and 1905. Rayon was produced just after the First World War and this helped, with other factors, to extinguish the silk industry in France

synthetic fibres in use today, such as plastics, directly copies the way in which silkworms, indeed all caterpillars, spin their silk. The batteries of spinnerets from which liquid silk is extruded and solidifies are the basis of today's machines which have fine nozzles and holes. Machines like these were designed as early as 1842 by an English silk-weaver called Louis Schwabe – of probable Huguenot origin – who experimented with extruding glass filaments.

Towards the end of the seventeenth century an influential silk merchant from Lyon, named Etienne Seignoret, was running the Royal Lustring Co. in Spitalfields. Lustrings was very popular; it was claimed at the time that there were about 670 looms in Spitalfields and ninety-eight in Ipswich (Suffolk) processing lustring silks, though this may have been a gross exaggeration. Despite being fined heavily for smuggling foreign lustrings into Britain, the wealthy Etienne Seignoret later doubled the capital of the Bank of England by investing heavily in the East India Co. (£14,187), sent money to the Protestant galley slaves in France, and participated in running the French hospital and Maison de Charité in Spitalfields. No more could be expected of a fellow countryman in a foreign country. Seignoret traded in Lombard Street with his partner René Baudowin and in 1695/6 his turnover was £9,000 per annum in silk and cochineal insects. On his death he was officially worth between £80,000 and £100,000.

Sir John Houblon (1672–1724) was the Huguenot who helped to found the Bank of England and was its first Director from 1713 to 1720. Mulberry trees still grow at the Bank. Houblon was a member of a Walloon family. Another influential Huguenot who became Governor of the Bank was Pierre Delme who also became Lord Mayor of London. He was worth a quarter of a million pounds when he died in 1728. Other prominent Huguenots of the City of London were the des Bouveries family and the Papillon family, of whom Thomas was Member of Parliament for the City between 1695 and 1700.

Another well-known group of refugees was the de la Pieres. They set up as silk-weavers in Canterbury (Kent) where there is still a De La Piere House today. John Peters (a corruption of de la Piere) still carries on the family name today. One of his predecessors, Francis La Pierre (sic), is thought to have made the state bed at Melville House, Fife, Scotland; it is lavishly adorned with Italian silks and velvet lined with Chinese silk damask.

The family fortunes of an ordinary Huguenot family, the Teulons, have been thoroughly researched[2] and reveal the sort of problems that the Huguenots faced. The Teulons's roots go back to the Cévennes village of Valleraugues (*département* of Gard) which lies in the shadows of Mount Aigoual. After the Revocation of the Edict of Nantes one of the Teulons was put in prison. Many people renounced their religion and were 'converted' and Anthony Teulons's only way to freedom was to volunteer for the French cavalry. This he did but soon deserted to the British troops which were in the region. With his brother, a pastor, they escaped to the coast and joined a boat to Cork in southern Ireland. Peter stayed in Ireland and became a Huguenot minister and Anthony went to Kent to set up a felt-making factory in Greenwich. In 1708 in the reign of Queen Anne, Anthony became a naturalized citizen. He also married a refugee girl from a neighbouring town in the Cévennes, Meyreuis, and had four children. He must have been a proud and resourceful man.

One of his daughters married a German immigrant from Coburg. Melchior Wagner was naturalized in 1709 and received a royal appointment as hatter to George I. The king himself had come over from Germany as a direct descendant of James I in 1625 to succeed to the English throne. The

T
H
E
·
S
T
O
R
Y
·
O
F
·
S
I
L
K

marriage may well have boosted trade at the felt-making establishment in Greenwich, since felt was the principal constituent of hats.[3] One of his sons, Anthony, took over the business.

Huguenots had by this time made their mark, not only by establishing themselves in prestigious positions including master silk merchants, but through their mastery of silk, and creating silk mills and silk-weavers' cottages. In 1985 the Huguenots celebrated their first three hundred years in England with a major exhibition; their influence on English silk and society had already been great.

NOTES

1. The word 'Huguenot' simply means French Protestant, perhaps named, it is thought, after the Medieval King Huguet of Tours whose ghost is said to roam the city.
2. The history of the Teulons was published privately in 1971 in a small booklet entitled *The Huguenot Refugee Family of Teulon*.
3. Felt was made from fur and wool often blended with a variety of animal fur such as camel hair, beaver, hare and rabbit fur. When compressed it had the advantage over cloth that it did not become threadbare.

CHAPTER 10

Silk-weavers, Cottages and Mills

Here Lys the body of Daniel Saul
Spitalfields Weaver and that's all.

Epitaph ~ St. Dunstan's Churchyard.

SILK-WEAVERS IN LYON

*L*yon has always been the silk centre of Europe, and has played a key role in manufacture and distribution of silk to the rest of Europe. It is well situated for trade; famous Italian silk came this way en route to north-west Europe, including Britain. It lies strategically on the mighty River Rhône which is navigable to the Mediterranean 290 km (467 miles) away to the south, exiting via the Camargue, a useful trade route not lost on the Romans.

Silk would have been traded through Lyon long before Louis XI issued letters of patent in the town on 24 May 1466, but there was only a handful of silk-workers then. The craft did not expand to become an industry until Francis I allowed Italians to work in the town in 1536. By 1544, twelve thousand people were involved in silk production and Lyon was establishing a name for fine silk.

Lyon's weaving quarter is the Croix Rousse, a hilly area close to the Rhône. It is a maze of close-knit houses, a stronghold of silk-weavers who were locally called 'canuts'. The silk-weavers were so named after the special canut machines for cutting the pile of velvets. The Croix Rousse is riddled with hidden tunnels so that workers could come and go without their competitors knowing what they were working on, such was the secrecy in the world of silk processing. There were other weaver strongholds in the districts of Le Forez and Le Vivarais.

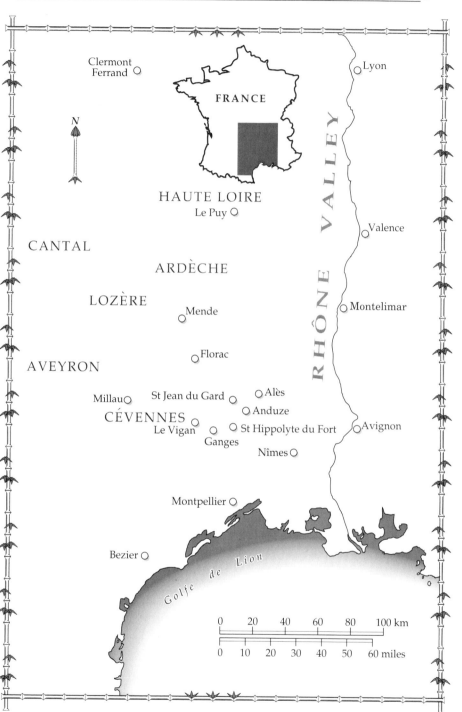

N

Clermont
Ferrand ○

Lyon ○

FRANCE

HAUTE LOIRE
Le Puy ○

CANTAL

ARDÈCHE

Valence ○

LOZÈRE

Mende ○

Montelimar ○

RHÔNE VALLEY

Florac ○

AVEYRON

Millau ○   St Jean du Gard ○   Alès ○

CÉVENNES   Anduze ○

Le Vigan ○   ○ St Hippolyte du Fort   Avignon ○

Ganges

Nîmes ○

Montpellier ○

Bezier ○

Golfe de Lion

The centre of the silk
industry in France,
Lyon, in relation to
its access to the
Mediterranean. The
other important
areas which served
Lyon were the
Ardèche, Gard and
Hèrault

0	20	40	60	80	100 km
0	10	20	30	40	50	60 miles

Silk-weavers,

Woodcut of oriental
silkworkers

Lyon profited in trade with the expansion of the French silk industry when
Henry IV and his minister Sully, together with a man called Olivier de Serre,
promoted the planting of mulberry trees throughout much of southern
France. Four hundred thousand trees were planted around Lyon, Dauphine,
in the Midi, and even as far north as Paris where the king established silk
weaving factories. These factories successfully produced silk gauzes and
shawls. In 1620 a new invention for automating the loom draw-strings was
invented by Dangon from Lyon.

Silk production continued until the Revocation of the Edict of Nantes in
1685. This sounded the death-knell for Huguenots in France. The Lyon
industry was paralysed. So too were Tours, Avignon and Nîmes. Three
quarters of a million people involved in the French silk industry emigrated.

Slowly Lyon regained its role as the silk centre of Europe. Other places like
the papal city of Avignon, tried hard to establish a big silk industry but they
were hampered by losing thirty thousand people to pestilence. Nîmes
profited by Avignon's misfortune but never made a success of its silk
industry. That left Lyon ruling supreme in the nineteenth century without
serious competitors.

Times were extremely hard and wretched for the silk-weavers of Lyon
in the early eighteenth century. A typical family had to live in a
6 sq m room which doubled up as a workshop for looms and living
quarters.

Cottages and Mills

ABOVE: Scores of filature buildings exist in southern France. They always had lots of tall windows to let in as much light as possible. Workers toiled long hours at machines under very institutionalized conditions. Built on barraged rivers, the water drove the mechanical equipment used for throwing and reeling silk. Later filature buildings and *magnaneries* relied on electricity. Many in France are now derelict, while others have been turned into *maison secondaires*. This one is at Peyregrosse, near Pont d'Hèrault, Gard

BELOW: The derelict filature of Pont de Salindres lies on the bank of the River Gardon, between Anduze and St Jean du Gard, Gard. Its majestic double-curved stairway recalls the golden age of silk production in the Cévennes at the end of the last century

Joseph-Marie Jacquard

Joseph-Marie Jacquard was born on 7 July 1752 in Lyon, son of a master worker in silk. Of eight children, Joseph-Marie and a sister were the only ones to survive infancy.

When he was twelve years old Joseph-Marie was apprenticed to his father and set to work pulling the loom strings ('tirer les lacs'), but Lyon was in turmoil. It had to be defended from troops of the Convention, and after 1793 the town fell. Joseph-Marie then served for several years in the regular army (rather than run the risk of being arrested and guillotined).

Returning to work in the silk industry, Jacquard invented an ingenious design which attempted to reduce the inconvenience of repeated pulling of loom strings. A patent dated 23 December 1800 did not induce immediate acclaim, but was taken up for weaving fish nets.

The Minister of the Interior invited Jacquard to Paris. Living at the Conservatoire des Arts et Métiers in Paris, Jacquard came across an ancient device for moving needles – an invention of Vaucanson's in 1745.

Returning to Lyon he continued with his experiments in automating silk-weaving. Jacquard had the foresight to see that Vaucanson's invention could be married up with a second device, a perforated card (a device to arrange the movement of the pins carrying the weft) invented by Falcon in 1734. The combination of the two, together with Jacquard's modifications, produced the Jacquard loom.

The significance of this discovery was that individuals could work by themselves and weave silk. Silk mills began to blossom with scores of Jacquard looms to a room.

Jacquard's great invention did not make him a fortune. He received the Legion d'Honneur in 1819 and was able to retire on a modest pension with his wife to Oullins where he died on 7 April 1834. Jacquard is today one of Lyon's most famous men and a statue of him adorns the Place de la Croix-Place.

Cottages and Mills

The invention of the Jacquard loom by Joseph-Marie Jacquard in 1804 transformed production patterns. It relied on a punched card which was inserted into the machine which read off the required design. By the mid-1830s most Lyon looms were Jacquard. The significance of the Jacquard loom was that it opened up great possibilities for design and pattern work. By 1881 there were more than 200,000 silk-workers in Lyon, benefiting from the new invention, and there were at least eighteen thousand Jacquard looms.

Despite the hardship endured by the ordinary silk-worker, the nineteenth century was the Golden Age of silk manufacture in southern France. Some details about the silk industry of Lyon were quoted in the *Courrier de Lyon* of 1840:

Raw silk annually consumed there is one million kilogrammes, equal to 2,205,714 pounds English, on which the waste in manufacturing is five per cent. As four cocoons produce one graine [grain] of silk, four thousand millions of cocoons are annually consumed, making the number of caterpillars reared (including the average allowance for caterpillars dying, bad cocoons, and those kept for eggs) 4,292,400,000. The length of the silk of one cocoon averages 500 metres, so that the length of the total quantity of silk spun at Lyon is 6,000,000,000,000 (or six and a half billions) of English feet, equal to fourteen times the mean radius of the earth's orbit; or 5,494 times the radius of the moon's orbit; or 52,505 times the equatorial circumference of the earth; or 200,000 times the circumference of the moon.

All seemed well until 1920, the year which marked the beginning of the demise of French-produced silk.[1] By then synthetic fibres such as rayon were entering the market. Lyon silk industries had to produce other materials to survive. They moved into synthetic fibres and by the 1950s a wide variety was available to the commercial houses of Lyon. However, their silk connections have never been severed and Lyon still controls much of the present-day market in silk.

In 1968, a total of 41,460 tonnes of fibre were processed in Lyon, 544 tonnes of it silk. Of other fibres there were 14,500 tonnes of rayon, 17,225 tonnes of 'fibranne', 1,065 tonnes of wool, 2,339 tonnes of cotton and 4,217 tonnes of various other fibres.

Lyon silk is still in great demand and is exported widely to meet the demand from various sources such as *haute couture*, boutiques, *supermarches*,

Silk-weavers,

In the middle of the eighteenth century everyone who lived in a typical hamlet such as this cévenol one near St Martial, Gard would have been involved in silk production. After the collapse of the silk industry, mulberry trees were pulled out and alternative crops such as vines and onions were grown

tapisier-decorateurs and *fabricants de siéges*. Highest on the list of users of Lyon material is West Germany, which used 132 million French francs-worth of material in 1968.

SILK-WEAVERS OF SPITALFIELDS[3]

Spitalfields, London was the centre of Britain's silk industry. Here they set up a community of their own. They established their own French church in 1743–4 and rows of weavers' cottages appeared. Wealthy silk merchants had their attics and lofts converted so that the workers could work upstairs. Some areas gradually became very seedy and were the setting for the exploits of Jack the Ripper in 1888. Much of the squalid housing was later demolished to make way for Commercial Road.

We are fortunate in having a good description of what life was like for a typical weaving family in the early nineteenth century. In 1840 the anonymous author of *Treatise on . . . Silk Manufacture* was most impressed with what he saw:

It sometimes happens that various branches of occupation in the silk

Cottages and Mills

Spitalfields Christ
Church was the focal
point for the French
Huguenots

manufacture are carried on under the same roof, by different members of the same family. It once occurred to the author of this treatise, in the course of his visits among the operative weavers in the district of Spitalfields, to visit a family consisting of a man, his wife, and ten children, all of whom, with the exception of the two youngest girls, were engaged in useful employments connected with the silk manufacture.

The father, assisted by one of his sons, was occupied with a machine punching card slips from figures which another son, a fine intelligent lad about thirteen years of age, was 'reading on'. Two other lads, somewhat older, were in another appartment, casting, drawing, punching, and attaching to cords the leaden plummets or lingoes, which form part of the harness for a Jacquard loom. The mother was engaged in warping silk. One of the daughters was similarly employed at another machine, and three other girls were on three separate looms, weaving figured silks, one by the aid of the mechanical draw-boy, the others with Jacquard machines.

An air of order and cheerfulness prevailed throughout this busy establishment that was truly gratifying; and, with the exception of

Many roads in the Spitalfields district of London show the garretted rooms in the roof with large and numerous windows to let in the maximum amount of light for working

ABOVE. Hand blocks were made for decorating polychrome dresses and furnishings. Made from several layers of wood glued together, with an outer hardwood surface, the design was carefully cut into the wooden block. Variations in the technique involved 'coppering', where copper or brass pins were beaten into the surface to make special effects, or 'felting', where areas of felt were inlaid into the block to give larger areas of colour. The person using the block had an assistant who made sure that the colour application to the block was uniform. The printer then applied the block to the fabric and finally tapped it to ensure that the fabric had taken up the colour. The next application of the block had to tie up accurately with the previous pattern which was applied. Each colour of the design had to be applied separately over the' previous pattern, ensuring accuracy at all times

LEFT. The famous Paisley pattern is an imitation of the cashmere design. In 1808 weavers in Paisley tried to recreate the pattern, aided in their attempts by the invention in 1818 of a '10 box lay' which enabled five shuttles to work in the loom simultaneously. Soon close copies of the Paisley pattern were being produced. Agents were sent to London to trace patterns of any new Paisley designs which had arrived from India. Eight days later shawls with these new patterns were available in London fully made up at £12 each instead of £70 – £100 for the originals. Exports were made to Turkey and Persia, and the cheeky Paisley weavers even tried exporting their Paisley shawls to India

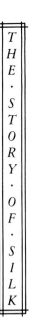

All silk-weaving companies had their own books of house patterns. Samples of block-printed silk were collected together as books for continual reference. Today they make fascinating studies of former techniques

Cottages and Mills

the plummet-drawers, all were clean and neatly clad. The particular occupation wherein each was engaged, was explained most readily, and with a degree of genuine politeness, which proved, that amid the harassing cares attendant upon daily toils of no ordinary degree, these parents had not been unmindful of their duty, as regarded the cultivation of their children's minds and hearts.

There was a huge concentration of silk-weavers in London. After the peak influx of immigrants in 1686–7 there were about fifteen thousand refugees estimated to be living in the City of London and areas to the east, with another eight thousand in Westminster and areas to the west. There were also refugee settlements in Chelsea, Greenwich, Wandsworth and Wapping.

Wandsworth, Bethnal Green and Merton in south London became famous for their weavers, and the firm of Toye, Kennet & Spencer became noted ribbon-makers there. Clean rivers were important for silk mills and places like Merton Abbey were well placed beside important waterways such as the Wandle.[3] A Huguenot burial ground was established at Mount Nod in Wandsworth. It is interesting to note that the terrible persecutions and hardship that the Huguenots had endured are reflected in the 'tears' motif incorporated in the Wandsworth Civic Crest still in use today.

The terror of the Huguenots is today still remembered in the badge of the south London borough of Wandsworth, which depicts a shield of a dozen tears. It was in this area that a lot of refugee craftsmen settled, some of whom were employed in dyeing silks in the clean waters of the River Wandle

Silk-weavers,

There was a proper teasel ground to the south of Spitalfields where Fuller's teasel was grown. The teasel heads were put on to revolving drums between which newly-made clothes were drawn. This 'fulled' up the fluff – a technique the Shetlanders still use today to make their soft pullovers. The teasel ground vanished when the area was used by the military as a training ground. One of the wealthy traders in 'Spittlefields' was Abraham Elton. He dealt in wool, wine, tobacco, copper, brass and glass and also owned the estate of Clevedon Court, Somerset, where today there is also a legacy of mulberry trees.

SILK-WEAVERS OF ITALY

Thomas Wardle had occasion to visit the silk-weavers of Piedmont in northern Italy, in the foothills of the Alps north of Turin, and has given us some interesting first-hand experiences of what it was like for silk-weavers there in the late nineteenth century. He found an extensive silk-reeling and -throwing establishment. Wardle was ostensibly there to have some treasured cocoons of the Tusseh silkmoth reeled, a task which was accomplished.

One of the filature factories was at St Cio, near Torre Pellice, where he was shown round a reeling room with one hundred young girls, reeling 'the small Piedmont cocoons of *Bombyx mori*'. Wardle found the occasion very interesting since the girls were singing old French songs in a dialect not even understood by the Italians. Apparently the mill owners had to learn this particular dialect in order to communicate with the girls. The French connection went back to the years of persecution when Provençal Huguenots fled across the Alps to Italy and settled there. There were French enclaves in the various Italian Alpine villages where French customs were maintained. The girls would spend several months of the year working and sleeping in the silk-reeling factories, working from five in the morning to eight in the evening. Then it was time for eating, singing and dancing, ready for another arduous day. After all the cocoons were processed the girls went back to their Alpine villages.

SILK-WEAVERS' COTTAGES

Weavers' cottages survive where Huguenots settled. Some places like

Cottages and Mills

Weavers' cottages at
Canterbury, Kent
show the traditional
use of maximum
amount of light, with
the inclusion of large
windows. The
building is now
within a pedestrian
precinct and is a
teashop

Silk-weavers,

Canterbury or Spitalfields are famous for their weavers' cottages. Unfortunately, many have been demolished to make way for redevelopment but others have been carefully restored and are open to the public.

Large weavers' cottages are fairly easy to recognize since they have one very obvious feature: large upstairs windows. Village, town and city streets tended to be close together. If you had to do a lot of needlework you wanted the most available light. Sitting downstairs did not give you the best light, since sunlight did not penetrate some of the rooms, in part due to overhanging first floors and the close proximity to the other side of the street. Some cottages were modified with an extra storey put on upstairs, while others were especially built.

In southern England weavers' cottages were often timber-framed. The Huguenots generally moved into existing buildings, but in places built their own; in the midlands the cottages tended to be of stone.

Producing silk was very labour intensive and attracted a lot of poor people. Special rows of cottages were made or attics and lofts converted very cheaply and simply. In Kent, cottages occur at Bearsted, Biddenden, Canterbury (where there are a number of fine examples), Cranbrook, Goudhurst, Meopham, Rye, Sandwich and Smarden. Alfriston (West Sussex) has one weaver's cottage still standing, while others were at East Grinstead and Winchelsea. In south-west England silk-weavers' cottages occur at Malmesbury, Melksham and Wilton, and at Yeovil in Somerset.

Some of the finest weavers' cottages are in London's Spitalfields, in such tiny and bustling roads as Brick Lane, Folgate Street, Fournier Street, Princelet Street, Scalater Street (derelict) and Wilkes Street. Cottages would have also stood in Weaver's Fields. The weavers' cottages in Fournier Street alongside Christ Church are typical. The long terrace of cottages is characterized by the upstairs windows which lie slightly back from the top edge of the houses. Some are still in a dilapidated condition, despite conservation work which is now in its second decade; others are finely preserved and look immaculate. There are plenty of other weavers' cottages around nearby corners.

The narrow roads and passages remind one of Medieval London. Many of the cottages are in a sorry state, and others are still used as squalid factories turning out clothing. However, several have been restored to their former Georgian splendour. Some have remained virtually intact with many of their fittings and these have been lovingly preserved. Early Dutch tiles surround the fireplaces, walls are hung with Chinese oyster-coloured silk, and chandeliers are wrapped in silk to match the walls.

Cottages and Mills

ABOVE: Weaver's garret in Spitalfields (5, Elder Street) before restoration

BELOW: Weaver's garret in Spitalfields after restoration; from Girouard *et al*'s *The Saving of Spitalfields*

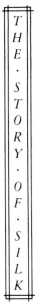

silk spinning

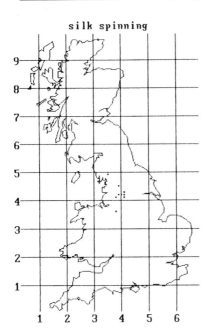

silk throwing

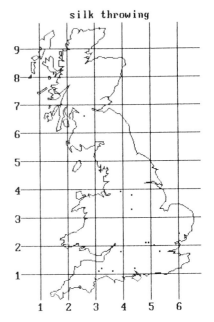

The distribution of
silk manufacturing in
Great Britain

silk weaving

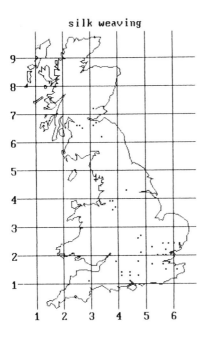

SILK SPINNING
Bradford
Brighouse
Congleton
Halifax
Huddersfield
Kandal
Lancaster
Rochdale
Skipton
Todmorden

SILK-THROWING
Aylesbury
Churchstanton
Derby
Glasgow
Leslie
Malmsbury
Sheffield
Sherbourne
Stockport
Stratford
St Albans
Taunton
Tring
Twyford

SILK-WEAVING
Alton
Aylesbury
Ayr
Battersea
Billeriacay

Bocking
Bonnington
Braintree
Canterbury
Chelmsford
Congleton
Dumfermline
East Ham
Edinburgh
Glasgow
Hadleigh
Hamilton
Haverhill
Henley
Ipswich
Kettering
Larkhill
Leeds
Letchworth
Macclesfirld
Maidstone
Malden
Malmesbury
Manchester
Northampton
Paisley
Perth
Salford
Selkirk
Southampton
Sudbury
Tiptree
Whitchurch
Winchester

Cottages and Mills

Further to the north, the tradition of building specially-designed weavers' cottages extended to Leek (Staffordshire), Macclesfield (Cheshire) and Kirkheaton, near Huddersfield (Yorkshire).

Other immigrant settlements

Silk-weavers moved north, east and west from Spitalfields early in the seventeenth century and established new colonies. By 1640, French churches were established at Southampton, Norwich, Canterbury and Dover. Dutch churches were at Norwich, Yarmouth, Colchester, Canvey Island and Sandwich Bay. The congregation of the French church at Southampton was made up entirely of serge-weavers as early as 1590.

Other waves of Huguenots departed Spitalfields in the early eighteenth century and set up enterprises in Edinburgh, Macclesfield and Sudbury. Many of Macclesfield's typical silk-weavers' cottages were built at this time. Many still survive, promoted by the Macclesfield Silk Heritage.

A century later in the 1840s 'freemen weavers' settled in the west midlands town of Hillfields and this soon became a centre for silk-weaving. Lots of weavers' cottages sprang up with upper storeys specifically made with large oblong windows; each window had between sixty and eighty panes. Upstairs was the loomshop. Between 1847 and 1859 other groups of three-storey cottages were built, each with a steam engine adjoining. The power plant occupied an outhouse and the power supply ran all the way round the three storeys of all the cottages. At Hillfields today there are sixty-seven cottages, all built as one triangle. The Quakers John and Joseph Cash, renowned for their name ribbons invented here, built several weavers' cottages adjacent to the local canal.

BRITISH SILK MILLS

Silk mills are dotted around Britain, often reflecting the routes of the Huguenot weavers. They range from silk mills in the south-west at Taunton to Paisley and Edinburgh, where kashmiri shawls were woven in the 1790s. It has been difficult sometimes to sort out silk mills from woollen mills. Almost certainly, silk was not always the major commodity processed, but may well have constituted a part when local produce or imported silks were available.

S i l k - w e a v e r s ,

Mills were used for twisting silk and gradually replaced hand-twisting which was often done in special workers' cottages. Many of these mills have now fallen into disrepair and some have disappeared altogether leaving a legacy only in street names. Others have been restored and are now open to the public.

The constant flow of water was found at the onset to be most satisfactory for driving the mills' complicated mechanical gear. Many silk mills were situated on a good source of water; so much the better if that water was of good quality for dyeing too. With the advent of steam engines and electricity the process of producing silk became much more efficient.

The East Midlands

Perhaps the most famous silk mill was Lombe's mill in Derby. It was so large – an eighth of a mile long – and so complex that it could never be reconstructed; it would take up too much of Derby's precious space. Unfortunately nothing of the mill remains except the foundations which are on an island site in the River Derwent. Today there is an impressive Industrial Museum on the river island site, and nearby a Silk Mill Inn, on the site of a similarly named inn.

John Lombe led a short but intriguing life. At the age of twenty in 1704 he took on a silk mill on the island site in the River Derwent at Derby, using imported Dutch machinery. All was well, except no one in England had mastered how to throw silk or double it. This was an Italian art, and the English could never match the Italians for quality. There was only one alternative for John Lombe. He went to Italy with the financial backing from his step-brother, Thomas, and industrial espionage then prevailed. John managed to find employment on the factory floor of a silk mill and, gaining everyone's confidence, drew plans of the Italian machinery for throwing silk. These plans were secretly hidden in bales of silk destined for England, loaded at Livorno by Thomas Lombe's agents and carefully retrieved in England. John managed to escape in time, even though his boat was pursued by a Sardinian man-of-war. The punishment for his deception would have been 'hanging by one foot from a gibbet until dead'. Everything seemed perfect thereafter; the new Derby mill began operation using the new technology in 1720 at a cost of £30,000, and England had its first thrown silk. However, tragedy soon struck. John Lombe died in 1722 when he was only twenty-nine. It was thought, but not proved, that he was poisoned by an

Cottages and Mills

It was here on an island near the centre of Derby that one of the most impressive of English silk mills stood, before it was gutted by fire. Today a museum stands on its site. Sir Thomas Lombe's silk mill was improved with technology secretly acquired from the Italians in a case of industrial espionage, for which eventually John Lombe probably paid with his life

Silk-weavers,

Italian woman who came to work at the Derby factory soon after it was built, since his death followed a period of intense internal pain. Perhaps the Italians eventually sought their revenge.

Lombe's machines were truly impressive and a masterpieces of the Industrial Revolution. The mill's water wheel drove 26,586 other wheels which had 97,746 movements. The wheel revolved three times each minute and for each revolution it moved 67,415 m (73,726 yd) of organzine silk thread. This worked out at 291,240,000 m (318,504,960 yd) per day.

In Staffordshire there was, and still is, an important silk mill at Leek. This was the Albion Mill, not open to the public but still in working condition. The creation of silk thread was the speciality of Leek in the seventeenth and eighteenth centuries. In the town there are silk-twisters' rooms recognizable by their long windows. Thomas Wardle, the noted expert and author on silk, lived in Leek and mentioned in one of his books a George Bermingham, silk manufacturer of Leek, in about 1890, as a very respected gentleman.

Congleton had its mills too. It was ideally situated on the River Dane and the first mill was established here in 1752. The main trade of the town in the nineteenth century was silk-spinning. Local weavers made ribbons and lace with cotton and silk binding.

In Cheshire the London Huguenots established Macclesfield as an important silk centre in the middle of the eighteenth century. One of the first mills was established there in 1743. Others followed quickly. Macclesfield was famous for its quality silk thread, its heavy woven Jacquards and button-making. It was also the first town to establish a water-powered yarn-twisting works, in 1743. The silk industry in Macclesfield did not reach its peak until the early part of the nineteenth century.

Macclesfield silk was controlled by just a few families, such as the Brocklehursts, Pearsons, Smales and Turners. There were literally scores of mills in the town. Forty-six Macclesfield mills have now been demolished, a sad plight for Macclesfield's magnificent historical heritage in the face of urban development. In the museum there is a photographic record – of revealing before-and-after pictures – of all its famous mills. The Macclesfield silk industry came to an end in the early 1870s due to competition from abroad and the introduction of man-made fibres. Now the silk trade of Macclesfield is a growing tourist industry. The Macclesfield Silk Heritage was set up in 1979 and is a thoroughly worthwhile venture.[4]

Not far away is Paradise Mill, preserved as a beautifully restored working mill, a time-warp from another century, complete with its twenty-six Jacquard looms and volunteers who grew up in the neighbourhood and

Cottages and Mills

worked some of the machines. It was built in 1820 and was the last to house a handloom silk-weaving business. The family firm of Cartwright and Sheldon ran Paradise Mill from 1912 to 1981 when it closed down. Although the last of the handloom weavers retired in 1981, there are still some silk products, such as ties, produced and sold.

Life as a silk-worker was hard at the best of times. Macclesfield men worked in the garrets, women worked in the evenings in outlying villages making silk buttons, and children were employed tying threads in the throwing mills. Weavers had to pay 'loom rent' for using the looms in their garrets. In the 1830s men could earn 7–9s. a week, but had to give back 6s. Women had to pay an additional 6d. for their trouble. The introduction of the Jacquard loom in the 1820s meant that fancy and cheap silks could be worked. Silk-workers worked a sixty-two hour week and earned 11s. for it.

Peace with France and the lifting of the 1826 Act banning imported French and Italian silk caused havoc in the silk towns of England. Imports flooded in and depressed the English industry. It threw Macclesfield families into poverty and destitution. Fifty per cent of the mills stopped working. The wealthy silk families were powerless to do anything, and were not much appreciated. People like John Brocklehurst kept some sort of spirit going by opening soup kitchens, but it cost him £70,000. In Crozier's 1947 book about the Brocklehursts, it is said that there were fourteen thousand employees in fifty-five factories in 1860, and only five thousand employees in thirty Macclesfield factories in 1885, such was the depressed state of employment.

The West Midlands

In Medieval times Coventry had wool and cloth industries but these have vanished completely today. Silk ribbons, tapes and hats manufactured in Coventry during the first half of the nineteenth century heralded a period of prosperity in the town. The village of Bedworth, now a suburb of Coventry, benefited from a silk industry being established there. Until about twenty years ago one of the early silk factories was standing near the centre of the town, with its living quarters on the ground floor and the silk shops with their long windows above. The building, a good example of nineteenth-century industrial architecture, has regrettably been pulled down.

A new town entirely for silk-weavers was established at Hillfields, near Coventry, where two thousand houses were constructed between 1840 and

Silk-weavers,

1860. Ludlow has a Silk Mill Lane, which suggests that there was a silk mill here. A weaving community grew up in Manchester from the 1780s and by 1830 there were twenty thousand looms producing low-grade silks. Free trade was promoted there by the Manchester School of Economists.

The North and Scotland

Silk mills occurred in Paisley, famous for its Paisley designs. These were named after the pine cone design which originated in Kashmir. Paisley dominated the shawl trade in Britain until a change in fashion ruined the industry in 1870.[5]

The great industrialist Samuel Lister made Bradford the centre of spinning. His development of various pieces of apparatus including the silk comb, which made the processing of silk much more efficient, and boosted production. His Manningham Mills employed twelve thousand people in 1900. Spun silk was mixed with local wool to make tough cloth, a technique not lost on today's entrepreneurs.

One of Scotland's newest mills is Welstead Mill in Caithness, opened in 1987. Predominantly producing tweeds it has diversified into mixing silks with its fabrics which now receive world acclaim, especially with the assistance of designers like Giorgio Armani, Vivienne Westwood and Jasper Conran.

London and environs

The Lewisham silk mills, in south-east London, were important in supplying silk for soldiers' garments. A royal small arms factory was taken over as a silk mill in about 1820 by a silk-throwster called Robert Arnold. Here imported skeins of silk were thrown which employed many young girls between the ages of nine and fourteen.[6] It is likely that the same Robert Arnold was the ribbon manufacturer on Cheapside, a stronghold of Huguenot fabrics.

Later in the nineteenth century Arnold's relations, the Stantons in Lewisham, were masters of twisting silk thread round very fine silver and gold thread. This was then exported to China and India to be embroidered into cloths. Gold bars used to be brought to Lewisham from Greenwich, carried openly on the back of a cart. It was squeezed and drawn out through rollers until it made a staggering 4,572 m (5,000 yd) of gold thread from

Cottages and Mills

each ounce of gold. One thousand troy ounces of silver were also brought from Greenwich and these cakes of silver were covered with gold leaf. The Stantons made all sorts of material from gold and silver skein threads, ribbons, braids, tinsel, cords, fringes and lace. A delightful story is recounted of how the employees of this factory made a special gold and silk girdle for a rich client from 22-carat gold wire and yellow silk 3 yd long, someone having to remain motionless from 08.00 to 14.00 while it was fitted and tailored.

Tring Park in Hertfordshire had its own silk mill. This is hardly surprising since the Park was owned by James I. He granted it to his elder son, Henry, Prince of Wales, for ninety-nine years and it later went to Charles I and his queen, Henrietta Maria. The mill was still there later when Walter Rothschild acquired the property. At Aylesbury, Buckinghamshire, there used to be a silk mill run by the Moscrop family.

East Anglia

With the large number of Huguenots, Dutch and Walloons in this area one would expect several silk mills. Norwich was famous for its shawls and crêpes with Kashmiri designs in the nineteenth century.

Hadleigh, eight miles west of Ipswich in Suffolk, had a silk-throwing mill early in the nineteenth century. This was during one of the better times for the town and the mill employed four hundred women and children. The town had always derived its livelihood from wool. It exported cloth as early as 1305 from its two fulling mills, and lindseys and kerseys from adjacent villages with those names. In 1618 James I gave Hadleigh its charter but this was taken away in 1687 due to exploitation by the mayor. There then followed a poor time for the villagers, the trade not picking up until the arrival of the silk mills in 1811.

The arrival of the Courtauld refugees from the Low Countries heralded the beginning of an important cloth empire, whose family name is still famous today. They had mills at Bocking and Braintree. Benjamin Warner & Co. also moved to Braintree in 1895.

There has been a recent revival of silk-weaving in Essex. The famous weaving family of Warners ceased trading in 1971 at Sudbury and Braintree and several of their looms and equipment were purchased by one of their aspiring apprentices, Richard Humphries. He set up the De Vere Mill at Castle Hedingham, and together with John Flizet, of the Lyon weaving school, now produces prestigious silks woven on 1830s looms.

Silk-weavers,

Old patterns have been meticulously copied on to cards for the Jacquard looms and copies of old designs are now being produced. De Vere silks have been used for the Speaker's bed in Westminster Palace, silk velvets for the Royal Trumpeters, strie cloths for the National Gallery, silks for the 'Treasure House' of the British Exhibition in Washington in 1985 and silks for royal palaces in Britain and in the Middle East.

Southern England

In central southern England perhaps the best preserved of all silk mills is that at Whitchurch, Hampshire. It was built on Frog Island in the middle of the River Test in the eighteenth century on the site of a former mill. Weaving has been known on this site since the Domesday survey around 1067. The mill, classified as of architectural and historical interest, is now restored with its own original water-wheel and is open to the public. For many years Lord Denning, former Master of the Rolls, has lived here and been responsible for the restoration. The mill has produced silks for Queen's Counsel gowns, and royal weddings.

Another Hampshire silk mill is in the precincts of Winchester Cathedral on the site of an old monastery; this mill is now being restored. There are several mulberry trees planted in the city gardens.

There is some circumstantial evidence that a silk industry was based at Wokingham, Berkshire, during Jacobean times and that a plantation of mulberry trees was established there. The last of the trees was pulled down in the 1970s.

A silk mill flourished for a short while near Sevenoaks, Kent, in the eighteenth century. It was established by Peter Nouaille, the third member of this Huguenot family with the same name. Peter Nouaille was born in 1723 and married Elizabeth Delamore in 1760, possibly of another Huguenot family. It was soon after this marriage that Sevenoaks silk mill was established on a small stream south of the town. Mill Lane is all that reminds one of this mill which produced crêpe silks. Peter Nouaille, with his father, Peter, are thought to have been the first people to produce crêpe in Britain. It was formerly imported from Bologna in Italy. The second Peter Nouaille, (b. 1693) was a Levant trader and married Anne, daughter of Jean Maillard of Spitalfields.

Cottages and Mills

This is a drawing from a photograph of the silk mill at Whitchurch, Hampshire, which stands on an island in the river, and which is open to the public. It shows the typical large windows to allow maximum light

South-west England

In Malmesbury, Wiltshire, there used to be two large silk mills in active use up to the beginning of this century, but they are now defunct. One of the mills, the Inner Silk Mill, stood on the River Avon. It became derelict but has now been modernized. It was originally built in the nineteenth century for the wool trade but was later used for silk-throwing and ribbon-weaving.

In the south-west there were at least two rival silk mills in Sherborne, Dorset, which had been there since 1753. One of the mills, of which little is known, was in the refectory of Sherborne Abbey. The other was Westbury Mill which was established by a Spitalfields throwster called John Sharrer. This mill was bought by the Willmott family in 1769, who then bought out the abbey silk mill. By 1885 silk-throwsting had replaced weaving. During the Second World War the mill was converted to glass fibre production. Lyme Regis may well have had a silk industry too, as there is a Silk Factory House there today.

Silk mills are also known from Taunton in Somerset, and Tiverton, Devon. In the 1860s a John Heathcote established a silk farm in Tiverton which was successful for a few years producing silk netting. It also had reeling machines. Heathcote's mill is still active today and produces embroidery threads.

NOTES

1. It was reported in the *Midi Libre* of 22 April 1990, that following the first crisis of the silk

Silk-weavers,

industry in the Cévennes, many people turned to licorice production. A current enthusiasm for collecting old licorice tins (illustrated in the article) has brought this fact to light.

2. Spitalfields is named after the church of St Mary Spital. Nice as it would have been, the word 'Spital' does not seem to refer in any way to the liquid silk secretions produced from the mouth of the silkworm. Hogenberg's 1600 map of London shows the whole area now occupied by Spitalfields, Shoreditch and Whitechapel illustrated by little fields, lanes and tree-lined hedgerows. Spital may refer to a poor house or Lazare house. Henry VIII used the Spital Fields for his gunnery practice and this activity is remembered today in the tiny lane called Artillery Lane which leads off Bishopsgate.

3. It is said that the first tie was originally a simple Macclesfield square folded in seven.

4. Much later appreciated by the designer, William Morris.

5. Charles Dewhurst, in his 1839 book, mentions that there was 'an ingenious silk manufacturer' in Paisley called Mr Andrew Wright.

6. Photographs of the mill as it was being demolished in about 1937 can be seen in Sylvia Macartney and John West's interesting booklet on *A History of the Lewisham Silk Mills* (*c.* 1980).

This is a silk embroidered wall hanging called 'Artichoke', as displayed at the National Trust property 'Standen' in Sussex. It was designed by William Morris in 1877, two years after he started a working relationship with silk-dyer Thomas Wardle, brother of Morris' manager, George Wardle. William Morris and Thomas Wardle both experimented successfully with vegetable dyes for their fabrics. A founder member of the Arts and Crafts Movement, Morris promoted the use of natural materials. In 1881 he was asked to decorate the Blue Room at St James's Palace, London where he created a woven silk damask for the curtains which he called 'The St James'. Pelmets were embroidered in pink, gold and green silk with a couched silk braid. There was more to link the Wardles and Morrises, since Mrs Thomas Wardle (later Lady Wardle) introduced William Morris designs into her husband's works

Macclesfield is the silk centre of Britain, with several silk companies surviving, and a fine museum which demonstrates the connections between the town, silk and the Huguenots

HERMÈS-PARIS

It takes two years to produce a celebrated Hermès scarf, from the selection of the silk from China to the finished product. Computers store an archive of over eight hundred designs and a shade catalogue of over two thousand colours. Only 300,000 scarves are produced each year

Now that silks are
becoming more
fashionable, they are
being incorporated
into other materials
such as woollens.
Here a range of
colourful samples
made in Scotland is
being shown off

191

T
H
E
·
S
T
O
R
Y
·
O
F
·
S
I
L
K

CHAPTER 11

The Industry Today

Weave troth with trust

S ilk is an increasingly chic commodity in the West, in great demand from designers. For a long while the price of raw silk from the East was very modest, but in the late 1980s China, the principal source of silk, increased the price to the rest of the world by more than 100 per cent. This large price increase has hardly affected the trade however, and silks are growing in demand. Some countries find it is worth promoting a silk industry since the natural fibre can be incorporated into wools and cottons.

There are over thirty countries in the world which now produce silk, but the overall leader, as always, is China. The silk industries in Japan and Korea are declining slowly. India still has the monopoly of tougher wild silks of which Tusseh is the best known, and a host of other countries dabble in silk production. Some, like France, have rejuvenated their defunct silk industry. In Latin America silk production is an increasing business.

Annual world production of silk is in the region of 59,000 million tonnes, and this represents only about 0.16 per cent of all textile fibres.[1]

China maintains its lead in the world by producing an average of 30,000 tonnes of silk each year. For raw silk it dominates the world market with 80 per cent, for 'silk goods' 40 per cent and for Tusseh silks 60 per cent. China produces about 1,000 tonnes of Tusseh silk each year.

The value of China's silk exports represents about $900 million per year. With the absorption of Honk Kong into China in 1997, silk exports from China will be much stronger since Hong Kong exports of finished goods have been of higher quality in recent years.

China's enormous work-force is a vital factor in its success. However, in the future India has greater potential to expand sericulture than China since

China heads the
world in the
production of raw
silk, although there
has been a slight
drop in its
productivity. Japan
enjoyed second
place, but has now
been ousted by
India. The USSR and
Brazil are expanding,
while Korea is
declining

Evolution of world raw silk production (tonnes × 1,000)

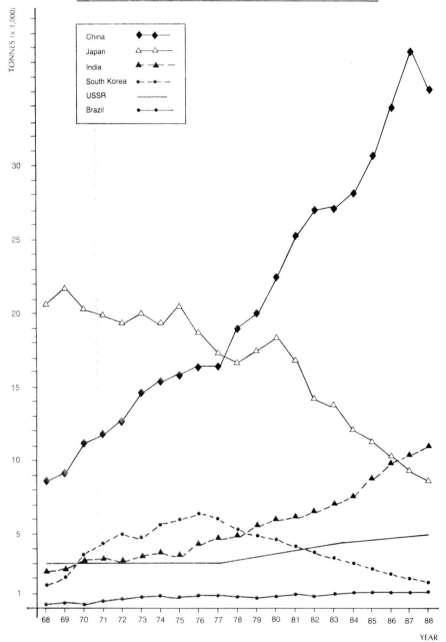

TONNES (× 1,000)

	China	◆ ◆
	Japan	△ △
	India	▲ ▲
	South Korea	● ●
	USSR	—
	Brazil	● ●

YEAR

The Industry Today

it has 146 million ha of land which can be cultivated for its 80 million people, compared to China which has 101 million ha of land for its 103 million people.

Over ten million farmers in China produce about half of the annual world production of 59,000 tonnes of cocoons per annum, and another half a million Chinese workers are involved in silk fabric production. There are about six hundred weaving mills in China and the whole silk industry is controlled by the China Silk Corporation, set up in 1982. Important research work is carried out at the Liaoning Province Sericulture Scientific Research Institute, near Dangong.

In the early 1980s Japan was the second largest exporter of silk in the world, but its production is decreasing. In the 1960s Japan was the largest producer of raw silk in the world but it ceded to China soon afterwards.

In 1988 Japan produced about 6,840 tonnes of raw silk. There are over 10,000 tonnes of raw silk stocks held by Japan and modern observers report that for political and economic reasons these are not likely to be released on to the international market.

The decline in Japanese silk production, despite Government promotion, is due to labour shortages and increased industrialization. The sericulture industry is highly mechanized with automatic twig- and leaf-harvesting, automatic feeding of leaves to caterpillars and automatic rotation of silkworm beds in controlled environments.

A typical Japanese farmer in a rural area might have a smallholding of about 5 ha (12.4 ac), most of which will be given over to mulberry plantations. The Japanese are extremely fussy about productivity and efficiency and follow all recommendations, especially on optimum spacing of bushes and irrigation procedures. Top quality leaf production results and this is reflected in the high quality silk cocoons.

In 1972 Japan began to experience a boom in silk sales since ordinary Japanese women were beginning to earn enough money to buy silk kimonos, the national dress of the Japanese, used at important ceremonies and festivities. Silk production and silk prices rocketed. Japan imported silk from China and Korea to satisfy demand but the boom was short-lived since western tastes in dress soon dominated the market. Today Japan still imports from China as well as from Brazil, where silk costs half that in Japan.

Today the city of Kiryu is the main silk centre of Japan, where computerized looms make exact copies of old designs. This new automation to Japan's industry has allowed it to become a leader in processing silks. The Empress of Japan is said to promote sericulture by feeding silkworms in the

T
H
E
·
S
T
O
R
Y
·
O
F
·
S
I
L
K

ABOVE: Muga
silkworms being
raised by villagers in
Assam, 1988

BELOW: Charka
reeling – an Indian
term for one of the
most primitive forms
of reeling, Assam,
1988

The Industry Today

grounds of the royal palace each spring. However, extensive use of synthetic diets for young caterpillars is now practised widely in Japan.

Because of the increasing development of Japan as an industrialized nation, it risks losing its second place for production of raw silk to India, which still has much available unskilled labour.

India has now taken second place for world production of raw silk through increased mechanization. It also has the advantage of producing a different range of wild silks to all other countries. India leads the world in the production of the rich yellow silk, called Muga; in fact it has the monopoly of this type of silk and produces most of it in Assam. India is second to China for Tusseh silk.

Indian sericulture is dependent upon a labour-intensive village industry. In 1986 there were 45,262 villages producing silk with 182,325 handlooms and 29,340 powerlooms, producing 7,029 tonnes of raw silk (from 217,839 ha (538,272 ac) of mulberry bushes), 464 tonnes of Tusseh silk, 352 tonnes of Eri silk and 52 tonnes of Muga silk. Indian silk goods are exported to over eighty countries of which 75 per cent go to western countries. Combined raw silk production from all sources is projected to be 10,900 tonnes by 1990. Better agricultural techniques have enabled India to produce 32.5 kg (71.6 lb) of raw silk from one hectare of land compared to 25 kg (55.1 lb) of silk from the same area ten years earlier.

Mulberry sericulture is practised today in the six Indian states: Karnataka, Andrhra Pradesh, West Bengal, Tamil Nadu, Jammu & Kashmir, Assam and Uttar Pradesh. Tusseh, Eri and Muga silks are centred on the states of Bihar, Madhya Pradesh, Orissa, West Bengal, Assam and North Eastern States. The state of Karnataka is most important since 80 per cent of all India's silk comes from there.

Silkworm-rearing and winding silk in rural India has changed little since earliest times. It is still undertaken by certain 'scheduled' castes and tribes in society, and provides work for 4½ million people in rural and forest areas.

All members of a family may be involved in different stages of silk production. Fifteen members of a typical family might make fifteen saris a year, each selling for 1,200–1,300 rupees each. Indian women, incidentally, practise thigh-reeling, which is the only time they really expose their legs from under their saris.

Raw Indian silk is never exported; it is reeled and spun before being exported as made-up material, saris, scarves, ties, fabrics, such as upholstery, cushion covers, bed spreads and the like. This enables many of the employees to work at home.

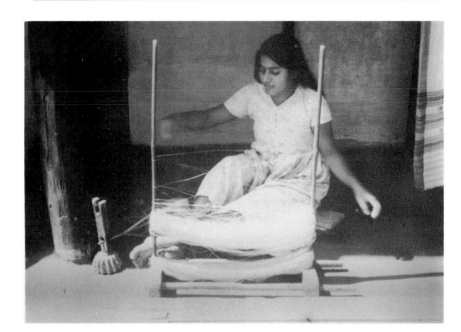

ABOVE: Hand skein-
winding in Assam,
1988

BELOW: Muga silk-
weaving in a shed as
part of a small
business in a village
in Assam, 1988

The Industry Today

In the Soviet Union, silk and cotton have been traditionally produced in Uzbekistan for hundreds of years and today 50 per cent of production of both comes from there. Productivity for the Soviet Union is thought to have risen from 2,800 tonnes in 1968 to 4,410 tonnes in 1982, and most is produced for the home market. The inhabitants of Uzbekistan adhere to strict Muslim rules, having been originally colonized by Turkish tribes. They are not allowed to wear pure silk, so their ikats are made of cotton (as warp) and silk (as weft).

Both North and South Korea produce silks, but quantitative information is both scarce and conflicting. South Korea certainly produces more than North and in 1986 produced about 2,088 tonnes of raw silk, some of which was exported to Japan.

Indonesia is increasing its production of silk with new developments on the main island of Java and on the south of Sulawesi. At present it imports more silk for processing (batik- and silk-weaving) than it makes and the aim of its new silk ventures is to reduce this dependence. Annual production of raw silk in 1985 was in the order of 20–40 tonnes of raw silk. There are about forty thousand hand-weaving looms at present and it is likely that the potential for sericulture in Indonesia will be realized rapidly, since it will provide employment for many of its 120 million people.

Brazil now holds sixth position for raw silk production, representing 3.5 per cent of the world market. It certainly has an increasing influence in the silk trade and has developed steadily since Italian immigrants brought silkworms to Brazil at the turn of the century. Brazil entered the silk market significantly in 1962. It saw great expansion in the 1970s, and probably raised production by 12 per cent between 1986/7 and 1987/8.

Silk production in Brazil is organized on a cooperative basis with six thousand workers. Selection of genetic strains, control of disease at the egg stage and early larval life is organized by the seven spinning mills in the country. Silk production takes place mostly in the states of São Paulo and Parana where the climate is temperate and the soil fine for cultivating mulberry trees. The mills send out the larvae after a week when they are in their second stage. The six thousand workers rear them and sell them back to the mill in the fifth stage. Cocoon-making and -processing thereafter is then centralized at the mill.

Seven to nine generations of silkworms each year are achieved in Brazil, suggesting a multi-voltine (multi-generation) race of silkworms. Temperature regulation of eggs may also be used to stagger 'generations'.

Brazilian silk is worth an annual revenue of $40 million and is exported to

The Industry Today

the USA, Japan, Formosa, Thailand, South Korea, Singapore, India and EEC countries.

Thailand's silk industry is, like China and India, labour-intensive and likely to benefit in the future while other countries mechanize. The industry employs about two million people directly and a further one million indirectly, and produces up to 900 tonnes of raw silk each year. Thai silk is unique in having a lot of knots and ties in it, and is very attractive when made up. There are over 300,000 thrown-shuttle looms and over twenty-three thousand fly-shuttle looms used in the country.

Taiwan's silk industry is a mere three hundred years old, compared to the sericultural legend of five thousand years for its neighbour on the mainland, and it was promoted at the end of the Ming Dynasty and established during the Ching Dynasty. The industry is now government-backed and is based upon a traditional village industry.[2]

Specialized districts for silk production were set up in 1973 in Miaoli, Nantou, Chiayi, Tainan, Pingtung, Taitung and Hualien. Coordination is through the Taiwan Sericultural Improvement Station in Kung-Kuan, a government organization, founded in 1897.

Recent advances in sericulture include increased mechanization, especially in mulberry field operations, selection of better silkworm and mulberry strains, and research and development on diseases. Taiwan's advanced sericultural expertise is exported to other countries including South Africa, the Phillipines, Indonesia, Colombia and Costa Rica.

In the late 1980s South Africa embarked on a sericulture scheme, with a silk pilot project at Gazankulu. This is a self-governing state in the district of Mahla. In 1988 there were already eight hectares of mulberry bush plantation, and Chinese technicians to supervise establishment. There is a small amount of military use of this silk farm since cocoons are shredded (using a paper shredder) to make silk wadding used in military duvets.

Elsewhere in Africa silk production has been a local and traditional occupation, for instance in Kenya silk is still produced at Kereicho, near Narok, where there are mulberry plantations and silkworm farms.

Europe used to be a major producer of silk but the collapse of the cottage silk industry in Italy and France has reduced the input of European silk into the world market to almost insignificant levels. Greece produces more silk than Italy (35 tonnes and 20 tonnes respectively) while Yugoslavia also produces about 10 tonnes each year.

The Comecon countries are the largest producers of raw silk in Europe:

The Industry Today

Soviet Union (4,400 tonnes), Bulgaria (200 tonnes), Romania (125 tonnes), Hungary (20 tonnes) and Poland (10 tonnes).

In the northern Turkish sector of Cyprus, weaving silk was a village craft up to the late 1960s, especially at places like Kharchia, East of Kyrenia. Growing silkworms and weaving were extensive. Silk production was undertaken on a serious basis last century, but this may well have succumbed to disease, according to Wardle who wrote about it in 1904. He mentioned that 'twenty five years ago, the disease [unstated, but it must have been the *pebrine*] which decimated Italy and France also destroyed the output of Cyprus'.

The story of the silk industry in Italy is of recent revival after a period of decline and consolidation. Italy was the first in the silk business in western Europe and has had a long tradition with the industry. Other countries covertly stole Italian loom designs and technology, while Italian silk-workers helped to establish the French and American silk industries.

In the 1960s there were fifty thousand people engaged in silk weaving, half around Milan, the rest around Como and Turin. Two areas which have experienced declines in the 1980s are Padua, which once (late 1880s) supported fifty-nine field stations throughout Italy, and Treviso near Venice. The sericulture research station at Padua used to be famous for its different coloured cocoons, while Treviso's sericulture cooperative died out by 1983.

Como is now the silk centre of Italy. There are several hundred firms producing more than a third of the world's textiles and a lot of the revival is due to a £1.5 million grant from the government to bring the cottage industry up to modern standards. Some firms, such as Ratti, which also has a plant in Lyon, even work for Japanese companies, printing their silk for traditional kimonos. Modern research has produced silks which can be washed in hot water without damaging their new colour-fast dyes. Ratti now employs one thousand people. Another typical firm is Mantero which, like the others, is managing to survive despite the Chinese putting up their silk prices by 100 per cent in the late 1980s.

The future of the silk industry worldwide could not look better. The silk industry will blossom forth in those undeveloped countries that cannot modernize rapidly because of lack of money; their unskilled work-force will produce silk at minimal cost to the employer, thus putting silk on the market which will produce a large profit margin. Developing countries will have to pay higher wages and fight harder in the market-place to sell this wonderful natural product.

The Industry Today

NOTES

1. A comprehensive survey of the silk market was produced by the Tropical Development and Research Institute in 1986 (Greenhalgh, 1986). It provides an overview of world silk production and analyses the capabilities of all countries. Its figures for world production of mulberry raw silk and green mulberry cocoons are current up to 1983.

2. *Taiwan Sericulture*: a colour brochure produced by the Taiwan Sericultural Improvement Station, 261 Kuan-nan, Kung-Kaun Mioali.

APPENDIX 1

Silk-weavers in the United Kingdom

All those listed are members of the Silk Association of Great Britain, except where marked with an asterisk*. There are twenty-two other UK importers of silk, not listed here.

Richard Atkinson & Co. Ltd
Nicholas Drive,
Michelin Road,
Mallusk,
Newton Abbey,
Northern Ireland
Tel: (02313) 43323
Silk-weaver,
silk tie manufacturer

Baltex Fabrics
Burr Lane,
Ilkeston,
Derbyshire,
DE7 5JD
Tel: (0602) 322403
Silk warp knitter

Brocklehurst Fabrics Ltd
Hurdsfield Mills,
Macclesfield,
Cheshire,
SK19 2QY
Tel: (0625) 22214
Silk-weaver

J. Comfort & Co. Ltd
10 Leake Street,
South Bank,
London,
SE1 7AN
Tel: (071) 928 1491
Silk tie manufacturer

Courtaulds Shamash
13–14 Margaret Street,
London,
W1
Tel: (071) 631 4912
Silk fabric converters

David Evans Group
Bourne Road,
Crayford,
Kent,
DA1 4BP
Tel: (0322) 57521
Silk-weavers and printers

Humphries Weaving Co.
DeVere Mills,
Queen Street,
Castle Hedingham,
Halstead,
Essex
Tel: (0787) 61193
Silk hand-weavers

P.N. Jones Trading Co.
18 Holly Grove,
Peckham,
London,
SE15 5DF
Tel: (071) 639 2113
Handloom silks

Appendix 1

Lister & Co. Ltd
Dress Silk Dept,
Manningham Mills,
Bradford,
BD9 4SH
Tel: (0274) 494188
Silk-throwsters and -weavers

Michelsons Ltd
105 New Bond Street,
London,
W1Y 1HM
Tel: (071) 408 2466
Silk tie manufacturer

Park Adam Ltd
River Mills,
Langley,
Macclesfield
Cheshire,
SK11 DE1
Tel: (02605) 2483
Silk-printers and -weavers

Stephen Walters & Co. Ltd
Sudbury Silk Mills,
Sudbury,
Suffolk,
CO10 6XF
Tel: (0787) 72266
Silk-throwsters and -weavers

Vanners Silk Weavers[*]
Gregory Mills,
Sudbury,
Suffolk,
CO10 6BB
Tel: (0787) 72396
Silks and polyesters

Worldwide Butterflies Ltd &
Lullingstone Silk Farm
Compton House,
Sherborne,
Dorset,
DT9 4QN
Tel: (0935) 74608
Silk farm, silk reeling

APPENDIX 2

Museums

The logo of the
Lullingstone Silk
Farm

UNITED KINGDOM

**Silk Museum, Heritage Centre and
  Museum Shop**
Roe Street,
Macclesfield,
Cheshire,
SK11 6UT
Tel: (0625) 613210
A bright, refreshing and professional look
at the silk industry in Britain, especially in
the Macclesfield area.

Paradise Mill Working Silk Museum
Park Lane,
Macclesfield,
Cheshire,
SK11 6TJ
Tel: (0625) 618228

Restoration of a prosperous working mill of
the 1930s complete with twenty-six
Jacquard looms in working order. Open
1400–1700. Closed Monday (except Bank
Holidays). £1.20 entrance fee.

David Evans & Co.
Bourne Road,
Crayford,
Kent,
DA1 4BP
Tel: (0322) 57521

A working mill which produces silks
exported throughout the world. Imported
silk bolts are processed to make colourful
flowing silk within eight weeks.

Appendix 2

Educational video on 'World of Silk'. Madder dyeing and silkscreen printing are specialities. Open Monday to Friday, 1030–1600. Coach parties welcome.

**Worldwide Butterflies Ltd &
Lullingstone Silk Farm**
Compton House,
Sherborne,
Dorset,
DT9 4QN
Tel: (0935) 74608

This is where the silk equipment from Zoë, Lady Hart Dyke's silk farm in Kent now resides. It is still used to produce English silk. Visitors see silkworm-rearing (in season), spinning and reeling. There is a unique exhibition on how English silk is produced.

FRANCE

La Maison des Canuts
Cooptiss Coopératives Ouvrières de Tissage,
10–12 Rue d'Ivry,
69004, Lyon
Tel: 78–28–62–04

Situated in the famous silk-weaving district of Croix-Rousse, this museum demonstrates the production of silk, weaving processes and looms, especially those of the famous Lyonais Jacquard. Open every day except Sunday, fête days and in August, 0830–1200 and 1400–1830.

Maison de la Soie
Place 8 mai,
St Hippolyte du Fort,
34, Hèrault
Tel: 66–77–66–47

Interesting display of silkworms (in season),

old looms, dresses, sericulture ephemera, educational video and commercial silk shop. This was the town in which Louis Pasteur stayed when coopted to work for the cévenols. His place of residence is nearby but is not open to the public.

Musée Cévenol
Rue Calquières,
Le Vigan,
30, Gard
Tel: 67–81–06–86

A municipal museum which includes the story of silk together with other regional interests. The area around the market town of Le Vigan was prominent in silk production last century.

Musée des Vallees Cévenol
95 Grand Rue,
St Jean du Gard,
30, Hèrault
Tel: 66–85–10–48

One of the most comprehensive museums in the region. Occupying one of the gateways to the Cévennes, St Jean du Gard used to be an important regional centre for silk production.

Other Museums with silk sections

Le Musée du Vieux Nîmes
Martine Nougarede,
Place aux Herbes,
3000 Nîmes

Musée Draguigan
Musée Arts et Traditiones,
89300 Draguigan

Appendix 2

Musée de la Soie
26200 Montboucher sur Jabron

Musée de la Soie
Montboucher sur Jabron,
26740, Montelimar

Musée Historique des Tissus
34 rue de la Charite,
69002, Lyon

NETHERLANDS

Atelier Ter Zijde Plantagebaan 199
Wouse Plantage Museum

Open 1000–1700 April to October.

INDIA

Banaras Silk Museum
28/21 Gyanbapi,
Varanasi,
221001

APPENDIX 3

Societies and Associations

Greenhalgh (1986) also offers a useful guide to addresses.

UNITED KINGDOM

Silk Education Service
Parkett Heyes House,
Broken Cross,
Macclesfield,
Cheshire,
SK11 8TZ
Tel: (0625) 613210

Caters for school parties and educational groups. Sells a variety of books, booklets and slide sets on silk (mail order leaflet on request).

Silk Association of Great Britain
c/o Rheinbergs Ltd,
Tonbridge,
Kent,
TN9 1RN
Tel: (0732) 351357

This is a voluntary trade group which supports the interests of most companies involved in the silk industry. It publishes a quarterly newsletter, *Serica*, in which UK silk statistics are published. The original silk association was put into liquidation in 1969. Members of the Silk Group formed the present limited company. 'The purpose of the Association is to promote, safeguard and further the use and appreciation of real silk and the interest of the British silk industry, to represent the industry to Government and Internationally and to provide a link between these institutions and members.'

FRANCE

Unité Nationale Séricicole
Centre de Cooperation Internationale en
Recherche Agronomique pour le Développement
(CIRAD),
25 quai Jean-Jacques Rousseau,
69350 La Mulatière
Tel: 7–78–50–41–98

This is the official sericulture body in France. It was formed in 1979 and hosts the International Sericultural Commission. It maintains a stock of *Bombyx* silkworms for research in France and abroad. It also runs a training programme, teaching, throwing and weaving, etc. for three month courses in Lyon in conjunction with the Higher School of Textile Industries of Lyon, the University of Lyon and the SICA Soie-Cévennes.

Appendix 3

International Silk Commission
20, rue Joseph Serlin,
69001 Lyon
Tel: 7–78–50–41–98

The Commission publishes the quarterly journal *Sericologia*.

**Société d'intérêt Collectif Agricole Soie-
Cévennes**
Monoblet,
30170 St Hippolyte du Fort
Tel: 66–85–29–09

Established in 1981 to revive the old cévenol silk industry. It aims, cooperatively, to produce 100 tons of silk a year, using four hundred 'growers' with 1,700 ha of mulberries. The key to its success has been the establishment of the Japanese bush mulberry 'Kokuso 21'. Silk production via SICA is already in progress in Gard, Hèrault, Ardèche and Drôme.

**Société d'intérêt Collectif Agricole
Ardelaine de Saint
Pierreville en Viverais**
Chambre d'Agriculture de L'Ardeche,
07001 Privas

Les Chemins de la Soie
Groupement pour la Connaissance et la Mise en Valuer du Patrimoine Ethnologique,
Filature du Pont de Fer,
30460, Lasalle
Tel: 66–85–24–44

Seeks to integrate agriculture, industry and crafts into a culture experience and to create a visitors' route through the region, taking in the rich silk heritage.

ITALY

**United Nations Food and Agriculture
Organisation (FAO)**
Via delle Terme di Caracalla,
0100 Roma

This branch of the UN promotes sericulture in developing countries and has published various manuals on mulberry and non-mulberry sericulture.

**Regia Stazione Bacologica Sperimentale
(Royal Sericultural Laboratory)**
Padua

Founded in 1871 it is the oldest sericultural institute in the world.

**Instituto Sperimentale di Zoologia
Agraria**
Via Lanceola,
6 Cascine del Riccio,
Florence

**Instituto Sperimentale de Zoologia
Agraria**
Via del Colli,
28, Padua

Assoziazione Nazionale Bachicoltori
Treviso,
Via Avogari,
27

INDIA

Central Silk Board
'Meghdoot',
95B Marine Drive,
Bombay 400 002

Central Silk Board
39 Mahatma Gandhi Road,
Bangalore,
560 001

Established by Act of Parliament in 1948. Publishes annual reports and various technical bulletins on all aspects of sericiculture. Has a network of sixty-five Research Extension Centres. Conducts farmers' training programmes.

Appendix 3

Central Oak Tasar Research Institute
Central Silk Board,
Central Tasar Research Station,
Ranchi – 834005

Provides research for development of the oak tasar culture. There are several regional tasar stations, including one at Ranchi (834005 Bihar) opened in 1964; the others include Batotoe, Bhimtal, Manipur, Lakha, Orissa and Jagadalpur. Mirza & Titabar (Assam) specializes in Muga and Eri silk culture.

Sericulture & Weaving Department (Hills)
Gauhati,
Assam

Regional Tasar Research Station
Bhimtal,
Uttar Pradesh

Silk & Rayon Textile Export Promotion Council
Resham Bhavan,
78 Veer Nariman Road,
Bombay, 400001

The Indian Silk Export Promotion Council
62 Mittal Chambers,
6th Floor,
Nariman Point,
Bombay, 400021

Central Silk Technological Research Institute (CSTRI)
Bangalore (Karnataka)

Conducts research on silk-reeling, processing and finishing.

International Centre for Training & Research in Tropical Sericulture (ICTRETS)
Sriramapuram,
Manandarada Road,
Mysore 570 008

Offers diplomas in tasar sericulture. Houses an important living collection of silkworm varieties.

THAILAND

United Nations Economic and Social Commission for Asia and the Pacific
UN Building,
Rajdamnern Avenue,
Bangkok 10200

This is a consultative organization for promotion of sericulture in the Far East.

JAPAN

The Japanese Silk Association Incorporated
Sanshi Kaikan 9-4 Yurakucho 1-come,
Chiyoda-ku,
Tokyo 100

Japan Silk Reeling Federation of Agricultural Co-operative Association
57 Kitanakadori 5-come Naka-ku,
Yokohama Kanagawa Pref. 231

Federation of Japan Textile Fabric Wholesalers' Organization
9-6 Nihonbashi Horidomecho 1-come,
Chuo-ku,
Tokyo 103

SOVIET UNION

Central Asian Scientific Institute for Sericulture
Sanish

Appendix 3

Ajerbaizan Scientific Institute for
  Sericulture (AJNISH)
Korovabad

BRAZIL

Fiacao de Seda Bratac
SA Rua Roberto Simonsen,
62–9 cj.91,
01017 São Paulo, SP

Kanebo Silk do Brasil
Via BR–369 Km 95,
86300 Cornelio Procopio, PR

Cooperativa Cafeiculturores e
  Agropecuristas de Maringa Ltda
Av. Prudente de Moraea 211,
87100 Maringa, PR

Kobes do Brasil Ind. e Com. Ltda
Av. Eugenio Coneglian s/n,
17500 Marilia, SP

Gunsan Fiacao de Seda
Almeda Santos 1800–130,
01418 São Paulo, SP

GLOSSARY

R obin Gwynn pointed out in his *Huguenot Heritage* that there was a galaxy of confusing names invented by the Dutch and Walloons in the Norwich (Norfolk) area at the beginning of the seventeenth century for their lace-making, ribbon-making and stocking-knitting. Many of these names are impossible to define by scholars today. Part of the reason for the diverse names was purely commercial, to make their products with foreign-sounding names more saleable. The English were not amused. The sorts of material being produced by immigrants in the Norwich area in 1611 were bays, bratoes, bussins, camientries, carletts, currelles, damaske, figuratoes, fustians, grograynes, lyles, serge de boyce, silk saye, striped tobines, tooys and tufted mockadoes! There were also different names for the same material, e.g. buffyn, a catalowne and the pearl of beauty were just one cloth. Textiles are often named after the place they were invented.

Arras for its arras
Avignon for its papal cloth or poplin
Baiae for its baize
Bokhara for its buckram
Calicut for its calicoes
Cambray for its cambric
Cashmere for its cashmere shawls
Cordova for its cordwain
Cyprus for its cypresse
Damascus for its damask
Damietta for its dimity
Drogheda for its druggets
Fostat (Cairo suburb) for its fustians
Friesland for its frieze
Gaza for its gauze

Gunninghamp for its gingham
Jean for its jean
Kersey for its linsey-wolsley
Lindsey (Norfolk) for its lindseys
Mantua for its mantuas
Masul for its muslin
Moors for their moir and mohair
Nîmes for its denim
Old Worsted for its worsted
Rennes for its rayne
Saracens for their sarsenets
Tarsus for its tabriz
Tartary for its tartarium cloths
Tucker-street, Bristol for its tuck
Tulle for its tulle

Alamode – A thin, light, glossy black silk
Antung – A Chinese silk fabric
Arras – A rich tapestry fabric

Arrasene – A material of silk and wool used in embroidery
Arrindy silk – Silk from *Philosamia cynthia*

Glossary

Bale – A variable weight of silk made from books of silk. Chinese and Japanese bales of silk weigh 55–65 kg (125–140 lb), Italian bales weigh 90 kg (200 lb)

Ballett – A small measure of thirty-two cocoons (eighteenth century)

Bandana – A silk, often a handerchief, typically tie-dyed to make white or yellow undyed areas and spots

Batman– An Armenian unit of weight of 8.5 kg (18 lb 12 oz)

Baves – A collection of silk threads as they are drawn off the cocoon, complete with their gum or sericin

Bells – Bell-shaped mounds of silk are made from the piling up of damaged cocoons which are useless for reeling; bells are used in quilting

Bisu – The old parts or husks of the cocoons left in the basin after reeling

Blaze – Short fibres on the outside of cocoons which do not take dyes

Bombasine (Bombazine, Bumbazine) – A black, twilled dress material, much used in mourning clothes, and made either of silk and worsted, cotton and worsted or worsted alone. Bumbazine (or satin cotton) was made from a mixture of silk and cotton wool

Book – A parcel of silk hanks weighing 2 kg. Japanese raw silk is packed in books of 25–30 skeins. One eighteenth-century definition was that three thousand cocoons make a book

Bouchon – A loop or nib on baves or threads

Brillante – A term used by weavers to describe the glossyness of finished silks

Brin – A single filament of silk drawn off from a cocoon, after degumming

Brocade – A woven material with raised figures or 'flowered' with silver or gold, often of Indian origin

Brocarts – A tissue which is heavily interwoven with gold or silver threads

Brocatelle – Linen, re-inforced, patterned furnishing silk

Calendering – A machine with rollers through which silks are passed to make a waved or watered effect

Calico – A plain white unprinted linen, not silk, named after an Indian town on the Malabar coast

Camlets – A light cloth of various materials, for cloaks, etc., originally a costly Eastern material of silk and camel's hair

Canuts – The name of the heavy cutting equipment used on velvets; also the name colloquially given to the silk-weavers of La Croisse-Rouge district of Lyon

Châle – A silk shawl produced in Paris in the early seventeenth century

Charmeuse – A silk satin fabric

Chiffon – A diaphanous silk-like muslin used in dressmaking about 1890

Cordonnet – A weakly-spun material made from waste silk, used for fringes and in lacemaking

Couched silk – Silk worked with embroidered threads all lying flat

Crap (Krap, Krapp, Kor-Krapps) – The first quality extract from the roots of madder used for dyeing silk red

Crape (Crêpe: French) – A thin, transparent, twisted raw silk with a crisped surface, often used for mourning clothes; usually has in the order of 2,000–3,500 twists of silk in every metre

Crêpe de Chine – White or coloured silks made from raw silk

Crêpe Lingerie – A Chinese 'brillante' silk, light and tight

Crêpe Marocain – A heavy Chinese silk with a very marked grain

Damask – A rich material of silk, wool and linen, woven with intricate designs, orginally made in Damascus

Decreusage – A French word meaning to degum silk

Denier – A unit of weight equal to about $8\frac{1}{5}$ troy grains, by which silk yarn was weighed and its fineness estimated in 1839. Another definition says it is a gram weight containing 9,000 m of silk thread. The Association International de la Soie defined a denier as the weight in demi-decigrams of the length of 450 m of silk. Twenty denier would equal a piece of silk 450 m long. Twelve denier is very fine. A bridal veil might be 9–11 denier and would normally be made by tricotage. Tissage would normally not be attempted with less than standard 20–22 denier

Diapause – A dormant stage the chrysalis enters to overcome winter; a sort of hibernation

Double Dutch throwing machine – An instrument for throwing silk, used before the circular Piedmontese machines came into operation

Douppion – The raw silk reeled from the cocoon

Ducapes – A strong, plain women's cloth

Eri silk – A silk from the caterpillars of the Eri silkmoths (*Philosamia cynthia* and *P. ricini*); thus, ericulture

Étoffe – A French word for fabric

Façonne – A figured silk

Fagara silk – Silk produced from the Atlas moth, *Attacus atlas*

Faille – A light, ribbed taffeta silk made in 1869

Felt – A cloth made from wool or fibre compresses, rolled or fulled to bind it together. The Huguenots of Wandsworth (SW London) made felt from a mixture of fine vicuna wool and rabbit wool

Ferret – A strong tape made from floss silk

Fibrillae – The specks on the surface of a yarn

Fibroin – The liquid silk produced by the silkworm which hardens in air and becomes viscous in hot water

Figurato – A cloth made of part silk and part white spun yarn

Filature – A building for the reeling of silk

Floss silk – The loose bits of silk from the outside of the cocoon

Foulard – A thin flexible silk

Frisons – The irregular pieces of silk reeled off cocoons before uniform silk is reeled off

Fulling (sometimes called **milling**) – The process of cleaning and thickening cloth by beating and rolling. Cleaning was sometimes done with Fuller's earth (a type of soil with cleansing

characteristics). Those involved in fulling were called fullers. Rolling, especially of felt hats for example, was done with mercury – thus 'mad as a hatter' – an occupational risk from mercury pollution

Frou-frou – The typical rustle of silks

Fustian – A coarse cloth of cotton or flax, the word probably originating from a suburb of Cairo

Fustic – The name of a variety of woods used for dyeing fabrics yellow

Galloons – Ribbons or braids for clothes and shoes

Gauze (Gaze) – Silk gauze, produced in Paris in the early seventeenth century, probably used on hats. The word is thought to have originated in Gaza in the Middle East

Georgette – A thin silk dress material, also known as georgette crêpe

Grenadine – A thin, gauze-like silk or woollen dress fabric, highly twisted organzine yarn; word perhaps originated in Granada (Spain)

Grogram – Coarse fabric of silk, mohair and wool, or these mixed after stiffening with gum. John Evelyn saw grograms being produced near Tours (France) in the seventeenth century

Grosgrain – A plain ribbed silk

Habutae – A plain woven Japanese silk fabric

Hank – A quantity of raw silk taken from a reel, then knotted loosely in a figure of eight

Heel – A device which divides the warp into two to make more colourful patterns

Holosericum – A Roman garment made of 100 per cent silk

Honan – A hand-woven Chinese wild silk fabric

Ikats – Coats or quilts with silk warp and cotton weft, dyed and woven on looms. The technical details were kept as trade secrets by the Jewish community in Uzbekistan (Soviet Union)

Jacquard – A type of loom which harnesses cloth for patterned weaving, named after Joseph-Marie Jacquard from Lyon, who invented it

Glossary

Kake – A unit of yield of cocoons in Japan

Kersey (Kersye) – A coarse, narrow cloth, often woven from wool with a long staple. Named after a village near Ipswich (Suffolk)

Kimono – The national dress of Japanese women, ('ki' meaning silk, 'mono' meaning the wearing of)

Lamé – A tissue with small amounts of gold or silken threads woven into it

Lampas – A glossy crêpe or a Chinese flowered silk (sixteenth century)

Lindsey – A cloth, named after a village near Ipswich (Suffolk)

Lutestring (Lustring) – A glossy silk ribbon used in dresses, or simply as a ribbon. Like alamodes, this kind of material was given a distinctive glossy appearance by a secret process perfected in Lyon (France). Lutestrings were also a speciality of Nîmes (Gard). At first lutestrings were exported from that region to the UK but the process eventually came to England in 1680, resulting in the formation of the Royal Lustring Co. in 1692. The following year all importation of lutestrings was banned in England. The company thrived until its major shareholder, Stephen Seignoret, was caught smuggling foreign lustrings and fined £10,000 in 1713

Magnanerie – A French word for a silkworm-rearing room or house

Mantua – A silk gown or petticoat, from the French *manteau*, and from the Italian town of Mantua

Mekhales – Intimately embroidered Muga silk skirts worn by women in Assam

Moches – A bale of imported raw silk

Mockado – A mock velvet cloth used in the sixteenth and seventeenth centuries, thus, perhaps, mockades; a corruption of the word mohair

Moiré – Faille or *Poulte de soie* whose sides are wrinkled, with reflective qualities. Also known in France as *Moiré d'Angleterre*

Momme – A unit of weight in Japan equivalent to 3.756 g

Mousseline – A very light silk

Muga silk – A silk produced from the Muga silkmoth (*Antheraea assamensis*)

Nagasaki – A figured silk made for printing

Nib – A lump in raw silk

Ninon – A sheer woven silk fabric

Noil – Knots of wool cleaned out of long staples

Organzine – A type of cloth made from a few silk threads twisted in the opposite direction to the main silk threads, sometimes to make the letter 'o'; (usually 400–800 turns each metre), thus also organdi, a kind of fine stiffish muslin

Passementerie – A French word for trimmings and elaborate braids

Petersham – A thick ribbed or corded silk ribbon used for hat bands

Photoperiod – The number of daylight hours which a caterpillar registers; below fifteen hours per day the caterpillar induces the chrysalis to enter diapause

Pirn – The spool which holds the weft yarn in the shuttle; two pirns per shuttle. See **quill**

Pirn winder – A piece of equipment which looks like a treadle spinning wheel used for winding silk on to the pirns. This was often a job for children to earn a few coppers. Later this was done automatically in a quilling machine

Poil – Highly twisted yarns

Pongée – A soft unbacked kind of Chinese silk

Poplin – This was formerly woven fabric of silk warp and worsted weft with a corded surface. It was originally made in the French town of Avignon, a papal seat, and the word stems from the French *popeline* and the Italian *papalina*. Now more commonly refers to heavy duty cotton with sheen, especially suitable for children's clothes

Poult-de-Soie – A fine corded silk

Prunella – A strong silk or worsted material used for graduate's, clergymen's and barristers' gowns

Quill – A Macclesfield (Cheshire) word for a pirn; thus, a machine for winding silk onto a pirn was called a quilling machine

Glossary

Reel – A wheel for reeling silk direct from cocoons, and then on to bobbins

Reeling – The process of reeling off the raw silk thread from cocoons softened in boiling water on to large wheels, and then transferring it to bobbins

Sacque – A loose kind of silk or train worn by Indians

Samite – A rich silk fabric of the Middle Ages sometimes interwoven with gold threads

Satin Duchesse – A very beautiful satin, thick, matt and irridescent

Satinettes – A material which looks like silk but was woven with a cotton warp and woollen weft, sometimes made from silk woven with cotton

Sericeous – Silky

Sericin – A gum secreted at the same time as the silkworm secretes liquid silk, used to stick the silk threads firmly together. It softens in warm water

Sericulture – The process of producing silk cocoons ready for reeling. The prefix 'ser' comes from the Greek (*sericum*, meaning silk), which comes from the Chinese. The true French translation is *sériciculture* but increasingly French people are using the English abbreviated *sériculture*

Schappe silk – A spun silk which has had 90 per cent of its sericin removed by fermentation

Scutching – A process of removing foreign matter and pupa remains from cocoons, using rotating blunt blades

Shantung – A Chinese wild silk fabric

Shot silk – A silk woven with different coloured warps and weft thread so as to make a tinted or irridescent appearance

Silk-reeling – The reeling of silk threads from the cocoon to the hanks

Silk-spinning – Spinning silk threads together

Silk-throwing – The process of winding silk from a skein

Silk-throwster – A person who converts raw silk into silk thread

Silk-twisting – The process of twisting together 2–5 silk threads to make a stronger thread from which to weave

silk. People who twisted silks were called 'twisters'. The word also refers to the twisting of another piece of thread on to an existing piece of warp. This was eventually done automatically

Skein (Skeane) – A quantity of silk (or cotton) wound on a reel and gathered into a loose knot. Cotton skeins consist of eighty turns of thread on a reel of about 137 cm (54 in) circumference. Many skeins were 914 m (1,000 yd). Aglionby (1699) recognized a 'skeane' as eighty threads in length without giving further details

Slubs – Irregular lumps in silk threads

Soie brut – Cleaned silk ready for manufacture

Soie grège – Raw untwisted silk complete with gum

Stamins – A material woven from coarse worsted often associated with Norfolk, famous for its worsteds

Staple – The length of pure natural fibres when teased out, for silk up to about 250 mm

Subsericum – A Roman garment whose warp was made of linen or wool

Suzanis – Special fabrics from Uzbekistan (Soviet Union), such as wall hangings, which embody intricate needlework and stitching; they often take several years to make and are especially noted as dowry gifts

Tabbi– The wavy appearance of silk, originally applied to striped silk, but later to wavy or watered silk. See calendering

Taffeta – A cross-woven stiff silk

Taffeta impermeable – An oiled silk

Tissage – The French word for weaving

Toile de Soie, Toile schappe, Toile doupion, Toile bourrette – Often referred to as linen or linen cloth, calico, ticking or oil cloth

Tram – Several silk threads which have received 100–150 twists per metre, always to the left

Tricotage – The French word for silk-spinning or knitting

Tulle – A silk fabric of fine silk bobbin net used for ladies' dresses, veils and

Glossary

hats; named after the town of Tulle in south west France where its manufacture was invented

Tusseh silk (Tasar, Tussore, Tusser, Tassah) – A tough silk made from the Tusseh silkmoth (*Antheraea mylitta*) and from *A. peryni*, *A. yamamai*. Tusseh is the Hindustani for shuttle

Velours (Velure) – A close-knit silk fabric; a pad of velvet for smoothing a silk hat. Velours de Genes, de Venise, de Florence are all velvets of Italian origin. Eight hundred small bobbins are used in making the fine pile of velours

Velvet – A closely woven fabric, usually of silk, with a short, soft nap or cut pile on one side

Vice redhibitoire – A Lyon term for mite-infested cocoons

Voile – A silk material woven with double or triple threads

Vole – A silk thread that is too fine and does not have sufficient resistance

Voltinism – A scientific term for the number of generations of insect each year; thus univoltine, bivoltine

Vrille – A defect of twisted silk threads

Warp – In weaving, the threads which pass lengthways along the loom and traverse the weft. A typical warp width has about fifteen thousand threads which all have to be tied up by hand

Watered effect – Rolling a heavy weight over silk to make water marks or wavy lines

Weft – In weaving, the threads which pass from left to right across the warp

Worsted – A type of thick cloth named after a little village north of Norwich; used in bombasines

Zoom – A Persian term for two bales of silk, each weighing 0.91 kg (2 lb)

Bibliography and References

Books on silk are scarce. In the nineteenth century the Sericultural Research Centre in Padua (Italy) boasted two thousand books on silk. There was a rash of books on silk published at the end of last century, which this list reflects, but precious few remain in libraries today.

It is worth bearing in mind that some of the Victorian naturalists were enormously productive; for instance Henry Dewhurst wrote at least twenty-nine books and Sir Thomas Wardle thirty-four books, many on silk in both cases. Interesting handbooks on silk culture have the habit of coming to light in antiquarian bookshops; few have been cited by anyone previously.

Important entomological libraries such as the Royal Entomological Society of London and the entomological library of The Natural History Museum, London, have only a handful of silk-related texts between them. However, a good source of information is The British Library which, apart from carrying all British published books, also carries some books on silk not published in Britain. The Cherokee Library in Atlanta (Georgia) is currently bringing together originals of eighteenth- century books published in the USA, including those on silk.

The 'Les Chemins de la Soie', a new government-backed organization in southern France, has gathered together a private library of books on silk, otherwise dispersed from defunct silk research stations in Montpellier, Alès and Var. They are also compiling a computer bibliography. For a comprehensive bibliography see Tocco's 1927 compilation which runs to no less than 3,850 entries. Those references cited here are enormously selective, and the author has seen most of them. They are nearly all books. Hardly any scientific papers are cited – of which there are many.

Several hundred books on silk, representing the collection of the Silk Association of Great Britain, were donated to the City of Westminster

Bibliography and References

Library in the 1960s. Most have now been dispersed or destroyed and only two books could be traced in early 1989.

Some of the more important works can be found in the following museums and libraries:

BCP   Bibliothèque Centrale de pret d'Indre et Loire. Loches, France
BL   The British Library
CML   Cherokee Museum Library, Atlanta, Georgia, USA
HL   The Huntingdon Library, San Marino, California, USA
LCS   Les Chemin de la Soie, Lasalle, France (private collection)
ML   Musée Historique des Tissus, Lyon, France
MNHNP   Musée National d'Histoire Naturelle, Paris
NHMLE   The Natural History Museum, London, Entomology Dept
RESL   Royal Entomological Society of London
RHS   Royal Horticultural Society, London
RS   The Royal Society, London
UNS   Unite Nationale Séricole, Lyon

Adrosko, R.J., *Natural Dyes and Home Dyeing*. New York, Dover, 1971

Aglionby, William, 'On ye nature of Silk, as it is made in Piedmont', Reg. Bk No. 9, p. 37. *Philosophical Transactions of the Royal Society* 1699, xxi, p. 183. RS

Aldemann, H.B., *Marcello Malpighi & the Evolution of Embryology*. Ithaca, New York, Cornell University Press, 1966. Several volumes. RS

Allen, F., *The American Silk Industry*. New York, Allen, 1876

Andre, E., *Élevage des Vers à Soie Sauvages*. Paris, Ficher, 1908. NHMLE

Anonymous, *Treatise on the Origins, Progressive Improvement and Present state of the silk manufacture*. London, Longman, Rees, Orme, Bram & Green, 1840. RESL [As factual and comprehensive as one could then achieve]

Arnold, J., *Queen Elizabeth's Wardrobe Unlocked*. Maney, 1989

Association pour le Développement de la Sériciculture en Cévennes, *Sériculture en Cévennes*, ADSC, 1978

Barham, H., *An Essay Upon the Silkworm*. London, Bettenham & Bickerton, 1719

Barlow, A., *The History and Principles of Weaving by Hand and Power*. Loir, London, Simpson Law & Co., 1878

Beaurepère, C-F., *L'Art d'élever les Vers à Soie dans le Département de la Côte-D'Or, et d'une instruction sur la Culture du Mûrier Blanc*. Dijon, Victor Lagier, 1833. LCS

Bibliography and References

Boitard, M., *Traité de la Culture de Mûrier.* 1828

Bolle, J. and Lambert, F., *La Sériculture au Japon.* Montpellier, Coulet et Fils, 1913. LCS

Bonafous, Matthleu, *De l'education des Vers à Soie d'après la methode du Comte Dandola.* 2nd edition, Paris, Huzard et Bohaire, 1824. LCS

Borah, W., *Silk Raising in Colonial Mexico.* Berkeley. 1943. BL

Borah, W., 'Silk Raising in Colonial Mexico', *Ibero- Americana*, Vol. 20, pp. 1–169. Boston & Los Angeles, University of California Press, 1940. HL

Boraiah, G., *Lectures on Sericulture.* Bangalore, Suramya Publishers, Bangalore, 1986. UNS

Borer, M.C., *The City of London.* London, Constable. 1977. BL [An excellent background book]

Bosseboeuf, Abbé L., *Histoire de la fabrique de soieries de Tours, des origines au XIXe siecle.*Tours, Paul Bousez, 1800. BCP

Boulger, G.E.S., *Familiar Trees.* London, Cassell, 1906

Boullenois, M. Frederick de, *Conseils aux nouveaux educateurs de Vers à Soie.* Paris, Bouchard, 1848.

Boyer, MM.F. and De Labaume, G., *De La Culture de Mûrier.* Nîmes, C. Durand-Belle, 1845. LCS

Brockett, L.P., *The Silk Industry in America. 1876. HL {A listing prepared for the centenial exhibition}*

Brooklyn Botanic Garden Record, Dye Plants and Dyeing. Vol. 20, Brooklyn, 1986

Bulletin Séricicole Francais. [A weekly periodical of the early 1900s, edited Monsieur Laurent de L'Arbousset of Alès, Gard, France, who was also the proprietor]

Bush, Sarah, *The Silk Industry.* Aylesbury, Shire Publications Ltd, 1987

Butler, E.A., *Silkworms.* London, George Allen & Unwin, 1927

Cambassedes, D., *Les usines de déchets de soie.* Montpellier, Coulet, 1889

Canada Bureau of State, *Synthetic Textiles and Silk Industry.* Ottawa, Canada Bureau, 1953. BL

Cansdale, C.H.C., *Cocoon silk, a manual for those employed in the silk industry and for textile students.* London, Pitman, 1937. BL

Carboni, Paolo, *Silk, Biology, Chemistry and Technology.* Translated by Karl Walter. London, Chapman & Hall, 1952. BL

Carron, M.A., *La soie brut en France.* Audin, Lyon, 1946

Castellet, C., *L'art de multiplier la soie ou traité sur les mûriers.* Aix, J. David et E. David. 1760.

Bibliography and References

Central Silk Board, *A Feel for Silk*. Bangalore, India, no date, but *c.* 1987

Central Silk Board, *Practical Handbook of Sericulture*. India, Bangalore, 1987. UNS

Centre National de la Recherches Scientifique, *Soieries Lyonnaises: 1850– 1940*. Lyon, Editions du CNRS, 1980. UNS

Charlot, G., *Essai historique sur la sériciculture de Chenonceaux*. Ladevèze, 1860. BCP

Charnley, F., Fargher, R.G., Hill, D.W. and Tippett, L.H.C., *Developments in the cotton, rayon and silk industry in Germany during 1939–45*. London, 1949. BL

Cheshire County Museums Publication, *The Last Handloom Weavers. Paradise Mill, Macclesfield*. 1987

Clark, H., *Textile Printing*. Aylesbury, Shire Publications Ltd, 1985

Clarke, J., *A Treatise on the Mulberry tree and silkworm and on the production and manufacture of silk, embellished with appropriate engravings*. Philadelphia, Thomas, Cowperthwait & Co., 1839. CML

Clouzot, H., *Le Métier de la soie en France: 1466– 1815*. Paris, Devambez, 1914. BCP

Cobb, J.H., *Manual containing information responsible for the growth of the mulberry tree with suitable directions for the cultivation of silk*. Boston, Carter, Hendrec & Co., 1833. CML

Collins, M.M. & Weast, R.D., *Wild Silkmoths of the United States, Saturniinae*. Collins Radio Co., 1961

Comité d'Organisation de l'Industrie Textile. Direction de la Soie. *L'Élevage du Vers á Soie La Culture du Mûrier. Note élémentaire et pratiques à l'usage des sériculteurs*. MNHN

Cornalia, Emilio, 'Monographia del Bombice del gelso (*Bombyx mori* Linn.)', *Nuovi Annali delle Scienze Naturali, Bologna,* Vol. 10, pp. 42–5. RS

Cox, Raymond, *Les Soieries d'art, depuis les origines jusqu'à nos jours*. Paris, 1914. BL

Crozier, M., *An old silk family, the Brocklehurst-Whiston Amalgamated Ltd*. Aberdeen, The University Press, 1947. BL [The book is covered with their own figured silk]

Dale, M.K., 'London Silkwomen of the fifteenth century', *Economic History Review*, pp. 324–5. 1933 [A fascinating historical account]

Dandolo, M. Le Comte, *L'art d'élever les Vers à Soie*. 2nd edition, Paris, Magnan, Blanchard et Cie, 1861. Translated from the Italian by Philibert Fontaneilles

Dandolo, Count, *The Art of Rearing Silkworms, translated from the work of Count Dandola*. London, John Murray, 1825.

Bibliography and References

Davidson, M.M., *Silk, its History and Manufacture.* Junction City, Kansas, J.B. Wadleigh, 1885. BL

Debernardi, G.B., *Il Filatorista Serico.* Torino, 1900. BL

Deschanels, M., *Les vers à soie en 1867.* Privas, Roure, 1869

de Serres, Olivier, *La Cueillette de la Soye.* 1599

de Serres, Olivier, *La Seconde Richesse du Mûrier Blanc.* 1633

Dewhurst, H.W., *A Familiar Treatise on the Natural History and Management of the Phalaena Bombyx mori, or Common Silk-Worm.* 2nd edition, London, Bennett, 1839, RES [A tiny volume with a lot of historical information, much repeated from elsewhere]

Duseigneur-Kleber, *Le Cocon de soie. Histoire de ses transformations, descriptions des races civilisées et rustiques. Production et distribution géographiques. Maladies des vers à soie. Physiologie du cocon et de fil de soie.* Paris, Rothschild, 1875. ML

Feltwell, J., 'The revival of the silk industry in the Basse-Cévennes', *Proceedings and Transactions of the British Entomological Society of London.* Vol. 16, 1983, pp. 24–9

Feltwell, J., 'Traditional rearing of silkworms in the Basses-Cévennes', *Proceedings and Transactions of the British Entomological Society of London.* Vol. 16, 1983, pp. 30–3

Flanagan, J.F., *Spitalfield Silks of the 18th & 19th centuries.* Leigh on Sea, F. Lewis, 1954. BL

Food & Agriculture Organization of the United Nations (FAO), *Manuel de Sériculture.* 3 Vols, I. Culture du mûrier. II. Élevage du ver à soie. III. Filature de la soie. FAO, 1975. UNS

Fraissinet, Ch., *Le Guide du Magnaguier ou L'Art d'Éleve des Vers à Soie.* Nismes (sic), J.B. Guibert, 1835 and later, Nîmes, Ballivet et Fabre, 1847

Franck, I. and Brownstone, D., *The Silk Road: A History.* London, Facts on File, 1988. [A very comprehensive account]

Gaddum, R.W., *Silk, How and Where it is Produced.* Macclesfield, H.G. Gaddum, 1947

Gallois, J., *Thèse Étude du Décreusage de la Soie du Bombyx mori.* Universitie de Lyon, 1965.

Ganswindt, A., *Dyeing Silk.* Greenwood, Scott, 1921. BL

Gardiner, B.O.C., *A Silkmoth Rearer's Handbook.* Hanworth, The Amateur Entomologist's Society, Vol. 12, 1982

Gilonne, G., *Soieries de Lyon.* Ed. du Fleuve, 1948

Girouard, M., Cruickshank, D., Samuel, R. and others, *Saving of Spitalfields.* London, The Spitalfields Historic Buildings Trust, 1989

Bibliography and References

Givelet, H., *L'Ailante et son Bombyx*. Paris, Libraire agricole de la Maison Rustique, 1861

Godart, J., *L'Ouvrier en Soie: monographie du tisseur Lyonnais*. Lyon, 1899. BL

Gomez Bustillo, M. and Fernandez Rubio, F., *Mariposas de la Península Ibérica*, Vol. 1. Madrid, Instituto Nacional Para La Conservación de la naturaleza, 1976

Gontier, J., *La Soierie de Lyon*, Lyon, C. Bonneton, 1985. BCP, CNS

Greenhalgh, P., *The World Market for Silk. London, Tropical Development & Research Institute*. London, Tropical Development and Research Institute, 1986

Grenvoul, H., 'Sériciculture 79', *Causses et Cévennes*, Vol. 4, Anduze, 1979

Gwynn, R., *Huguenot Heritage. The History and contribution of the Huguenots in Britain*. London, Routledge & Kegan Paul, 1985. [An historic publication]

Haberlandt, F., *Der Seidenspinner des Maulbeerbaumes seine Aufzuchtund Seine*. Wien, Krankheiten, Druck und Verlag Von Carl Gerold's Sohn, 1871. LCS

Hanyum, Gao., *Soireries de Chine*. Nathan, 1987

Hart Dyke, M.Z., *Silk Farm*. London, Westchester Publishers, 1948. [A less well-known book, for children]

Hart Dyke, Z., *So Spins the Silkworm*. London, Rockliff, 1949. [A well-known and anecdotal book]

Hook, B., *The Cambridge Encyclopaedia of China*. Cambridge University Press, 1982

Hooper, Luther, *Silk, its Production and Manufacture*. London, Pitman, 1927

Hughes, S., *Washi. The World of Japanese Papers*. Kodansha International, 1978

Japanese Silk Association, *Introduction à l'élevage du Vers à soie*. 1968. ML

Johnson, Emma B., *Silk culture in Louisiana & in the Southern States*. New Orleans, Southern Knight Press, 1882. BL [Poor, except for regional information]

Jolly, M.S., *A Decade of Tasar Research, 1964–74*. Bombay, Central Silk Board, 1974

Jolly, M.S., Chowdhury, S.N. and Sen, S.K., *Non-Mulberry Sericulture*. Bombay, Central Silk Board, 1975

Jouanny, J., *Le Tissage de soie dans les Bas-Dauphiné*. Grenoble, 1931. BL

Kenrick, W.M., *The New Orchardist or an account of the most valuable varieties of fruit adapted to cultivate in the United States from the latitude 25–54 etc.* Boston, Carter, Hende & Co., 1833. CML

Bibliography and References

L'Arbousset, M. Laurent de, *Cours de Sericulture Pratique*. Alais, C. Castagnier, 1893. LCS

L'Arbousset, M. Laurent de, 'L'Avenir de la culture du Mûrier', *VI Congrès International d'Agriculture, Paris, 8 juillet, 1900*. Paris, Masson & Cie, pp. 630–40

L'Arbousset, M. Laurent de, *On Silk and the Silkworm*. Translated E. Wardle. Leek, Eaton, 1905

Lafont, F.D. and Rabino, H.L., *L'industrie sericole en Perse*. Montpellier, Coulet et Fils, 1910. BL, LCS

Legay, J.M., *Physiologie du ver à soie*. Paris, Institute National de la Recherche Agronomique, 1960. ML

Leggett, William F., *The Story of Silk*. New York, Lifetime Editions, 1949. BL [A digest of facts]

Leon, J. de, *Sericultural Leaflets*. Jerusalem, Department of Agriculture and Forestry, 1932. BL

Leon, J. de, *Sericulture in Cyprus*. Tel Aviv, Omanuth Erez, 1933. LCS

Lions, —, *Guide pratique sur l'éducation des vers à soie et sur le choix que l'on doit faire de la feuille de mûrier pour les élever*. Librarie de Jurisprudence de Dorier, 1843. ML

Liu, G.K-C., 'The Silkworm & Chinese Culture', *Osiris*. Vol. 10, pp. 129–93, 1952. BL

Loiseleurs-Deslongchamps, M., *Nouvelles considerations sur les Vers à Soie pour servir à l'histoire de ces insectes*. Paris, Huzard, 1839. LCS

Lombe, Sir Thomas, *An Impartial Inquiry into the State of Georgia*. London, 1741

Lower, E.S., *Chemicals and Chemistry in the Production of Silk*. 1970. [May be purchased from the Silk Education Service, UK]

Luppi, G., *Dictionnaire de Sericologie*. Lyon, Charles Mera, 1878. LCS

Macartney, S. and West, J., *A History of the Lewisham Silk Mills*. Lewisham Local History Society, 1979. [26pp booklet, fascinating research]

Maillet, E., 'Plantations de mûriers blancs et élevages de Vers à soie dans le Lochois de 1760–1782', *Société des Antiquites du Tours*. Vol. 36, 1971

Maillot, E. and Lambert, F., *Traite sur le ver à Soie du Mûrier*. Montpellier, Coulet et Fils, 1906. LCS, NHMLE.

Malpighi, M., *Dissertatio epistolica de Bombyce*. Edited by H. Oldenburg. MS presented to the Royal Society on 18 February, 1669. RS

Malpighi, M., *La structure du Ver à Soye, et la formation du poulet dans l'oeuf. Contenant deux disserations en forme de lettre*. Paris, 1686. BL

Malpighi, M., *Mèmoire on the Silkworm, De Bombyx*. 1678. ML, RS

Bibliography and References

Malpighi, M., *Opera Postuma, quibus prefixa est ejusdem vita a seipso scripta*, London. 1697

Mason, F.R., 'The American Silk Industry and The Tariff', *The American Economic Association Quarterly*, Vol. 11, No. 4, 1910, pp. 1–182. BL, HL

Matsui, Shichiro, *The History of the Silk Industry in the United States*. Howes, 1930. NHMLE

Mikkers, J.C.M., *Zijdeteelt in Sint-Michielsgestel 1829-1955. Streekarchivariaat Langs Aa en Dommel*. 1982.

Millward, R. and Robinson, A., *The West Midlands*. (Landscape of Britain Series.) London, Macmillan, 1971

Mozziconacci, A., *Le Ver à Soie du Mûrier*. Paris, Libraire Hachette, 1921

Mukerji, Nitya Gopal, *Handbook of Sericulture*. Calcutta, Bengal Secretariat Press. [In Hindustani and in English]

Museum of London, *The Quiet Conquest, The Huguenots 1685– 1985*. 1985

Mutti, G., *Report on the culture of silk and the growth of the mulberry tree in Bengal*. Bombay, Public Document, 1838. BL

Nencki, Lydie, *Colorants végétaux sur soie*. Paris, Dessain et Tolra, 1985

Nunez Ortega, A., *Apuntes sobre el cultivo de la Seda en Mexico*. Brusselas (sic), 1883. BL

Ozil, Hervé, *Magnaneries et Vers à Soie. La sériciculture en pays Vivarois et Cévenol*. Villeneuve de Berg, Candide, 1986. ML, BCP

Padilla, Victoria, *Southern California Gardens*. Berkeley & Los Angeles, University of California Press, 1961. RHS

Paillot, A., *Traité des Maladies du Vers à Soie*. Paris, G. Doin & Co., 1930

Papion, R., *Mémoire sur la culture des mûriers et les récoltes de soie*. Foulquier, 1809

Pasteur, L., *Études sur la Maladie des Vers à soie*. Vols 1 and 2. Paris, Gauthier-Villas, 1870

Pigorni, L. and Teodoro, G., *Lezioni di Biologica Applicata alla Sericoltura*. Vol. 1. La Lititipo Editrice Universitaria, 1921

Pitaro, Antoine, *La Science de La Sétifère ou L'Art de produire la soie*. Paris, J-P Roret, 1828 RESL

Pommier, H., *Soierie Lyonnaise 1850–1940*. Paris, Centre National Recherche de la Scientifique, 1980. BCP

Quajat, E.D., *Dei Bozzoli*. Verona, Fratelli Drucker, 1904. LCS

Randot, Natalis, *Rapport sue les soies*. Paris, Imprimerie Nationale, 1885. LCS

Reali, G., Meneghini, A. and Trevisan, M., *Bachicoltura Moderna*. Bologna, Edagricole, 1985. UNS

Reynier, E., *La soie en Vivarais*. 2nd edition, Marseille, Lafitte Reprints, 1981

Robinet, S., *Expériences sur la ventilation des Magnaneries*. Paris, 1848

Robinet, S., *Manuel de l'éducateur de Vers à Soie*. Paris, Libraire Agricole de la Maison Rustique, 1848

Robinet, S., *Mémoire sur la filature de la soie*. Paris, Madame P. Huzard. 1839

Robinet, S., *Mémoire sur l'industrie de Vers à soie*. Paris, 1846

Robinet, S., *Recherches sur la production de la soie en France*. Paris, Millet MM et Robinet, 1843–6, 95 pp. LCS

Rodgers, F., *Derby Old & New*. Wakefield, EP Publishing, 1975

Roman, Leopold, *Manuel de Magnanier, application des Theories de M. Pasteur, à l'Education des Vers à soie*. Paris, Gauthier-Villars, 1876. LCS

Rothstein, N., *18th Century Silk designs in the Victoria and Albert*. London, Thames & Hudson, 1990

Roxburgh, William, 'Account of the Tusseh & Arrindy Silk-worms of Bengal', *Transactions of the Linnean Society of London*. Vol. 7, 1802, p. 33

Scober, T., *Silk and Silk Industry*. London, Constable, 1930

Schützenberger, M.R., *Matières colorantes comprenant leurs applications à la teinture et à l'impression et des notices sur les fibres textiles les epaississants et les mordants*. Paris, Victor Masson, 1867

Secretain, Ch. and Schenk, A., 'Guide du Bon Sériciculteur', Alès, Claparède, Station Séricicole d'Alès, *Bulletin Technique Séricole*, No. 3, 1943

Sena, A.N., *Properties of Silk*. Calcutta, 1937. BL

Seringe, N.C., *Description et Culture Mûrier*. Paris, Victor Masson, 1855. LCS

Silbermann, H., *Die Seide ihre Geschichte, Gewinnung und Verarbeitung*. Dresden, Von Gerhard Kuhtmann, 1897. LCS

Silk Association of Great Britain, *An Exhibition of British Silks*. London, Silk Association, 1912

Silk & Rayon Users Association, *The Silk Book*. W.S. Cornell Ltd, 1951

Skinner, C.M., *Myths & Legends of Flowers, Trees, Fruits and Plants*. Philadelphia & London, Lippincott Co., 1913. RHS

Stallenge, W., *Tracts on Silkworms 1603–1609*. 1609. Three books bound together:

1. Silkewormes for the making of silke in this Kingdome. Whereunto is annexed his Majesties Letters to the Lords Lieftenants of the severall Shiers of England tending to that purpose. The Perfectus of Silk-Wormen and their benefit with the exact planting, and artificiall handling of Mulberrie trees whereby to nourish them, and the figures to know how to feede the Wormes, and to winde off the Silke. And the firt manner to prepare the bark of the white Mulberrie make fine linnen and

Bibliography and References

other works therof. Done out of the French original of D'Olivier de Serres Lord of Pradel into English, by Nicholas Geffe Esquier.

2. With an anexed discourse of this owne, of the meands and sufficiencie of England for to have abundance of fine silke by feeding of silke-wormes within the frame; as by apparent proofes by him made and continued appeareth. For the general use and universall benefit of all those hios Countrey men which embrace them. Never the like yet here discovered by any. Au despit d'enuie.
    Published by Felix Kyngston, London. 114 pp.
    {Introduction by Nicholas Geffe}

3. *Mémoires et Instructions pour l'établissement des Meuriers; & Art de faire la Soye en France.* 3 figs, Paris, près de Carnes, Imprimeurs Ordinaire du Roy, Jamet & Pierre Mettayer, 32 pp., 1603. BL

Station Montpellier, *Traité du Vers à soie.* Montpellier, C. Combet, 1878, (Station sericiculture de Montpellier. Mémoires et documents sur la sériciculture.) ML

Stevenson, A., *Observations on the Culture of Silk. c.* 1840

Sutton, A.F., 'Alice Claver, silkwoman of London and maker of mantles and laces for Richard III and Queen Anne', *The Ricardian.* Vol. 5, 1980, pp. 243–7

Tanaka, Y., 'Studies on hibernation with special reference to photoperiodicity and breeding of the Chinese Tussar-Silkworm', *Journal of Sericulture, Japan.* Vol. 19, p. 358

Temple, R.K.G. *China, Land of Discovery & Invention.* Wellingborough, Patrick Stephens, 1986

Tocco, Roberto, *Bibliografia del Filugello (Bombyx mori Linnaeus) e del Gelso (Morus alba Linnaeus).* Milano, Casa Editrice Dott. A, 1927. LCS

Toyo Trading Co., *Introduction à l'élèvage du Vers á Soie.* 1968. UNS

Trimoulet, M. Henry, *La sériciculture et descriptions du nid d'un Bombyx exotique.* Bordeaux, Coderc, Degreteau et Poujol, 1865

Vaschalde, J., *Les industries de la Soie.* Paris, PUF, 1972. UNS

Verson, E. and Quajat, E., *Il Filugello e l'arte Sericole.* 2 Vols, Padua, Stazione Bacologica Sperimentale di Padova. 1896. Vieil, L., *Recherche sur la Soie.* Lyon, 1891. BL

Vieil, L., *Sériciculture.* Paris, Boulliere, 1905

Vignon, L., *La Soie au point de vue Scientifique et Industriel.* Paris, 1890. BL

Wardle, T., *Handbook of the Collection Illustrative of the Wild Silks of India, in the Indian Section of the South Kensington Museum, with a Catalogue of the*

Bibliography and References

Collection and Numerous Illustrations. London, George E. Eyre and William Spottiswoode, for Her Majesty's Stationery Office, 1881. RESL [A unique account, well illustrated]

Wardle, T., *Kashmir, Its New silk industry with some account of its natural history, geology and sport, with notes of a visit to the silk producing district of Bengal in 1885–6*. London, Simkin, Marshall, Hamilton, Kent & Co., 1904. BL

Wardle, T., 'Obituary', *The Textile Mercury*, 8 January 1909. BL [With photograph]

Wardle, T., *On The Entomology and Uses of Silk; with a List of the Families, Genera, and Species of Silk Producers, Known Up to the Present Date*. North Staffordshire Naturalist's Field Club and Archaeological Society, after 1889. RESL

Wardle, T., *On the present development of the power loom weaving of silk fabrics at Lyon*. Manchester, W. Harris, 1893

Warner, F., *The Silk Industry*. Manchester, Dranes. 1921

Webb, J.J., *Industrial Dublin since 1698 and The Silk Industry in Dublin*. Dublin, Mansel & Co., 1913. BL

Whitby, M.A.T., *A Manual for rearing Silkworms in England with a brief Notice on the various species of this insect and on the cultivation of the Mulberry Tree*. London, John W. Parker, 1848

Whiter, J.S., *The Silk Industry of Great Britain*. London, Issued for private circulation, 1882. BL

Whitfield, R., *The Art of Central Asia. The Stein Collection in the British Museum (Natural History), Volume 3: Textiles, Culture and Other Arts*. London, Kodansha International Ltd, in cooperation with the Trustees of the British Museum, 1985

Wickens, H., *Natural Dyes for Spinners and Weavers*. London, Batsford, 1983

Williams, C., *Instructions in Silk Culture, Mulberry Trees, the silk worm, market for cocoons*. Minneapolis Beach, Marian B. van Antwerp, 1895. HL

Williams, P.E., *Treatise upon the Cultivation of the White Mulberry Tree, and the Art of Rearing silkworms in England*. Norwich, Bacon & Co., pre-1848

Woodcraft, B., *Abridgements of the Specifications relating to Spinning*. London, 1866

Wyckoff, W.C., *The Silk Goods of America, a brief account of the recent improvements and advances of silk information in the United States*. New York, Silk Association of America, 1880. HL

Yigal Yanai, *Susani – Central Asian Embroideries*. Tel Aviv, Haaretz Museum, 1986

Yo-San-Fi, R.O.K., *Sur L'Art d'élever les Vers à Soie au Japon*. Onekaka-Morikouni. Translated by J. Hoffmann, Paris, Bonafous, 1848

Index

References to illustrations are in italic.

Index

Index

Index

Index

Index

Index

Springfield, 136
Staffordshire, 181, 184
Stallenge, William, 18–19, 41, 47,
    87–8, 92
Stantons, 186
Stein, Aurel, 12, 128
Stockings, silk, *127*, 143, 145
Stowmarket, 109
Strensall Common, 139
Strings, silk, 137
Subsericum, 10
Sudbury, 187
Suffolk, 103
Sulawesi, 197
Sumatra, 122
Surgery, silk in, 136
Surrey, 103
Sussex, West, 178
Swammerdam, Johann Jacob, 45
Swiss Development Cooperation (SDC),
59
Switzerland, 161
Sycamore, 76, 97
'Sylkewymmen and Throwsterres', 104
Syrian silkmoth, 59
Syringa, 76, 97,

T'ai-Yuan-Fu, 11
T'ang dynasty, 128
Taffeta dress, 150
Tagetes sp., 120
Taiwan, 91, 95
    Sericultural Improvement Station, 198
Taking the silks, 112, 140
Tartars of Kalachan, 6
Taunton, 181, 189
Tan dynasty, 11
Telescopes, silk for, 138
Templars and Hospitallers, 78
Terminalia alata glabra, 60
Tessinari family, 14
Teulon, Anthony, 164
    family 164–5
Texas, 93–4
Texan mulberry, 73, 94
Texas root kno nematode, 98
Thailand, 95, 198
Threads, silk, *127*
Thrown-shuttle looms, 198
Tiverton, 189
Tobacco, 24
Tours, 88–9, 167
Toye, Kennet & Spencer, 175
Tradescant, John, 23, 108
Treaty of Shan-yuan, 12

Tree of heaven, 62, 97
Treviso's sericulture, 199
Tring Park, 187
Tulip tree, 109
Tulipomania, 30
Tuileries garden, 88
Tun-huang, 128
Turfan region, 128
Turin, 176, 199
Turkey, 10
Turkhmak, 120
Turmeric, 121
Turners, 184
Tusseh silkmoth, 8, 28, 59, 60, *61*, 97,
    129, 176, 191, 195
Tutbury Castle, 150
Tutbury, Michael, 58
Tweedie, Michael, 58
Tyre, 115
Tyres, silk, 139

Uncaria gambir, 122
Unquomock silk mill, *31*
Urtica dioica, 119
Uses of silk, 123–56
USSR, 192
Uzbekistan, 13, 117, 120, 122, 197

Vallerauges, 164
Vancouver, Captain, 32
Var, 90
Vaucanson, 170
Vaucluse, 44, 90
Venice, 158, 199
Versailles, 14, 146
Vetron, Monsieur, 18
Vickers, 139
Victoria, Queen, 115, 152
Vincennes, royal farm, 97
Virginia, 22, 23–5, 117–8, 151, 152
Virginia Co., 22, 87, 92
Viscum alba, 98
Vivares, 88
Von Le Coq, Albert, 12

Wagner, Melchior, 164
Wales, William, Prince of, 155
Walloons, 187
    family, 164
Walter, Archbishop Hubert, 101
Waltham Abbey, 114
Wandle, river, 132, 175
Wandsworth, 104, 175
    Civic Crest, 175, *175*
Wapping, 175

Wardle, Thomas, 58, 115, 176, 184
Ware, river, 101
Warner, Benjamin, 187
Warwickshire, 103–4
Washington, 188
Washington, George and Martha, 152
War of Independence, 29
Wars of the Roses, 14
Weaver's Fields, 178
Wedding dresses, silk, 150
Wellingtonias, 109
Welstead Mill, 186
Westbury Mill, 189
Western Han period, 132
West Midlands, 185–6
West Sussex, 103
Westminster, 143
Westminster Abbey, 101, 151
Westminster Palace, 188
Whelk, Common, 115
Whitby, Mrs, 52, 83
Whitchurch, 188–9
White mulberry, 81–92
    identification, 81
    origins, 87
    propagation, 91
    varieties, 81–6
Wightwick Manor, 99
William and Mary, 140
William Prince & Son, 30
Willmott family, 189
Wilson, Ernest, 94
Wiltshire, 189
Winchelsea, 161
Winchester Cathedral, 188
Windsor, 148
Woad, 115–16
Wokingham, 188
Wolsey, Cardinal, 146
Wooton, Lord, 108
Worldwide Butterflies Ltd, 84, 155
Wu-hsi, 12

X'ian, 6

Yangchow, 11
York, 78, 101, 139
York, Duke of, 148
Yorkshire, 181
Young, Dr, 109
Youxian, Dr Feng, 136
Yugoslavia, 95

Zithers, 137